Designing Social Architecture

Designing Social Architecture

Spaces, Relationships, and Communities in the Philippines

Fuyuki Makino

LEXINGTON BOOKS
Lanham • Boulder • New York • London

Published by Lexington Books
An imprint of The Rowman & Littlefield Publishing Group, Inc.
4501 Forbes Boulevard, Suite 200, Lanham, Maryland 20706
www.rowman.com

86-90 Paul Street, London EC2A 4NE

British Library Cataloguing in Publication Information Available

Library of Congress Cataloging-in-Publication Data

Names: Makino, Fuyuki, author.
  Title: Designing social architecture : spaces, relationships, and
    communities in the Philippines / Fuyuki Makino.
  Description: Lanham : The Rowman & Littlefield Publishing Group, Inc.,
    [2022] | Includes bibliographical references and index. | Summary: "In
    Designing Social Architecture, Fuyuki Makino examines how experimental
    methods in modern architecture have helped form micro-relationships,
    social networks, and social structures among inhabitants of Manila,
    Philippines, and considers whether the architects' aim to promote
    certain social behaviors was successful or not"-- Provided by publisher.
  Identifiers: LCCN 2022004483 (print) | LCCN 2022004484 (ebook) | ISBN
    9781793649515 (cloth) | ISBN 9781793649539 (paperback) | ISBN
    9781793649522 (epub)
  Subjects: LCSH: Architecture and society--Philippines--Manila. |
    Architecture, Domestic--Philippines--Manila. | Architecture and
    anthropology--Philippines--Manila.
  Classification: LCC NA2543.S6 M345 2022 (print) | LCC NA2543.S6 (ebook) |
    DDC 720.1/030959916--dc23/eng/20220324
  LC record available at https://lccn.loc.gov/2022004483
  LC ebook record available at https://lccn.loc.gov/2022004484

I dedicate this book to my parents, Tadashi and Keiko. I greatly appreciate them for inspiring me to ask important questions, think critically, and live ethically.

Contents

List of Figures

Preface

My first fieldwork in the Philippines, conducted in 1998, was in an area called Metro Manila. After that, while fleshing out my research's theme, I did fieldwork in depressed areas of the Philippines, Mexico, and Cambodia. During this time, I thought about the essence of scholarship. The essence of scholarship is not just learning established knowledge, but the mental and physical activity of creating new knowledge, as well as using that knowledge in daily life.

In recent years, many social science disciplines, including cultural anthropology, have required a concrete return from academic achievements to society. However, the difficulty of applying academic research results to the real world is a major issue. Regarding the application of cultural anthropology, I thought about the nature of the field of cultural anthropology, which captures the actual situation of life, as well as the fields of architecture and urban planning, which create living spaces. From there, I pursued the theme of fusing anthropology and architecture. While investigating the relationships of people in depressed areas, the people who lived there urged improvements in their areas of residence. I thought that anthropological knowledge would be of great help to living spaces, shared spaces in communities. In such an environment, I have been exploring the possibility of practical application of cultural anthropology. I think it's natural to learn architecture for concrete applications, that is, for the purpose of drawing and proposing community plans with my own hands. After attending a school for architecture, I gained practical experience and in the field of community development. This book summarizes the results of fieldwork conducted in Metro Manila from both anthropological and architectural perspectives.

The research field is the squatter area of Metro Manila. I conducted anthropological fieldwork and architectural surveys in the area, challenging interdisciplinary areas across disciplines. I conducted community planning surveys and individual interviews on housing and living patterns for rural-to-urban migrants in Metro Manila. I also considered how the residents perceive the city. As a practical application of anthropological fieldwork, I challenged the international architectural design competition and disaster recovery program sponsored by the Philippine government. These various experiences are the basis of this book.

The title of this book includes the phrase "social architecture." What is social architecture? Architecture has always been a part of society. In the field of architectural design, social architecture refers to not only livability and safety, but also social environment. Moreover, it means a collaborative program designed to involve members of the community. Architects expect the architecture they create to change human behavior. There is one more item to add to the social architecture I consider in this book. I think that architecture, and specific architectural forms or styles that have existed in society for a long time itself, functions as a tool for deepening mutual understanding among people. These long-established forms or styles have their own meaning, and people have shared the worldview and recognized the community by experiencing and reading the space. For example, Cunningham points out the symbolism of the house (Cunningham 1973). I think furthermore that architecture is not just a thing created jointly by architects and communities, but that the act of architecture itself promotes mutual understanding between individuals with different ideas. In this book, I aimed to establish a social architecture that upholds these meanings by a method called "architectural anthropology." I wanted to present a new perspective on anthropology and architecture and rethink social architecture thereby.

I hope and believe that this book will help people with different social backgrounds to understand each other and create new values together.

Acknowledgments

In carving out this new discipline, Professor Yasushi Kikuchi guided the project in the right direction with useful advice. Supervisors in the Graduate School of Asia-Pacific Studies at Waseda University and teachers in the Art and Architecture School at Waseda University also provided support and assistance. Professor Kikuchi offered guidance toward the essence of anthropology as an academic discipline in the field since the fieldwork in the impoverished areas of Metro Manila in 1998. Junkichi Watari, a senior scholar in Philippines studies, provided countless suggestions regarding traditional houses in the Philippines. Moreover, approaching this subject from the two angles of architecture and anthropology stems from the powerful influence of Yoshiaki Akasaka's view on architecture.

Further, architecture has retained a unique perspective, unprecedented in other disciplines, by giving visual form to ideas. Although contributing humanities and social sciences research results to society is challenging, during repeated ventures into the fieldwork, many teachers offered guidance on the importance of reinvesting research results via an approach where residents are the central concern. This study owes a great debt to them.

This book is underpinned by fieldwork conducted in Metro Manila. During this fieldwork, Professor Mary Racelis from Ateneo de Manila University Institute of Philippine Culture; the Foundation for the Development of the Urban Poor, an NGO in the Philippines; the Urban Poor Associates, and TAO-Pilipinas, Inc., provided considerable support. The study is also highly obliged to the San Agustin homeowner's association (HOA), Macoda HOA, Samarima HOA, and Daang Tubo residents for participating in the fieldwork and measurement surveys. Professor Jurg Helbling, supervisor during the study abroad on the doctoral program at the University of Zurich Graduate School, provided an important opportunity to revise views on the impoverished areas of Metro Manila from a pluralistic perspective. Further, Professor Shinji Hirai, a friend since college and professor of the Center for Research and Higher Education in Social Anthropology in Mexico, furnished the methodology for solving present-day anthropology problems via regular research-update sharing, which infused depth to the discussion based on global trends in anthropology.

Finally, the study owes a debt of gratitude to supportive family members throughout the decision-making process: children, who are always full of life; parents, brothers, and sisters; and extended family members.

Introduction

This book highlights the collaboration between anthropologists and "others" in the emergent method of anthropological practice. It considers the potential to realize cultural understanding through sustained practices based on the cyclical process of "reading, presenting, and making." Moreover, the study examines architectural practices as ethnography (i.e., architectural ethnography). Ultimately, anthropological fieldwork results are contributed to society through reading, expressing, and constructing architecture. This point also expresses my own way of thinking about social architecture: that it is important that deepening mutual understanding with others through building activities is recognized as a new meaning of social architecture. And mutual understanding contributes to the creation of new values for people.

The study investigates poor areas of the University of the Philippines and three areas where Community Mortgage Program (CMP) development projects are being implemented. In particular, the study focuses on the following two areas. First, it focuses on micro-relationships such as family and inhabitants in poor urban areas and considers the existence of new human networks and social structures evoked from spaces with narrowness, density, and adjacency. Second, to understand the concept of residents and human networks, the study presents the notion of "visualized architecture" to illustrate the inner image. Visualized architecture is a shared framework aimed at a mutual understanding between anthropologists and residents.

The first half of this book describes the basic ideas of architectural anthropology. Next, I present the framework of "visualized architecture," which represents the internal images of its inhabitants. Internal image here means a spiritual, concrete form, or a particular event or scene that resembles the spiritual image of psychology. For example, even in poor urban areas, the lifestyle, spatiality, and worldview of the area of origin are even projected onto the living space and architecture. This approach revisits the visual images of housing and communities used in improvement projects in poor areas of Metro Manila as a framework for mutual understanding between outsiders (NGOs, anthropologists, researchers) and residents in the poor area. After that, I will focus on the relationships and attribution created by extreme narrowness, crowdedness, and adjacency of the houses. The book's second half discusses the possibilities for interpretation of residents' spatial consciousness and social structure. I will also discuss specific ideas for the architectural application of anthropology.

Chapter 1 introduces the basic idea of architectural anthropology and reviews the perspectives and discussions proposed in the architectural domains of cultural anthropology. Those who began studying anthropology after the 1990s needed to understand what self-criticism in anthropology was in that earlier period. This chapter outlines the historical situation surrounding anthropology in order to clarify the position of architectural anthropology. It also outlines the history of housing research methodologies, reviews the concepts and trends of urban analysis, and explains the perspective of architectural anthropology.

Chapter 2 presents a framework for cross-cultural understanding within the cyclical process of "reading, presenting, and making" architecture in the broad sense. Specifically, I will examine the effectiveness of the framework of "visualized architecture" by organizing images of communities and housing obtained from workshops in urban poor areas. An appropriate and accurate framework is one of the communication methods between anthropologists and residents. Having a common frame greatly expands the possibilities of mutual understanding. In this chapter, I consider the practical consultation process in urban planning and architecture and consider the possibility of using image-sharing as a communication tool.

Chapter 3 examines informal settlements within the University of the Philippines as a case study of reading architecture in the broad sense. Their spatial features, forced upon inhabitants, are extreme narrowness, crowdedness, and adjacency, which deprive them of normal life functions and engender new communal living places. In this chapter, I will clarify the reality of human relationships created by places with these spatial characteristics. The case study will be five residences that were actually surveyed at the University of the Philippines. From the survey results, I will verify the living style in these small dwellings from a microscopic perspective derived from the actual living conditions and measurement surveys. Regarding the relationships between residents, I analyze the relationships between adjacent dwellings, the collaboration in building dwellings, and the human relationships in shared spaces.

Chapter 4 examines several upgrading projects conducted in impoverished areas, where self-build practices were incorporated under the CMP method, resulting in substantial improvements to the environments in the informal settlements. In this chapter, I will focus on the composition of the resident population, their response to small living spaces, and the transformation of the sense of belonging from the investigation of kinship organizations. I also explore the spatial characteristics that create new relationships between residents and between residents and communities. In addition, I discuss the role of NGOs. The regional coordinator of the Foundation for the Development of the Urban Poor (FDUP) is able to deal directly with the local population in all processes, from beneficiary screening to land delivery. It is very important for NGOs that residents trust them.

Chapter 5 discusses the emergence of spaces, relationships, and communities in impoverished urban areas regarding the fieldwork in the informal settlements and the three areas where CMP projects are being conducted. I capture the relationships between residents from the perspective of the "face-to-face" living space with the extreme narrowness, crowdedness, and adjacency of the houses, which is characteristic of architecture in urban poor areas, and I reveal the existence of loosely connected urban relationships that preserve individual heterogeneity.

Chapter 6 describes examples of efforts to improve living space in architecture. By reviewing these historical efforts, we can gain useful insights for the improvement of housing in poor areas. The housing improvements that modern architects have been working on address various social problems that exist in developed countries. Since the latter half of the nineteenth century, there have been major changes in economic activities and social systems in Western countries. Many of the social problems created by rapid industrialization overlap with the items needed to improve housing in poor areas in developing countries today. The focuses here are improvements in hygiene, environment, economy, function, and society. The various architectural methods that have been tackled so far provide great clues for housing improvement in poor areas.

Chapter 7 examines the broad potential of architecture via critical mutual understanding between the researcher and subjects, based on two case studies of collaborative endeavors with CMP residents and a disaster recovery program. By sharing anthropological achievements between residents and anthropologists through visual images, anthropological analysis, such as understanding of social structure, can be linked to concrete architectural plans. The Proposal for Metro Manila Poor Areas in case study 1 is an early attempt to apply anthropological research to architectural planning. This proposal places multiple core units within the community. Based on the core unit, the aid side and the recipient side work together to improve the living space. Also, regarding space sharing by multiple families, it is important to strengthen ritual kinship and community relationships. The core unit must provide the impetus for creating urban relationships. Case study 2 describes an ideal process for building in collaboration with residents. It focuses on the Disaster Recovery Program conducted by the Philippines National Disaster Coordinating Council Civil Disaster Office. Based on a proposal that includes materials, design, and construction methods, the intent is to face current global urban problems and seek solutions by means of architecture.

The rapid progress of globalization in the twenty-first century is accelerating the concentration of population in cities. In the world's largest cities, there are many densely populated and poor areas, and there is an urgent need to improve the living space. At the same time, in these big cities, the influx of different cultures is mixed, and new social structures and spatial perceptions are being reorganized while embracing traditional values. Even as virtual relationships permeate, there are always places where people meet in real life, and a common sense of belonging is shared among those who share this living space. Living spaces, especially in urban poor areas, are associated with extreme narrowness, crowdedness, and adjacency. Residents have no choice but to live their daily lives while relying on each other. In other words, in today's urban setting, people living in neighborhoods are based in a shared space while also retaining relationships and a sense of belonging that do not share a physical space.

Most of the discussion surrounding people and places presented in this study draws heavily on prior anthropological discussions. In particular, the view that residents read their house as a book is important. Moreover, attempts to analyze houses dynamically per the structuralist approach (i.e., the discussion surrounding the symbolic approach to houses and criticism thereof) are essential. Given these discussions, the strategy of explicating human relations in informal urban settlements from the perspectives of places characterized by narrowness, crowdedness, and adjacency, common to the informal settlements described in this book, emerged through interaction with residents. From the in-depth examination of actual life in informal settlements, architectural anthropology arguably assigns primacy to the ephemeral aspects of place and neighborhood that envelop a certain location at a certain time. This perspective illuminates human relations as gradually aroused by houses or shared community spaces, unlike the typical duality of farming villages and urban areas or the conceptual approach regarding contexts already embodied within the house.

Architectural anthropology attempts to realize the possibility of cross-cultural understanding within the context of sustained practices, per the cyclical process of "reading, presenting, and making" architecture in the broad sense through anthropologist–architect collaboration. Architectural anthropologists, visualizing a basis for mutual collaboration via the common framework of architecture—seek to contribute anthropological fieldwork results to target societies through the cyclical process. Though the target societies are not limited to any settlement type, this study focuses on informal settlements inhabited by socially vulnerable individuals, known as "slums." Rather than constructing preexisting ethnographic practices within the dimensions of anthropology, architectural anthropology attempts to engage with architecture in the broad sense while actively committing to the target society to reconstruct the framework of anthropology.

Chapter 1

Reflection—Architectural Anthropology

This chapter first examines the history of cultural anthropology as an academic discipline and logically examines current challenges facing the field. Next, it reviews perspectives and discussions in the architectural domains of cultural anthropology. Research in cultural anthropology has focused on various human activities. Accordingly, since the discipline's infancy, anthropologists have examined diverse spaces in which humans live, including the range of unique dwelling types that people inhabit, shared spaces in communities, and housing structures and arrangements. However, cultural anthropology, with related disciplines such as geography and history, has treated "architecture" as a component of "culture," and has not addressed architecture as a central concern. Even when houses have been discussed individually, it has only served as a means for describing "culture."

CULTURAL ANTHROPOLOGY: CURRENT CHALLENGES

Accordingly, the 1980s proved to be pivotal for cultural anthropology. Cultural anthropology could not provide a cross-disciplinary paradigm, such as structuralism. Anthropology researchers in the late 1990s noted "a crisis in anthropology" and "ethnographic writing" (Clifford and Marcus 1986, 3; Rosaldo 1989, 38). The venture into anthropology coincided with the dawn of a new anthropological study era and a period of experimentation, where cultural anthropologists began to take on new challenges.

Various critiques of the pre-1980s forms of cultural anthropology have mostly focused on the identity of the individual presenting the culture. That is, the political aspects and power relations of the representative individual were problematic. Where anthropologists described culture, the patterned descriptions of "others" in the ethnographies generated from their research results were problematized. Culminations of the cultural anthropology critique can be seen in *Writing Culture*, by James Clifford and George E. Marcus, and *Culture and Truth*, by Renato Rosaldo. However, given that much of the critique emerged from within, the cultural anthropology discipline is essential in maintaining its soundness via a self-cleanse.

In the 1990s, anthropology received an injection of new perspectives from researchers outside the United States and Europe, such as Asia, Central and South America, and Africa, that studied people, thus making various new attempts to highlight culture. From the 1990s, anthropologists have been required to clarify how their concerns were formed within the society to which they belonged and their positioning, intentions, and purpose in the target society. Moreover, it was necessary to clarify the positions of their own society as well as the target and international societies, and any wider regional communities, to comment on their relative political dimensions. Complete objectivity is of course not possible, but it was necessary to devote a lot of time to honest ethnographic writing, at least aiming for a perception or veneer of objectivity.

The numerous criticisms concerning researcher positioning prompted a gradual fall in comprehensive cultural theory studies that sought to attain cross-cultural interpretations from universal, objective perspectives. Instead, researchers began compiling ethnographies offering detailed descriptions of individual cultural phenomena. Studies have since addressed separate themes, such as tourism, development, women, nationalism, identity, disasters, refugees, and migrants. In recent years, researchers have faced even stronger demands to contribute their research results to society. Considering that anthropology once contributed to the legitimization of imperialism and colonialism by Western powers, researchers arguably have a strong awareness of the importance of appropriately contributing anthropological study results to source societies.

Given the new form of cultural anthropology, this study naturally adopted a research stance with a constant awareness of objectivity toward the target society. In particular, in surveys of socially vulnerable people (e.g., slum dwellers), surveys at field sites or with NGO and government officials spotlighted the perceptions of and treatment by the local people.

FROM SELF-CRITICISM TO COLLABORATIVE WORK

Although the scope of cultural anthropology overlaps with political science, philosophy, linguistics, sociology, and cultural studies, the discipline has two main characteristics: fieldwork (i.e., participant observation) and ethnographies to present research results. The basic fieldwork method involves conducting surveys over an extended period while living with residents at the field site. From visible living spaces to intangible customs and imaginary worlds, cultural anthropologists compile a detailed account of life in the target society. Underpinning this approach is the principle of cultural relativism, which asserts that no local cultures are superior to others and compels us to recognize each other's values. Thus, cultural anthropologists made an early break from Eurocentrism, supporting the development of Western modern science while also playing a reformative role as ethnographers. Subsequently, in the 1980s, cultural anthropology was forced to change from several angles, and its core practices of "fieldwork" and "ethnography" were called into question.

Regarding fieldwork, a cultural anthropologist suddenly arrives in a community as a member of an NGO. Even though this varies depending on the study location, concerning the informal settlements of Metro Manila in the Philippines (the focus of this book), the anthropologist was anything but objective or neutral. Subjective behaviors and assertions somewhat influenced the target society, no matter how insignificant they were. Moreover, informal settlement surveys were often conducted with government officials or university affiliates. That is, informal settlers knew the anthropologist was cooperating and affiliated with the powers that be; thus, the fieldwork was conducted with this knowledge. At the field site, the study employed the services of an interpreter, held workshops, and visited each family with the community leader. Hence, it seems only natural that the researcher should have a certain influence on the political dynamics of the society under study.

Previously, cultural anthropologists wrote ethnographies as though they were invisible. However, it is inconceivable to remain completely objective regarding the study subjects. Primary sources obtained through cultural anthropological fieldwork mainly comprise narrative descriptions, which may differ per researcher. Thus, a study is non-repeatable. Hence, this study explores the practice of anthropology as a social science, to rid the discipline of humanistic elements after the rise of structuralism. However, if the anthropologist's subjectivity is overemphasized and objectivity toward the target phenomena is insistently denied, cultural understanding is only possible in subjective terms, and a common basis for cultural understanding is overlooked. Therefore, what steps should cultural anthropologists take to secure research objectivity? This challenge remains today as anthropology employs trial and error, having shelved the issue of objectivity temporarily.

The objectivity of cultural anthropologists had already been criticized by Western anthropologists and social scientists, including Clifford Geertz (1973), Edward W. Said (1978), and Pierre Bourdieu (1977). However, Clifford and Marcus, in *Writing Culture* (1986), first criticized the conventional model of cultural anthropology. They argued that ethnographic texts, previously regarded as reports on objective facts, comprised jargon exclusive to anthropology and the authors' political stances. Rosaldo's *Culture and Truth* (1989) also made a similar point: that the descriptions presented by cultural anthropologists confined culture to a closed system, treating it as unchanging, bounded, and self-contained. Rosaldo noted that classic norms had an enormous effect on how anthropologists represented fieldwork results in ethnographies. He identified views influenced by classic norms, examined actions to reconsider them, and proposed that ethnographers represent modern society through a more diverse range of descriptions. Through diverse representations, societies would be positioned more open-endedly globally. As the movement of people increased at unprecedented rates, these new methods of describing societies became necessary.

Since the new research direction was highly critical of the old ethnographic style, the new generation of scholars who sought to widen the horizons of cultural anthropology enthusiastically accepted it. However, more conservative cultural anthropologists widely criticized it. A prime example of this criticism is highlighted in Steven Sangren's discussion in *Current Anthropology* (1988). Sangren criticized Said's *Orientalism* and *Writing Culture* and defended traditional ethnography (1988, 407). In his translation of Clifford's *Routes* (2002, 418), translator Yoshitaka Mouri summarized the criticism against postmodern cultural anthropology primarily comprised the following points:

- Postmodern cultural anthropology is based on textual criticism and reduces the cultural anthropology problems to problems of rhetoric and description in ethnographies.
- It transforms the social practices of the target society into fantasy; thus, the descriptions of cultural anthropologists become autogenous and internal.
- Cultural relativism, which overemphasizes the agency and creativity of field subjects, denies the possibility of social reform.
- By rejecting existing ethnographic descriptions written from the historical perspectives of cultural anthropologists, real-world political and ethnical involvement is lost.

Mouri argued that such criticism fails to properly grasp the direction of postmodern cultural anthropology. He noted that postmodern cultural anthropology approaches the political aspects in ethnographic descriptions and strengthens ethnographer involvement in modern society. Clifford may seem to have raised a more fundamental question common to many disciplines by focusing on the act of "writing culture" rather than its content and questioning the power systems involved in this practice. Accordingly, even if a researcher has a genuine academic interest in a certain research area, this interest would have developed within the restrictions of a certain society and period. For whom are ethnographies written? There should be constant awareness that ethnographies were and still are written more for the societies to which anthropologists belong than for those they describe. Ethnographic descriptions are often treated as a means of supporting authority in the society to which the researcher belongs. For example, some ethnographies are written mainly for submitting a doctoral dissertation. Clifford and Rosaldo's ethnography criticism and proposal for reconstructing the discipline attempted to overcome academic politics in cultural anthropology.

NEW PRACTICES OF REPRESENTATION

In *Routes*, Clifford (1997) proposed a new way of interpreting fieldwork. Rather than the preexisting, narrow concept of long-term participant observation, Clifford saw fieldwork as something closer to travel, which includes a multiplicity of practices involving a large amount of movement. He further proposed the new concept of "everyday practices of dwelling and traveling" under dwelling behavior. Moreover, Clifford questioned whether applying that concept might make it possible to focus on those outside the scope of prior research and develop new descriptions of aspects that went unnoticed during the long-term stays. Thus, Paul Gilroy's *Black Atlantic* (1995), published around the same time, seems to depict the "everyday practices of dwelling and traveling" of black people in the modern period, and is among the first instances of such efforts.

Cultural anthropology has long explored the form cultural anthropological practice should take in the future, the form in which field experiences in the target society should be examined, and how the results should be treated. The attempt involves the possibility of realizing cultural understanding through joint endeavors and incorporating informant perspectives into certain research results in addition to those of anthropologists. It hinges on the notion that ethnographies that can reflect both perspectives might pave the way beyond subjective analysis, reaching a degree of objectivity. Rosaldo's discussion notes cultural anthropological practices based on collaboration. He highlights that the analysis agent must be repositioned over time, arguing for gaining relative knowledge via an agent-subject exchange of dialogue, discussion, and interpretations.

Ethnographic films contain clues to the new practices of representation in cultural anthropology, which were early attempts to present culture. They can be traced to the era of documentary films in the early days of cinema. Similar to the advent of photography, the invention of a medium to record whole movements over time (video recording) provided a highly effective means of "recording vanishing culture" or "rescuing" culture (salvage anthropology), a key concern of cultural anthropology at that time. Although problems existed surrounding the filmmaker and cast identities, various attempts were made to overcome the problem regarding ethnographic films, well before cultural anthropology films. For example, Robert J. Flaherty's *Nanook of the North* (1922) is a famous example of an early ethnographic feature film. It was created using agent-subject dialogue and exchanges. When making films in those days, it was necessary to develop the negative immediately after filming, which was conducted in collaboration with the Inuit featured in the film. In Flaherty's case, this unintended development, necessitated by technological problems at the time, ultimately provided an important clue in addressing the issue of identity. Subsequently, experimental films of the Russian avant-garde[1] and John Marshall's "sequence films"[2] sought to overcome problems regarding the presence of the filmmaker's identity.

Clifford was also interested in the humanities as a place for cultural anthropological output and discussed travel diaries and poetry as possible mediums. Per Mouri's commentary on *Routes* (2002), Clifford's first publication was a study of Maurice Leenhardt (Clifford 1980; 1982). Mouri noted that this ethnography had a strong dimension of collaborative work with the people of New Caledonia and was actually appropriated by locals as a piece they wrote. That is, this ethnography touched on the fundamental element of fieldwork currently needed.

Further, Clifford wrote an essay about museum exhibitions (1997). Comparing four museums around Vancouver (the Museum of Anthropology at the University of British Columbia, Kwagiulth Museum and Cultural Centre (now the Nuyumbalees Cultural Centre), Royal British Columbia Museum, and U'mista Cultural Centre), he identified differences in how tribal communities were represented by the state and the tribes and verified the various power relations that arose when a certain culture is presented. The discussion also addressed how native communities accepted the "art-culture" system of museums in the position of power. Clifford focused on the dominant narrative of national culture formed by the nation-state and its relationship with tribal cultures, arguing that the museum as a facility cannot be restricted to the Western functions of collection and exhibition, and it is, instead, possible to emphasize the narratives of native communities represented by places in which they live, using these as continuations of indigenous traditions. That is, items exhibited by native communities are not treasures (from an already vanished past) to be salvaged but comprise a dynamic mode of living currently practiced in the native communities. The new museum concept aptly captures the perspective of the native communities. Many exhibits now collaborate with Native American artists and tribes, and prior exhibitions involved collaborative work with indigenous curators. Clifford notes that the four museums in his study employed unique methods to combine discourses on art and culture and politics and history. They simultaneously compete and are complementary against a background of changing historical perspectives, unequal cultural descriptions of the tribes, and an unequal balance of economic power.

The cultural understanding realized through such collaborative work does not provide a single clear answer. However, a new intellectual framework can be developed by pushing the boundaries of cultural anthropology and collaborating with other fields and disciplines to explore the possibilities of cultural understanding. It is important to note that architectural anthropology is one strand of such developments in cultural anthropology.

HOUSE RESEARCH IN ANTHROPOLOGY: EARLY PERSPECTIVES

House research in anthropology has undoubtedly been greatly influenced by the dominant ideas and paradigms of each period. The dominant cultural paradigms during the early years of cultural anthropology were evolutionism and diffusionism. In the late nineteenth century, Western powers advanced into Asia, Africa, and South America, establishing colonies over a wide area. Since colonization was an invasion of another country, various logics were constructed to justify these invasions. For example, social Darwinism was formulated, and eugenics was imported from the original biological scholarship to the social sciences. The colonists were purported to be superior to the colonized people, and it was said that colonial rule would lead to the development of economic and political foundations for the modernization of the colonies. Based on this idea, there was unilateral control over local residents and imposition of culture, and the exploitation of local resources was deemed justified. Modern thought is emphasized as the background of such theories, new paradigms were needed to establish a theoretical basis to legitimize colonial policies. Cultural evolution was one of these new paradigms, which also developed in response to the demands of an evolutionary-thinking era and free economic competition established via the industrial revolution. Naturally, research on houses, a central component of culture, was conducted within these paradigms. People need to be fully aware that their opinions and ideas are influenced by their era. With this in mind, this section refers to the theory of homes in anthropology. Satoh summarized prior house discussions within anthropology from the architectural history perspective. Housing classification and analysis methods during the infancy of anthropology are outlined below, referring to Satoh's classification system (1989b).

In *Ancient Society*, Lewis H. Morgan (1972) analyzed houses and house forms through the evolutionary perspective. Morgan saw houses as a form of culture that evolves in a single direction, from savagery to civilization.

Cultural evolution assumes that all cultures develop unitarily through several stages, from primitive to civilized states. The historical phenomena of humanity have an underlying commonality that transcends regions and peoples, and the reason diverse cultures exist is that the pace of each culture's evolution differs, placing different peoples at different stages in this process. This concept was developed by applying theory of evolution to culture; it associated areas considered "underdeveloped" (primitive) with the state of the West before the industrial revolution and placed European civilization at that time at the apex of evolutionary development. In its original form, evolutionism recognized the equal potential for human development in every culture (Spencer 1858). However, as Western modernization advanced, the evolutionary approach was integrated with ethnocentrism, and the original tenets of the theory changed.

Friedrich Ratzel (1896) propounded the theory of cultural diffusion. His theory sought to explain culture through the movement of populations and the spread of cultural items. Leo Frobenius further developed this approach. He grouped areas with shared cultural features into singular *Kulturkreise* (culture circles), reasoning that each cultural feature is diffused within its *Kulturkreis*, and attempted to trace the routes by which cultural traits were diffused. Further, in his research on cultural forms, Frobenius introduced evolution into his concept of *Kulturkreis* (1900). He explained why various forms of material culture exist within a single *Kulturkreis* by incorporating the *Kulturkreis* concept and cultural evolution into his examination of change in building practices.

Fritz Graebner (1911) and Wilhelm Schmidt widened these diffusion routes to encompass the whole world, developing the *Kulturkreis* theory. In *Peoples and Culture*, Schmidt and Koppers (1970) noted that although the cultural traits constituting a *Kulturkreis* coalesce into a single entity, these features are continuously detached and integrated into the diffusion process, thus showing that new *Kulturkreise* contain elements that overlap temporally and spatially with old *Kulturkreise*. Moreover, he noted that houses were also connected to society, an observation in which cultural evolutionism theories and *Kulturkreis* were simultaneously invoked. Schmidt divided culture into primitive, primary, and secondary development phases and indicated that social organization (marriage regulations and kinship organization) and material culture (houses) were related in each phase.

At that time, research culture methods centered on locating written materials in as many cultures and peoples as possible, including materials compiled by government officials assigned to colonies and notes on church missionary work. Researchers established causal relationships by discovering similarities between seemingly unrelated phenomena and described cultural dimensions of the world. Evolutionism and diffusionism shaped every aspect of these pan-cultural perspectives, and house research around that time played a role in this trend. Although various disputes arose between evolutionism and diffusionism, these effectively lost their meaning with the advent of the functionalist approach in the 1920s.

STRUCTURED SPACES

So-called functionalist anthropologists, such as Bronislaw Malinowski (1922) and Alfred R. Radcliffe-Brown (1931), developed the antihistorical approach.[3] During this period, cultural anthropology underwent a major methodological transition. The historical study method, which emphasized the interpretation of materials, gave way to more empirical fieldwork methods. Central to this change was the view that describing culture through phenomena experienced firsthand could lead to a more accurate cultural understanding than the study of materials.

The Savage Mind by Claude Lévi-Strauss (1969) is often quoted regarding structuralism, yet the roots of structuralist thinking in cultural anthropology have deeper origins. The current perspectives of cognitive anthropology and symbolic studies had already been introduced in 1903 in an essay by Émile Durkheim and Marcel Mauss, titled *On Some Primitive Forms of Classification: Contribution to the Study of Collective Representations* (1980). Moreover, the perspective of Durkheim and Mauss was also adopted in Dutch structural anthropology, as anthropologists at Leiden University developed structural analysis from the 1920s. P. E. de Josselin de Jong advanced the symbolic approach to houses and attempted to explain Indonesian social structure through similarities with the spatial housing structures (De Josselin de Jong 1987). For example, he considered it possible to connect the dual division principles within dwellings (such as "inside" and "outside" spaces) to the dualistic mentality of inhabitants[4] and the dual organization of society (Satoh 1989a: 118).

Willem H. Rassers (1959) and Hans Scharer (1963) noted resemblances in structure analysis, spatial division, and orientation concepts by analyzing the dual organization house principles. Bourdieu considered housing structure to be based on systems and shared principles that govern dwellers' worldviews (1970). In *Tristes Tropiques* (1977), Lévi-Strauss identified the relationship between the social structure of the Bororó in South America and the spatial structure of their villages. Japanese scholars also contributed to this trend, through publications such as *Juukyo-kuukan no Jinruigaku* (The Anthropology of House Space) by Naomichi Ishige (1971), *Sumai no Genkei I* (Original Types of Dwellings I) by Seiichi Izumi (1971), and *Sumai no Genkei II* (Original Types of Dwellings II) by Takamasa Yoshizaka (1973). The perspective that sought to discern analogies with larger cosmological orders (macrocosms) within house-space analyses (microcosms) results was patternized and widely reported in research on house symbolism from the 1970s (Cunningham 1973; Bourdieu 1973; Feldman 1979; Muratake 1971).

CRITICISM OF ARCHITECTURAL SYMBOLISM

Right and Left, edited by Rodney Needham (1973), integrated a series of exemplary essays on symbolic dualism. Although the book was ground-breaking for explaining dualism to the general reader, it also encountered a great deal of criticism within anthropology. As house research culminating in structuralist conclusions began to be produced in larger quantities, research on house symbolism was criticized because researchers merely applied arbitrary analytical concepts to the target culture (Satoh 1989b, 94). P. T. Suzuki (1984), who specialized in the study of Indonesian houses, noted that in Jerome A. Feldman's structuralist report (1979), Feldman's object of analysis was restricted to official houses, such as chief and courtesy houses, and excluded those of commoners. Moreover, various other village elements had been sacrificed to imply that the settlements reflected specific dualist spatial concepts. That is, the structuralist approach concerned with identifying correlations between the social structure, worldviews, and order of a certain community and the architectural order of its houses were heavily criticized for aggregating culture, an essentially pluralistic concept, into a monistic framework through patternized reports.

From its early form, where house spaces were connected to certain social structure types, structural analysis of house spaces expanded into meta-fields such as religious views and cosmology. Moreover, the pairs of opposing characteristics used to explain house structures were freely selected from information obtained through methods such as questionnaires and diagrams developed by the observers, as such classification criteria were arbitrary and wide-ranging. Since dichotomous classifications can be established for any society, they are easily selected as points of similarity in various phenomena. However, research models that arbitrarily applied social structures to dichotomous spatial dwelling concepts were strongly criticized for their abstraction of various other items and phenomena that did not fit the model (Sugishima 1988, 200–2).

Thenceforth, scholars began to consider that "if analysis methods based on patternized idea systems are unable to clarify the level and standards of involvement of the researcher, then they are highly defective as methods of describing specific cultures" (Satoh 1989b, 93). Similar questions were raised regarding the ethnographer's involvement in visual anthropology analysis. Timothy Asch (1971) proposed the sequence film as a method of minimizing filmmaker involvement. This approach gave weight to the spontaneously occurring interrelationships among human beings and sought to maintain the order of events while reducing overediting; narration was either unused or restricted to concise explanations. Per Paul Hochings (1981), the sequence film occupied a central position between ethnographic film and writing. The sequence film was initially conceived when, in 1970, Marshall filmed a hunter-gatherer tribe in the Kalahari Desert (1973); the genre placed importance on interrelationships among people over a relatively short period and involved shooting footage of the detailed interplay within these relationships. Subsequently, many questions about the sequence film were raised, which presented naked realities and objectivity in visual form. For example, it was pointed out that there is subjectivity in the selection of the subject to be photographed and its behavior. Therefore, calls were made to publicize details of the filming process and clarify the subjectivities of the film cinematographer and editor (Hochings 1980, 19). This view is also connected to an essential problem with symbolism theory. Just as the debate on symbolic analysis in a society is influenced by the anthropologist's society and worldview, film cannot completely rule out the bias of the filmmaker. However, the filmmaker sought to produce an honest ethnographic film by publicizing the filming process and presenting the degree of its arbitrariness.

AFTER STRUCTURALISM

Bourdieu emphasized that rather than developing a monistic structuralist interpretation of houses, inhabitants view their house as a book while interpreting it unconsciously per period and place (1970). In response to Bourdieu's argument, Henrietta L. Moore noted that the same space takes on different significance per the unique contexts emerging via the behaviors of individual residents (1994, 71–85).

Yamaguchi's discussion overlaps with Bourdieu's notion of the house as a "book." Per Yamaguchi, residents seek clues to decoding the world and understanding culture in their house (1983, 27). Dan Sperber (1979) considered a similar perspective: The various symbols in houses function like books that must be read by the residents, allowing for diverse interpretations.

Lévi-Strauss's "house-based society" theory (1982) is also relevant. It focuses on the notion that in a given society, the house is inherited as an immaterial asset and analyzes the house as an object of rights and obligations. For Lévi-Strauss, the "house-based society" was restricted to hierarchical societies. Many overlaps exist between this perspective and the Japanese family system.

Janet Carsten and Stephen Hugh-Jones analyzed the temporal relationship between construction processes and house styles and changes in family and kinship organization, addressing physical aspects, where the house is considered an accumulation of items, and external aspects of design and structure (1995, 36–42). Carsten noted that family reorganization due to events such as births, marriages, and movement of relatives is intimately connected to the house reorganization.[5] Further, the authors touch on the fact that certain houses accumulate spiritual powers and assets; the relationship between the decorative elaboration of the house's facade and identity, wealth, and power of its inhabitants; and the fact that houses are symbolic vehicles that strongly encourage the recollection of powers and prerogatives (1995, 12).

Waterson insisted that that one cannot accurately understand the house without understanding how it is imagined according to inhabitants (1990). Hence, the house is no longer a reified object, but an invisible entity fused to the image of indwellers. Stephen Sparkes and Signe Howell objectified the "house as image" notion (2003). Images of houses as living spaces vary among societies; Sparkes and Howell explored how the house influences daily behavior and morality formation in society. This perspective, where real spaces are integrated with images, also overlaps with Kevin Lynch's concept of "image-ability" discussed in the following paragraph. Waterson argued that life is maintained by living things and, in some societies, houses (1990, 115–37). Waterson demonstrates how houses are living entities via examples of small island communities in Southeast Asia, where houses are seen as having their own "vital force." This vital force is drawn from various sources, accessed by converting the natural power of trees and the spiritual power of nature through relations with ancestral spirits. The house's life force is reproduced as humans inhabit it; it dies when its inhabitants leave.

Compared with conventional research on the symbolic aspects of houses, analysis of the relationship between architecture and humans subsequently diversified through the injection of situational and temporal dimensions.

INTEREST IN DESCRIBING URBAN AREAS

In the late 1960s, anthropology developed a keen interest in urban areas, where modernization had progressed the furthest. In the former colonies that gained independence after World War II, and in the developing world generally, modernization and industrialization advanced. Given the large-scale population movement from rural to urban areas and transnational labor migration, anthropologists shifted their research focus from small-scale rural societies to urban population centers. By this time, Robert Redfield (1941) and W. Lloyd Warner (1976) had provided a direction for urban research in their examinations of communities in the United States. However, after population flows back and forth into and out of urban areas accelerated from the 1970s, anthropologists began to engage fully with urbanization issues, opening up the new urban anthropology field.

Aidan Southall's *Urban Anthropology: Cross-Cultural Studies of Urbanization* (1973) was a pioneering study in urban anthropology. His discussion highlighted problems that remain important in urban anthropology, such as changes in resident and family relationship roles due to urbanization, migration patterns, hometown association roles in urban areas, and social ties within ethnic groups. Traversing the early view of urban anthropology that changes in urban environments weaken social ties among families and ethnic groups in immigrant societies, William L. Rowe noted the maintenance of family ties and the reconstruction of family relationships in urban areas (1973), which became the basis for present-day migration studies. This research on urban migration included studies where individual spaces were introduced as examples illustrating the behavioral principles of urban areas rather than the symbolic aspects of houses and urban spaces.

TRANSNATIONALISM AND CROSS-BORDER MOVEMENT

From the 1990s, anthropology began to analyze urban areas via transnationalism, borrowed from economics and international relations.

Although transnationalism is an analytical concept for describing phenomena associated with the large-scale globalized movement of people, as signified by the term, the specific act of crossing a national border is an important element when applying it as a concept. In the late 1970s, many Latin American and Mexican immigrants engaged in "return migration" from America to their place of origin. This phenomenon became an important contemporary research topic in urban anthropology and migration studies. Until then, it was considered that, in the long term, immigrants to the United States were assimilated into the urban areas to which they migrated. However, in actual practice, many immigrants also migrated to their place of origin. The main reason for this return migration was not the economic failure of the immigrants in their new urban homes but rather the strong ties they held to their families and communities in their birthplace.

In the late 1980s, a new form of immigration emerged. Rather than dwelling permanently in urban areas or returning completely to the place of origin, "the livelihoods of migrants and their families are not necessarily bound to one location and it is not unusual to move back and forth between the destination country and the home country" (IOM 2017, 15). A phenomenon was reported where migrants, most notably to the United States from Latin America, frequently and continuously visited their home countries. Thus, riding the wave of globalization via the large-scale expansion of transportation systems and rapid development of information technology, this phenomenon spread worldwide. Hence, the concept of transnationalism was employed to accurately conceptualize this new migration type, whose protagonists were neither "permanent migrants" nor "temporary sojourners." Glick Schiller, Basch, and Blanc-Szanton defined transnationalism as "the processes by which immigrants build social fields that link together their country of origin and [. . .] settlement" (1992, 1). Moreover, when they examined the definition of transnationalism, the new definition broadly followed the original (Basch 1993, 7–9). Michael Kearney, who critically examined transnationalism research in anthropology and sociology, also invoked Schiller's definition, defining transnationalism as phenomena that "transcend one or more nation-states" (1995, 548). Moreover, Portes, Guarnizo, and Landolt provided a similar definition as "occupations or activities that require regular and sustained social contacts over time across national borders" (1999, 217–18). In response, Steven Vertovec emphasized the "multiple identifications" and "multiple networks" elements, which, though indicated, were not clarified in Schiller's definition, where transnationalism is "multiple ties and interactions linking people or institutions across the borders of nation-states" (1999, 447).

Vertovec divided the perspective of transnationalism into six major strands: as a "social morphology," "type of consciousness," "mode of cultural reproduction," "avenue of capital," "site of political engagement," and "reconstruction of place and locality." Vertovec also linked the "type of consciousness" strand of inquiry to his discussion of diasporas, noting migrants' identifications with multiple places or areas, notably "place of origin and place of settlement" and "rural and urban." Uesugi examined these transnationalism studies and identified four core elements of the transnationalism concept in the domain of anthropology, namely (1) transcendence of one or more nation-states, (2) long-term continuity, (3) regular and frequent back-and-forth, and (4) formation of multiple identifications and networks (2004).

Next, this chapter considers the meaning of "transcending one or more nation-states," one of the core elements of transnationalism. The English term "transnationalism" has several equivalents in Japanese. The word "*ekkyo*" focuses on the notion of crossing national borders, whereas "*kokusaika*" and "*minsaika*" are closer to "internationalism." Moreover, since these translations cannot fully convey the meaning of transnationalism, the foreign term can also be directly transliterated into the *katakana* syllabary.

In cultural anthropology and sociology in Japan, the term *ekkyo* is sometimes used to mean simply crossing national borders; however, it is also employed in globalization, deterritorialization, and multiple identification discussions (Tokoro 1999). Given migrants' frequent and continuous border crossing, multiple networks across national borders are maintained, and new identifications are created, where places of settlement and origin overlap. Accordingly, it is necessary to accommodate within the concept of transnationalism the situation where immigrants' awareness of crossing national borders diminishes.[6] Once such free movement is possible, numerous similarities can exist between internal and transnational migration phenomena. "Continuous and repeated," "maintenance of multiple networks," and "new identifications" core elements are similar to those of phenomena identified by interpreting rural–urban migrant relations in internal migration studies (Matsuda 1996).

CONNECTIONS WITH ARCHITECTURE: NEW INTEREST IN LOCAL HOUSES

Regarding architecture's approach to the anthropological domain, following the 1964 publication of *Architecture Without Architects* by Bernard Rudofsky, the field of architecture developed an interest in local houses and communities.[7] This development concerned the historical background of the field in that modern architecture failed to produce a new design language. In Japan, in 1965, a Sachi-machi design survey[8] in Kanazawa was employed by a research team from the University of Oregon, and it thereafter became somewhat in vogue to concern oneself with local houses. In the 1970s, several design surveys were conducted to develop new design motifs. The most notable examples include a village survey by the Hiroshi Hara Laboratory (2006) and a spatial survey by the laboratory of the architect Mayumi Miyawaki, at Hosei University (2003).

Although the houses and architecture of various societies were surveyed through fieldwork in Japan and overseas, as survey methods at the house level were refined, researchers gradually began to distance themselves from conventional perspectives on ethnic architecture and traditional village spaces; that is, participant observation surveys to uncover the significance of houses in people's lives. The fieldwork methods were distinct from conventional fieldwork in the anthropological sense, which emphasized mutual exchanges with residents and prioritized refining the field surveying system.

Ethno-architecture is a field largely confined to ethnic architecture studies, which opens up new research anthropology domains from the architectural history perspective. Satoh compiled a four-volume series called *Shirīzu Kenchiku Jinruigaku: Sekai no Sumai o Yomu* (Architectural Anthropology Series: Reading Houses of the World; 1998–1999), which discussed aspects such as house styles, structure, and meanings. This work identified certain problems with architecture's devotion to ethnic houses since the usage of design surveys. Per Satoh, the understanding of houses through surveys between several days and several weeks leads to a hackneyed understanding of culture due to its bias toward surveys of architectural structures conducted in relatively short periods. Further, beginning with Indonesia, Funo surveyed house environments, urban history, and spatial principles in the wider Asian region and presented the characteristics of Asian architecture based on in-depth surveys of living spaces (1991). Although this approach of analyzing lifestyles and dwellings of ordinary citizens through fieldwork from the fields of architecture and urban planning has much in common with the anthropological study method, the degree of mutual exchange with inhabitants is limited.

CONNECTIONS WITH URBAN
SOCIOLOGY AND URBAN STUDIES

Before urban lifestyles were integrated into anthropology, sociology, particularly urban sociology, already attempted to elucidate aspects of urban areas through detailed interviews centered on fieldwork activities. Robert Park and Ernest Burgess formed a research group comprising political scientists and sociologists, later known as the Chicago School, which valued fieldwork surveys as a research method. The group addressed various urban problems, such as migration, living environments, and labor, caused by urbanization in Chicago that began at the dawn of the twentieth century. Per the assumption that the urban development process expands concentrically from the city center toward the suburbs (Park, Burgess, and McKenzie 1925), they proposed an assimilation theory that many immigrants would one day adapt to urban culture. Park moved to the University of Chicago in 1914 and retired in 1936. It is interesting to note that the publication of Malinowski's *Argonauts of the*

Western Pacific (1922) coincided with the period in which fieldwork was established as a research method. Lewis Mumford's *The Culture of Cities* (1938) offered an analysis centered on urban history from the medieval period to date, along with descriptions from fieldwork. William Whyte (1943) conducted a survey of Italian communities in a central Boston slum, where he identified urban structures characteristic of deprived urban areas by examining the activities of local politicians and various people in the communities.

The turning point from examining the formation of a single city and inhabitants' houses in-depth to describing migration on a global scale was Saskia Sassen's global city hypothesis in *Global City* (1991). This text, which interpreted larger-scale movements of people and changes in big cities due to globalization, noted the bipolarized exploitative structures caused by class differences within the city. Subsequently, urban studies flourished as its center shifted from Chicago to California, buoyed by studies such as Mike Davis's (1990) analysis of the political processes of Los Angeles and Edward Soja's (1996) discussion of the significance of space and urban change per an interdisciplinary approach with human geography. The transformation of urban social study into an approach for interpreting urban areas via internal problems, such as culture, gender, and class, and disparities and connections with surrounding areas influenced various academic approaches to urban areas beyond disciplinary boundaries, including cultural anthropology. In recent years, researchers have comprehensively interpreted the relation among urban areas, societies, and people from a global environmental perspective. For example, initiatives by the Japanese Research Institute for Humanity and Nature in megacity domains adopted an interdisciplinary approach, drawing on economics, policy studies, urban planning, architecture, environmental studies, sociology, and anthropology and holistically addressed urban areas from various perspectives (Matsumura et al. 2016).

CONNECTIONS WITH JAPANESE FOLKLORISTICS: HOUSES AS MATERIAL CULTURE

Cultural anthropology considered houses as symbols of cosmologies (views of the world and the universe) connecting individuals and society and considered it possible to understand individuals and society by examining houses in-depth. However, as researchers noted the limitations of the symbolic approach to houses and the challenges involved in understanding present-day urban areas through conventional methods to examine traditional settlements, a new research strand emphasized material culture and focused on the personal belongings found inside the house. An example was *Seoul*

Style 2002, a special exhibition held by the Japanese National Museum of Ethnology. Given the problem of identifying individuality and difference in the homogenous house spaces common to urban areas, this approach sought to understand inhabitants and interpret worldviews and diverse qualities of society through personal possessions.

Hakuboukai (Research Group of Whited Thatching) was composed of architects such as Sotoh Kouichi and Wajiro Kon, and folklore scholars such as Kunio Yanagita, pioneered the notion of focusing on the items inside houses. Since its inception in 1917, architects associated with Hakuboukai have collected house sketches and floor plans, while Hakuboukai folklore scholars have conducted ethnographic studies such as village histories and collections of folktales and folk beliefs. However, the association was disbanded with the death of Satoh, although Kon continued to study folk dwellings and published *Japanese Folk Dwellings* (1922). Further, similar perspectives were adopted by Nihon Seikatsu Gakkai (Japan Society of Lifology), Communication Design Institute (CDI), and Gendai Fuzoku Kenkyukai (Research Association of Contemporary Culture), advancing Kon's approach. Studies on everyday items conduct exhaustive surveys on various house tools, referred to as "durable consumer goods." However, items urbanites possess are generally sold and distributed as products. In practice, a few features distinguish ownership items. Studies on material culture have sought to understand individuality by conducting interviews on aspects such as the acquisition routes and significance of possession of durable consumer goods.

HOUSE ANALYSIS PERSPECTIVES

In cultural anthropology, various methods of analyzing houses have been proposed as ways of understanding culture. Each analytical method involves subjectivity and discretion. Thus, it is impossible to grasp the whole picture of the relationship between houses and humans via a particular method. This section discusses notable points on house research given these limitations.

From Static to Dynamic Understanding of Houses

The symbolic approach to houses held that invisible meanings govern the spatial housing structure, and the same logic operates regarding other cultural aspects. A characteristic of the symbolic approach is that it considers it possible to grasp the whole picture of "culture" through houses. Thus, studying culture through houses assumes an unchanging, static society exists in the house background. However, small-scale communities, the traditional targets of cultural anthropology, feel the globalization effects, which can no longer be ignored. Recent house research has yielded various perspectives on the relationships between houses and communities. Such research has associated houses with the dynamic aspects of social groups and observed close relationships between social-group reorganization and house transformation. What these studies have in common is their attempt to uncover associations between the process of change in house forms and social groups and inhabitants. When studying houses, it is necessary to consider the complex, reciprocal relationships between houses and inhabitants. The dynamic aspects of houses must be considered, focusing, for example, on questions such as what processes occur when inhabitants choose the house location, how the house design is determined through interaction with inhabitants, and when and why inhabitants change the house form.

Researcher Involvement and Relative Understanding

When subjecting houses to anthropological analysis, the question of who oversees analyses and interpretations remains a vital theme. In the discussion of houses, the analytical indicators regarding inhabitants and anthropologists are rarely specified. However, if pairs of opposing characteristics employed in the analysis of houses are selected randomly, the reference to researcher identity is unavoidable. However, when this position is carried to its logical conclusion, it becomes impossible for either the researcher (anthropologist) or the subject (inhabitant) to interpret the house and even more impossible for the researcher to convey an understanding of the house to others.

This book presents the idea of employing "visualized architecture" to consider how inhabitants interpret meanings embodied in the house and how they can be shared with third parties. It then examines the possibility of realizing mutual critical understanding while acknowledging the problem of identity. Researchers and inhabitants interpret the house from different perspectives. Unless these perspectives for relative understanding are maintained, it is impossible to interpret houses as real-world phenomena that evolve.

Worldwide anthropological studies today cannot ignore globalization's influence. Two important elements that sustain transnational people's houses are the indirect communication unbound by place and time facilitated by the spread of the internet and the virtual social spaces not shared in real space. However, direct, face-to-face communication remains constant, even in urban contexts. The next chapters consider the direction of architectural anthropology given the above discussion.

NOTES

1. Dziga Vertov was a Soviet documentary film director and a pioneer of the documentary style along with Flaherty. From 1922, he developed the Kino-Pravda (literally "film truth") series, adopting a style that captured everyday natural experiences. His works depicted people in locations such as marketplaces, bars, and schools and included visual expressions that illuminated social problems.

2. Marshall was an ethnographic filmmaker who pioneered and practiced the "sequence film" method (1973). *The Hunters* (1958), the first of his major works, greatly influenced visual anthropology in the early years. Another important film was *A Kalahari Family* (2002), which documented 50 years of a hunter-gatherer community in the Kalahari Desert from the 1950s to 2000.

3. The historicist criticism at that time did not always reject the notion of diachronic change. According to Lévi-Strauss, both anthropology and history adopted a similar approach by studying societies distinct from the researcher's home society. The difference was that anthropologists were concerned with analyzing phenomena not yet recorded in writing. Lévi-Strauss argued that, even when analyzing synchronic changes, there remained an inevitable need to rely on historical descriptions. (Lévi-Strauss [1958] 1963)

4. Based on their analysis of totemism in Australian aboriginal and Native American societies, as well as the Chinese divination system, Durkheim and Mauss concluded that the criteria for classifying phenomena and spaces were not essential inborn qualities but aspects modeled on social relations. Accordingly, studies must investigate the classification systems in target societies to understand the societies. This proposition is also relevant to Lévi-Strauss's *The Savage Mind.*

5. According to cases studied by Carsten and Hugh-Jones, parents extend and remodel the house when a child marries. The married couple also frequently move to another house after marriage. Moreover, when a child is born or dies or the household is reorganized, the house is often lifted off the ground and carried to a new location by neighbors and close relatives. Carsten noted that while the house is dynamic in the sense of physical mobility, so too are relationships between houses and family or social structures (Carsten and Hugh-Jones 1995, 107).

6. Some social systems materially dilute people's awareness of crossing borders, where special cross-border visas are issued to people living in border regions, such as those of Southeast Asia, and ethnic minorities for whom movement is a central part of life.

7. It is interesting that the period where the focus of architecture shifted from urban to rural and small-scale societies coincided with that where the focus of cultural anthropology shifted in the opposite direction from closed and small-scale societies to urban societies where networks are complexly intertwined.

8. The term "design survey" was first introduced to Japan in 1966 in a survey conducted in Sachi-machi, Kanazawa City, by a research team from Oregon University (Oregon University 1966).

Chapter 2

Circulation—Places That Engender New Knowledge

RECONSTRUCTING THE FRAMEWORK OF ANTHROPOLOGY

This chapter first considers the meaning of "architecture" in the context of architectural anthropology to conceive a framework for cross-cultural under-standing within the cyclical process of "reading, presenting, and making" architecture in the broad sense. The word *architecture* was originally trans-lated into Japanese as *zoka* (house building) before the current term *kenchiku* (architecture) was adopted by Ito (1894). As *zoka* suggests, importance was placed on the practice of building structures. In Japan, much interest has been devoted to the technical aspects of architecture, demonstrated by the fact that the study of *kenchiku* belongs to engineering. However, *kenchiku* is an abstract concept with theoretical and ideological dimensions.[1] Architecture as an abstract concept refers to the spaces between hard structures—walls, floors, and roofs—and buildings they comprise. Simultaneously, architecture also includes the meta-concept of the will and structure that constitute things.

Although the material aspects of architecture tend to be emphasized, this book interprets architecture in architectural anthropology as architecture in the broad sense; that is, as a phenomenon that includes buildings as visible entities and spaces that develop within or between these buildings; places formed through face-to-face encounters, such as meeting places and spaces nearby; architecture and spaces as mental images; and human relations that unfold within dynamically changing spaces.

STAKEHOLDER RELATIONS IN
CULTURAL ANTHROPOLOGY

First, this chapter reviews the state of relations among the people involved in conventional cultural anthropology before doing the same for architectural anthropology. Conventional cultural anthropology has three stakeholders: (1) others, (2) anthropologists, and (3) readers and audiences who consume the anthropologist reports. The anthropologist establishes hypotheses and themes related to a subject of academic interest and conducts fieldwork in a society populated by others. Based on the fieldwork results, the anthropologist then constructs an argument and conducts analysis from a cultural lens. Denote this process as "creation," as it produces a new intellectual framework for understanding "others." Anthropologists must thereafter consider the organizations to which they belong, their position, and any political dimensions or power systems that may have shaped the framework to analyze "others." Next, the fieldwork results are translated by the anthropologist into the mother tongue and publicized as an ethnography. This process also requires a consideration of various problems that arise when translating study results into linguistic form, including who the translation is for and who the agents and objects of the analysis are. Through the translation, the fieldwork results are "distributed," primarily within academia. Next is the knowledge relay from academia to society at large (readers and audiences). Conversely, the results were rarely returned to the fieldwork subjects—others. Notably, when returning the fieldwork results to the field site, the results must be publicized in the local language; if the anthropologist wishes to reach a larger audience, the results must also be presented in various languages, such as Spanish and French. Since ethnographies and the content they present attempt to understand and explain "others," cultural anthropology practices are effectively "consumed" by readers and audiences.

The systems that guarantee anthropological practices, represented by the ethnography, were based on the idea that the anthropologist is an academic scholar, and readers and audiences belong to the same society as the anthropologist (or at least understand the culture of the anthropologist). If the fieldwork results presented in the ethnography are recognized in academia, the anthropologist is acknowledged as a scholar given this achievement and becomes a member of the academic community who participates in reproducing this system. Ethnographies and other research results in anthropology to realize intercultural understanding have been supported by the construction of a common filter based on the intellectual framework developed in the modern Western context within academia. Alternatively, rather than working as an anthropologist in academia, the researcher may opt to conduct developmental and environmental activities in places near the field site. Nevertheless, even outside academia, if the anthropologist survives as a researcher in the broad sense, conveying findings to readers and audiences from the same culture remains the same, even despite a wider audience.

This chapter outlines the people involved in the framework of architectural anthropology. Architectural anthropology has two stakeholders: (1) others and (2) anthropologists. In principle, the third stakeholders of conventional anthropology—the readers and audiences of the same culture as the researcher—fall outside of this framework. The anthropologist begins by conducting fieldwork on architecture in the broad sense in the others' society and constructing a new theory based on the fieldwork results. Simultaneously, the others also interpret architecture in the broad sense as an active participant in the research process. The work between others and anthropologists constitutes a mutual critical interpretation. What mediates between the two parties is the shared framework of visualized architecture introduced in the following section. Next, architectural ethnography is distributed in places where others live via collaboration. Architecture exerts a social impact on society over a period. The others and anthropologists participate in social activities by collaborating on architectural drafts, plans, and construction processes. Previous readers or audiences now consume architectural ethnography by visiting and experiencing architectural spaces firsthand. Thus, it is no longer possible for those involved in architectural anthropology to confine their work to academia. Hence, to create, distribute, and consume architecture in the broad sense alongside others, the anthropologist must be actively involved in others' lives and the shaping of their communities. That is, architectural anthropologists, insofar as they aim for intercultural understanding, are anthropologists and social activists, who, having accepted that they cannot be an insider, must at least become a long-term running partner to the others.

THE ARCHITECTURAL ANTHROPOLOGY METHOD

Architectural anthropology is a proposition for a platform where new knowledge is created by combining academic and nonacademic knowledge and rearranging the three-party framework employed in conventional anthropology. The proposal concerns the creative process, seeking to discover an ideal form of intercultural understanding within this new knowledge framework. It is essential to accept the researcher-subjects repositioning along the temporal continuum of creation, distribution, and consumption to facilitate the internalization of the framework of visualized architecture for others and anthropologists. Regarding the framework effectiveness, despite a recognized need for further empirical evidence, visual expressions do allow for nonhierarchical discussions at the working level with valid transmission effects as a shareable communication tool.

The method of collaboration between anthropologists and others in architectural anthropology comprises three phases. The first phase involves reading architecture in the broad sense via fieldwork. Anthropologists interpret residents' families, social structures, urban awareness, various daily life customs, and diverse house forms. Rather than focusing exclusively on architecture as a built form, they grasp the dynamic aspects of houses during long-term participant observation of architecture in the broad sense. Simply put, they elucidate the contexts embodied in preexisting houses and interpret the dynamic changes where spaces shared by residents, within the houses themselves and in the community, engender new human relationships.

The second phase involves sharing interpretations of architecture in a broad sense. The fieldwork results in phase one are shared with others, and the shared framework of visualized architecture is employed to enable mutual critical interpretations. The third phase constructs architectural ethnography via visible architecture in concrete forms based on the mutual sharing of critical interpretations in phase two. The anthropologist is actively involved in the local society and engages in architectural practices (e.g., architectural proposals, plans, the construction process, supervision, and finance) in collaboration with others. Through the practical process of creating architecture collaboratively, concrete forms that generate new interpretations are created in the society of others. The architectural ethnography developed in the third phase is a foundation for supporting inhabitant lives and is conveyed to phase one of the next cycle as new content to be read as architecture in the broad sense. This method of architectural anthropology is a recursive process from phases one through three.

THE HOUSE AS PART OF A LARGER SYSTEM

There are three reasons for choosing to focus on houses when examining architecture in the broad sense. First, houses can be studied comparatively since houses and shared spaces exist in any group or society. Second, house spaces accommodate basic living activities (e.g., sleeping, cooking, and eating); thus, they are important for examining specific human relationships and social structures. Third, houses comprise the largest portion of the many built forms in society. Moreover, it is important to consider how houses function as a component of social structure.

Consider the case of House A. Assume that all everyday activities regarding House A occur inside the house. Winter life in frigid regions is one such example. In this case, it would sometimes be sufficient to only survey House

A. Next, consider another case: House B. Assume that some of the everyday activities of House B take place inside the house while the majority are spread across society outside the house. Urban life is a good example of this. In this case, the relationship between subjects and House B cannot be grasped simply by studying House B. The house is part of a larger society, including the surrounding environment, the community, and the urban area. A direct mutual influence exists between the important aspects and individual houses. For example, when people select a house, they also select a specific site, neighborhood, and wider urban area simultaneously while selecting house features. By including the housing environment in the examination and description of the everyday life process and consideration of when, where, and how these processes are conducted, it is possible to grasp the House B conditions.

When we consider how the wave of globalization impacts people's lives today, it is no longer common to settle in a certain community and stay there for life. For example, the informal settlements discussed in this book are home to a large number of migrant workers. However, the houses these people have constructed and inhabited could include (1) traditional rural houses in their hometown where they lived since childhood, (2) houses in informal urban settlements in urban areas in which they live now, or (3) houses in the suburbs provided through housing improvement projects operated by organizations such as NGOs. Thus, it is necessary to examine these three types of houses simultaneously.

READING ARCHITECTURE IN THE BROAD SENSE

The basic theme when reading architecture in the broad sense is the interaction between people and architecture. In short, the approach considers what kind of human cultural components emerge explicitly as architectural features and when, in what form, and on whom that architecture exerts its influence.

In considering this point, we must more clearly identify the cultural components at play. Amos Rapoport (2005) considered the main reason that characteristics of relations between people and the built environment could not be clarified is the excessive abstractness and generality of the term "culture." He argued that by dismantling this abstract concept into more concrete elements, it is possible to map the interaction between people and the built environment clearly. As examples, Rapoport recommended components, such as kinship, family structure, roles, social networks, status, and identity as concrete and observable expressions, and categories, such as worldviews, images, norms, lifestyles, and activity systems as even more specific cultural expressions. He asserted that these dismantled components exert differing degrees of influence on the built environment per the period and social conditions. These components can be further dismantled into smaller ones, allowing for easily connecting environment and culture via subdivision.

However, this method has a major problem. It assumes that culture can be dismantled into specific components, which independently influence the construction of environments. Cultural anthropology typically assumes culture to be interpreted not as a tree structure, where it can be dismantled into specific components, but as a "semilattice" structure (Alexander 1965, 58–62), where each component is interrelated. The dismantled components are not independent but interactive. These component groups are not absolute: new (existing) components might be added (removed) depending on the study. It is challenging to establish how multiple components influence a built environment as an objective criterion. Even if it is possible to grasp the relationship between kinship or family structure and the built environment for a specific family, it is impossible to generalize the complex relationships between people and the built environment by merely focusing on associations between discrete cultural components and houses. Next, regarding individualization and generalization, consider how the interactive components of culture exert influence per the following three perspectives: (1) examining individual cases via anthropological and architectural surveys, (2) anthropologically and sociologically analyzing groups of cases, and (3) examining the trade-off relationships among the components in play in the formation of built environments.

Examining Individual Cases through Anthropological and Architectural Surveys

This perspective surveys cultural components, such as kinship, family structure, roles, social networks, status, and identity, through anthropological participant observation and seeks to understand the relationships among individual components, restricting the focus to particular families. This view is where anthropological participant observation is most valuable. Meanwhile, through architectural field surveys of individual houses, the researcher grasps aspects such as the plan, elevation, cross-section of the house, design features, the construction method and process, neighborhood relations, land management methods, and the use forms of the house. These visible surveys are commonplace in architecture. Grasping the spatial properties of houses as physical sensations through architectural surveys is extremely effective when conducting interviews with subjects. By combining the two fields through participant observation and spatial surveys, the researcher can grasp the relationships between people's behavior and the spaces they inhabit. Including seemingly unrelated house components, particularly during primary surveys, and striving to be exhaustive when gathering information are important.

Anthropologically and Sociologically Analyzing Groups of Cases

Cultural anthropology is fundamentally characterized by its focus on deriving general properties from individual cases in the target area through long-term fieldwork by participant observation. Moreover, sociological, statistical methods are sometimes integrated with trend analysis based on quantitative analysis of questionnaires and large data sets already in the public domain. Individual behavior forms are wide-ranging, and it is challenging to draw generalizations from short-term surveys. What begins to transpire during longer field periods are the higher structures through which generalizations can be drawn from the individual cases. For example, the movement processes of individual migrants are wide-ranging. However, nostalgia, a powerful force urging migrants to return to their hometowns, becomes an indicator for interpreting a certain group. When examining groups of cases, a long survey period is required.

Examining the Trade-Off Relationships among the Components in Play in the Formation of Built Environments

Various economic and social circumstances are complexly intertwined in the formation of house environments. Certain cultural components are sought in the formation process, whereas others are sacrificed. Examining the trade-off relationships among these components can help explain the mechanisms underlying the formation of house environments. For example, there is a trade-off relationship between a building site and house size. When selecting a convenient site in the city center, residents with limited economic means are naturally forced to choose collective housing. Moreover, it is challenging to obtain a site and space with room to spare. However, since the area is more accessible due to various means of transportation, frequent back-and-forth travel between the city and remote locations may be possible, enabling closer relations with the home town. Houses, in particular, are highly personal and social. It is necessary to go beyond merely ascribing housing choices, structures, and use forms to the individual, consider the economic and social components behind these choices, and closely examine trade-off relationships.

By comparing (1) and (2), we find that there are similarities and differences between the individualized and collective perspectives. Moreover, (3) examines the antinomic relationships surrounding the formation of house environments, thereby questioning the kinds of cultural components sought to a greater degree and the kinds sacrificed. Introducing perspective (3) into the discussion of survey results based on (1) and (2) can enable the researcher to organize the complex interrelationships among the various components.

THE FRAMEWORK OF VISUALIZED ARCHITECTURE

This section considers the framework of visualized architecture an important medium by which others and anthropologists share mutual interpretations in the second phase of architectural anthropology. The idea of visualized architecture was conceived during workshops for locals conducted as part of a project to improve impoverished areas. By sharing anthropological results obtained through fieldwork and the interpretations of the residents themselves through the framework of visualized architecture, a foothold is established from which to carry out architectural practices (architectural ethnography) in the third phase. Visualized architecture is the concrete visual expression of architecture in the broad sense; that is, "places where people meet and the spaces nearby," "inhabitants' views on their dwellings and urban awareness," and "the architecture and spaces as mental images." More specifically, it consists of two-dimensional (drawings, sketches, flat graphics), three-dimensional (models, architectural forms), videographic (continuous sequences), and specialized (cartographic and diagrammatic expressions) expressions. The specialized expressions are related to all three of the preceding visual expressions. Diagrams are separate entities from the spaces people experience, and a great deal of information is lost relative to real spaces. Nevertheless, the incompleteness of this information transmission narrows the information conveyed and encourages effective communication. That is, the "framework of visualized architecture" can be used as a communication method to provide a common framework for researchers (anthropologists) and subjects (residents). Further, this chapter considers the possibilities and problems of mutual sharing by focusing on the fact that these visual expressions were highly effective when working on improving impoverished areas.

SIGNIFICANCE OF VISUALIZED ARCHITECTURE IN ANTHROPOLOGY

David Harvey's (1989) "time-space compression" became a phenomenon, experienced firsthand due to the expansion of globalization. The notion of questioning the superiority of places has also been advanced in cultural anthropological research, and the reorganization of concepts for interpreting relationships between people and their environments is currently underway. Specifically, due to the rapid development of transportation and information technology, "placeness" is no longer an important component in the manifestation of identity, ego formation, and construction of relationships. The perspectives of architectural anthropology regarding architecture in the broad sense have also shown considerable interest in human relations detached from living spaces, with many studies attempting to reconstruct the concepts of community, state, and identity around keywords such as diaspora, homelessness, migration, and globalization. For example, there have been attempts to reconstruct concepts that originally included local dimensions, such as culture and identity, by seriously questioning the method of interpreting migrants within the dichotomous framework of rural villages (the place of origin) and urban areas (the place of settlement) and displacing the foundation of culture in a transition from "dwelling" to "traveling" (Clifford 2002, 53). Further, by applying the economic concept of transnationalism to the field of anthropology, researchers have explored new methods of study, including attempts to interpret human relationships that cannot be understood within preexisting frameworks such as the state and community.

However, where people share places of living—houses and spaces as concrete-built environments—and encounter each other, relationships are constant. In conventional anthropological house studies in traditional village communities, importance was placed on grasping general trends in society by comparing the differences that arise through the study of community house styles. As noted above, such studies assumed independent societies built upon tradition and included the notion that social structures must reflect built forms in real space. This perspective is not exclusive to anthropology and can also be seen in the architectural approach. Similar perspectives can also be seen in the early surveys of townhouse research conducted by Uzo Nishiyama from Kyoto University (Sumida & NPO Uzo Nishiyama Memorial Library 2007) the design survey of Sawai-machi in Kanazawa City by the University of Oregon, that of Japanese private houses by Mayumi Miyawaki (Miyawaki and Miyawaki Seminar 2003), and surveys of overseas settlements conducted continuously from the 1970s by Hiroshi Hara (Hara Laboratory, Institute of Industrial Science, the University of Tokyo 2006).

The design surveys amid a crisis in modern cities, where traditional values were being torn apart and disordered by market forces and development, progressed uniformly. They examined a certain spatial form and clarified the social and cultural backgrounds and human relationships embedded in that form. The approach held that if it was possible to grasp the correlations between a spatial form and a social structure, constructing spaces befitting the social structure is possible, even if the society changes later. This co-relationality between space and structure is also connected to Chizuko Ueno's observations regarding spatial imperialism (2002; 2004).

While recognizing the validity of the view that specific social structures and worldviews are embedded in houses and community spatial structures, architectural anthropology focuses on real human spaces and the face-to-face relationships among families and inhabitants. It develops suggestions regarding the dynamic human relationships engendered by our concrete, visible environments. When we seek to understand urban areas through impoverished districts, correlations between spaces and social structures are not easily affirmed. As discussed in later chapters, most Filipinos are devout Catholics, and many houses in the Philippines contain crosses and statues of the infant Jesus (Santo Niño) or the Virgin Mary. While this could highlight an association between inhabitants' worldviews and spatial structure, in informal settlements, people are spiritually and economically impoverished. In particular, most settlements examined in this book comprise bricolage shelters, pieced together from various scrap materials. Some houses are built from concrete blocks through gradual renewal, yet the built environment remains distinctly temporary since residents do not know when they might be evacuated. Thus, it is challenging to establish mutual relationships between built social structure and structural forms. Moreover, although architectural measurement surveys are an effective method of house research when one wishes to represent houses accurately in diagrammatic form, the insight that can be gleaned from the physical structures of houses examined in this book is limited.

The framework of "visualized architecture" allows for interpreting urban concepts held by inhabitants and the new dimensions of human relationships unobserved in-house surveys and similar approaches. By grasping the new social structures of residents through fieldwork and researcher-subject idea sharing, mutual interpretations including both perspectives can be obtained.

IMAGE AND VISUALIZATION

This section summarizes various ideas on images and visual representations. Although imagination resembles the concrete experience of perceiving objects, scenes, or events, things experienced are imperceptible to the senses (McKellar 1957; Richardson 1969; Finke 1989). Normally, the words *image* or *imagine* refer to the mental representations of objects or the act of mentally representing objects. However, these words also commonly refer to intuitive or sensory behavior in connection with an object.

In fields such as sociology, social psychology, and organization theory, "image" is a concept akin to "behaviors and attitudes" (Boulding 1956). For example, when a person is asked, "What is your image of Japan?" and the answer is, "Diligent people," the meaning of the word "image" is not of a concrete entity but rather one that is connected to the behavior of a group of people. Further, regarding "image analysis" in art history, the subject is not a mental representation but a concrete image, such as a drawing on paper or canvas, a concrete support medium, a photograph, or a video (Wakakuwa 2000). Icons are similar concepts. They are devotional paintings or statues and objects of reverence that depict Christian gods, angels, and saints. The discipline that studies aspects such as the history, spirituality, and culture of icons is called iconology,[2] pioneered by Aby M. Warburg and developed by Erwin Panofsky and Ernst H. J. Gombrich (Rampley 2001). Iconology is important in image analysis. Although the study objects were originally paintings and sculptures, iconology now applies to subculture[3] fields such as photography, video, and film, encompassing a wider range of objects, including architecture and urban forms (Wakakuwa 1990).

EXTERNAL AND INTERNAL IMAGES

Michael Neuman classified images into two types: the "external image" (W) and the "internal image" (Y) (Neuman 1996). The external image (W) is regarded as an outward representation, an abstraction of reality, representing subjects in forms such as photographs, videos, and symbols. The external image (W) is a visual projection of a concrete form. The internal image (Y) is a mental, concrete form or specific event or scene, similar to mental images in psychology.

Although the internal image (Y) is perceived as a mental representation in the mind's eye, the objects that arouse the image can be categorized into "concrete forms that exist (places)" (A) and "symbols" (C). Internal images (Y1) aroused by concrete objects that exist (A) have less divergence from reality since they capture actual states. In contrast, since internal images (Y2) via symbols (C) do not capture concrete forms, they are greatly influenced by preexisting concepts and social conventions to which the subjects belong. Internal images aroused by symbols diverge from their actual forms under the influence of other similar elements.

Next, consider concrete forms (Y1') and (Y2'), a visual representation of an internal image (Y1) and (Y2). Per Neuman's definition, the external image (W) is an abstracted projection of reality. Thus, (Y1'), a concrete form re-represented through an internal image (Y1), is excluded in this concept. However, the internal image (Y1) originally stems from reality, making it challenging to clearly distinguish between the abstracted representation of reality (W) and the concrete visual representation of the internal image induced from reality (Y1'). Hence, the entire visual construct form (Z). Visual representations W, Y1,' and Y2' are part of form Z. The following outlines the specific methods of representing form Z.

- Two-Dimensional Expressions: This is a form of representation projected onto flat support. The representation method varies per factor (e.g., period, area, and membership group). The view that distinguishes between two-dimensional expressions without depth occurs on the surface of the support. Those that evoke a sufficient sense of depth differentiate representation forms via the terms flat, spatial, and cosmic worlds (Yahagi 2000). As general image representations, two-dimensional expressions include paintings, drawings, sketches, and flat graphics.

- Three-Dimensional Expressions: This is a three-dimensional concrete form, such as a sculpture, model, or origami pop-up. In fields related to the symbolic study of houses (e.g., anthropology, architectural history, and semiology.), three-dimensional expressions are effective as complementary materials supporting theories on the relationship between spatial and social structures.

- Videographic Expressions: Videographic expressions incorporate the concept of sequence (continuity) in two-dimensional representations, supplying an additional dimension of time. People conduct their lives while observing changing scenery and continuous sequences. The word sequence includes a sense of continuity and boundary-crossing and indexes the space that connects the inside and outside. In our lives, we move across a wide variety of boundaries (e.g., in our houses and shared spaces)—unconsciously traversing the internal and external. Videographic expressions are a good way of depicting such social dimensions.

- Geographical and Architectural Expressions: They represent ideas through certain shared procedures that only specialists can understand. Architecture includes methods of expression such as plan, section, elevation, and isometric. Knowledge and experience are required to decode specialized expressions and represent real forms through abstraction. As noted, diagrams are separate entities from human spaces, and much information is lost relative to real spaces. Sharing specialized knowledge can compensate for the information transition incompleteness.

IMAGE EXPRESSIONS IN ARCHITECTURE AND URBAN AREAS

Now, consider visual images in the domain of architecture. Architects have variously responded to the question of how to form images of the built environment and express these visually. Gregory Bateson (1972) held that if we can only interpret the world through our movement, then it is natural to use movement sequences that make use of the dimension of time as an expression of cities and architecture. Similarly, Gordon Cullen's (1971) serial vision technique provided a method for realizing sequential spatial experiences.

If the movement route is depicted sequentially, a visual-spatial experience is formed.

Discussing the city image, Kevin Lynch (1960) attempted to visualize residents' internal image of a city. Lynch defined the city as "an object perceived by its inhabitants," referring to internal images shared by most citizens as "public images," and developed a visual representation of public images regarding Boston, Jersey City, and Los Angeles. He asserted that the city image could be attributed to its physical forms and classified them into five elements—path, edge, district, node, and landmark—and sought to derive effective principles for city design.

Modern architects used drawings and models—three-dimensional expressions—as effective means of representing images. In the unbuilt architectural initiatives, visual materials are often the final product as designers experimented with methods to express their ideas fully. In experimental architecture, examples include Richard Buckminster Fuller's *Dymaxion House* (1930) and Frederick Kiesler's *Endless House* (1924).

Le Corbusier, a pioneer of modern architecture, founded and edited the architecture journal *L'Esprit Nouveau*. Understanding the importance of sharing images through the media, he spread many visual images, from urban plans to structural models, throughout society. His contribution was lauded as follows:

> Through these achievements, Le Corbusier not only succeeded in constructing his own thoughts and devising planning principles but also spoke heart-to-heart with thousands of young engineers and succeeded in directing this young enthusiasm toward a clear objective. Perhaps it is these matters that make his publications stand out as the most valuable contribution. (Sutamo 1953)

Le Corbusier's publications were effective as a method of sharing ideas with society. Ludwig Mies van der Rohe refined modern architecture's prevailing ideology, specializing in a visual expression style that presented images using fewer elements. The Archigram architectural group emerged in modern times. While creating drawings, Archigram represented images through various media forms. Notable examples include Warren Chalk's *Capsule Homes* (1964), Michael Webb's *Drive-in Housing* (1966), and David Greene's *Living Pod* (1965). Since unbuilt architecture is not intended to be realized, the models and diagrams constitute important final products. John Hejduk, the young Daniel Libeskind, and Zaha Hadid were also well-known unbuilt architects.

PREMODERN DRAWINGS

This section considers the state of architectural drawings[4] of the built environment in the premodern period. Drawn images of urban areas and architecture can be broadly divided into the following three types: (1) Images of architecture or urban areas that existed at the time or previously, (2) Images of actual architectural forms to be built thereafter, (3) Experimental architecture not intended to be realized (unbuilt architecture).

Regarding external images (W), per Neuman's definition, (1) images of architecture or urban areas that existed at the time can be interpreted as abstracted representations of reality and images of architecture that existed in the past as "visual representations of internal images aroused by symbols" (Y2'). Further, (2) and (3) are visual representations of internal images and mainly belong to (Y2'). In (1), even if we restrict our search to post-Renaissance images, the architects of the day left behind an enormous volume of drawings. In the late Renaissance, drawings included in Andrea Palladio's *The Four Books of Architecture* (Palladio 1965) depicted architecture that existed at the time and expounded Palladio's architectural works and theory of architecture. Eighteenth-century architect Giovanni Battista Piranesi left behind more than a thousand drawings, the principal motif of which was ancient Rome (Piranesi 1748). In (3), there is a series of prints by Piranesi called "Imaginary Prisons," (Piranesi 1761) which left a strong mark on philosophy and literature.[5] Étienne-Louis Boullée (1784), Claude Nicolas Ledoux (1804), and Jean-Jacques Lequeu (1800), known as visionary architects, left behind countless drawings not intended to be built.

VISUAL IMAGES IN THE CONSULTATION PROCESS

In urban planning, drawings and model expressions are often used because of the need to convey urban-area images accurately to the locals. Jürgen Habermas (1984), John Forester (1989; 1993), Patsy Healey (1997), and E. J. Innes (1998) research the theoretical aspects of the consultation processes surrounding built environments. Cooperation, citizen participation, and communication activities are some of the keywords employed in these studies. In particular, the approach where space-specific visual expressions promote communication is effective in consultation processes at the working level. The following sections examine the role of visual images for consensus-building processes in architectural design and urban planning.

LINGUISTIC PROPERTIES AND
CULTURAL RELATIVITY

Per Mikhail M. Bakhtin, drawings are a basis for true interactive discourse. Bakhtin (1981) argued that using drawings, language containing a mixture of technical terms at once becomes a unified cultural whole that facilitates integrated communication, showing the linguistic properties of drawings and their effectiveness in promoting understanding and sharing information among those involved. Edward Robbins noted that a "drawing serves as the memory of architectural conversations between the client and architect, engineer and architect, or builder and architect" (1994, 37). Further, "the drawing is used to cement and contract agreements between individuals involved in different aspects of the making of a building and serves as a memory of those agreements." In addition to the social functions, he discussed the significance of legacy drawings (Robbins 1994, 37).

Between people who lack a common cultural discourse, drawings enable the sharing and transfer of nonlinguistic content through visual expressions per elements such as concepts and ideas. Thus, drawings can also be considered a form of language. Of the various discussions on the linguistic aspects of drawings, the chief concern has been the ambiguity of drawings. Robbins considered that "while [a] drawing is in general ambiguous, it must work, at certain points in architectural practice, as a clear and direct communication" (1994, 38), arguing that drawings, despite their ambiguity vis their visual wholeness, serve as a communication tool for promoting mutual understanding. Conversely, Stefanie Dühr (2007) noted that when drawings are used, many differing images exist simultaneously among viewers, highlighting the problem that images are perceived through a multiplicity of readings by individuals. The ambiguous nature of images and the relativity brought from individual interpretations cannot be denied.

ROLE OF THE IMAGE

Beginning with the assumption that "behavior is governed by the image," Boulding (1956) considered the role of the image in society, economic life, and politics. He argued that numerous preexisting images encapsulate people, and fixed images acquired through perception are greatly influenced by preexisting concepts and social conventions of society. He then presented a discussion of the cultural dimensions of the image. The notion of associating images with decision-making behavior has been applied in anthropology since the 1970s. Boulding argued that when we make decisions, we imagine several potential futures and noted that correlations exist between images and real behavior. For example, in the international aid activities conducted by the Institute of Cultural Affairs (I), residents' behaviors regarding initiatives to improve impoverished neighborhoods were significantly changed by adjusting future images in more desirable directions, thus clarifying the influence of images on actions.

Further, Robbins (1994, 5) saw drawings as expressions of ideas and emphasized that their social uses must be analyzed along with discussions of representation methods and linguistic dimensions. When considering the role of the image and discussing drawing effectiveness as a communication method, an important task for the future is to examine themes such as the extent to which drawings—as conceptual, subjective, ambiguous expressions—can unify societies and the extent to which they can directly shape the real world while recognizing cultural relativity.

SHARING VISUAL IMAGES IN CONSENSUS-BUILDING

This section examines how visual images have been used in consensus-building processes.

Drawings in Policy-Making and Planning

Dühr noted that, in spatial planning on the wider European scale, cartographic visual expressions effectively convey key components of urban plans to residents (2007). Per Dühr, rather than sharing visual representations as final drafts, clarifying differences in opinion among residents and between residents and governments facilitates consensus-building between the two. In policy-making and planning, strategic spatial planning focuses on maintaining and promoting collaboration with residents through consultations centered on visual expressions. Moreover, case study research has examined the usefulness of visual expressions in consensus-building, including Barrie Needham's (1997) study of Friesland in the Netherlands and Neuman's (1996) study of southern Madrid.

Neuman studied urban plans for an area of southern Madrid called the *Gran Sur* (Great South). Seven municipalities comprise the *Gran Sur*: Mostoles, Alcorcon, Leganés, Getafe, Pinto, Fuenlabrada, and Parla. In the 1980s, Madrid's urban plan changed significantly as the top-down, centrally administered planning process was replaced by a more level process that allowed for multilateral consultations. The essential feature was that it incorporated the "use of visual images" in the planning procedure. Prior images of southern Madrid bespoke poverty and underdevelopment; however, they were swept away by new a new image, aroused by designations such as the *Gran Sur* and metropolitan Madrid, under the revised urban planning objective of redeveloping the region as a new living base in the suburbs of the capital. The *Gran Sur* image presented by urban planners to shed society's negative image of the southern region also functioned effectively in consultations with the *Consejería de Política Territorial* (Department of Territorial Policy).

The *Gran Sur* image was conceived in 1986 by Felix Arias, director of the *Oficina de Planeamiento Territorial* (Regional Planning Office). Initial drawings indicate the strategy of avoiding extreme overcrowding in Madrid and dispersing residents into the suburban municipalities. The initial plan for the metropolitan south was not aimed at widespread development encompassing all seven municipalities; it was originally a strategy for controlling each area. However, Arias saw that the southern area needed to detach itself from Madrid and establish its own unique identity, stressing the need for access roads traversing the seven municipalities. The drawings representing the internal image for the development were redrawn and reproduced by Arias after each round of consultations on the *Gran Sur*. Through this long-term process, the image of the *Gran Sur* garners support among residents and is a factor in the widespread acceptance of the plan. By only presenting broad representations that left room for interpretation, he allowed residents to read images flexibly, bringing settlement to the discussion and illustrating the essential role of drawings.

Drawings in Architecture

Robbins analyzed the social functions of drawings via interviews with architects. He emphasized the importance of drawings as a means of conveying ideas, noting that, "Conception and development of the design are most usually illustrated through drawing." Further, "most articles about theoretical aspects of architecture consist of words and drawings. At times, drawings alone are used to express the ideas of important architectural theorists" (Robbins 1994, 5). Moreover, while the drawing "provides a common mode of discourse with which to deal with the many in order to deal with complex aspects brought to an architectural project by the many different actors who are a part of any architectural making," it is also "used to order and structure the social interactions and social relations of the many actors who participate in a design project." It then "sets social hierarchies, defines a social agenda, and provides an important instrument through which the social production of architecture is organized." In other words, drawings do not always encourage equal social discourse but can sometimes play conflicting roles where power relations are at work.

In planning the Menil Collection, architect Renzo Piano traveled to Israel with his client, where he conducted various information-sharing research activities. During the trip, in completing his design, Piano held discussions via many drawings and left behind numerous drawings depicting his ideas and highlighting plans regarding a roof structure that illuminated the gallery space in soft, natural light. The roof structure was an important part of the design process for Piano, and the roof drawing provides a comparison of the Kibbutz Museum in Israel and part of the roof structure at the Menil Collection. Moreover, other drawing shows notes detailing each room's functions based on the client's intentions in the Treasure House and gallery design. These drawings were used until the end of the design process to share ideas between the client and the design team, substantiating the architectural plans.

In the Pulross Care Center Project, architect Edward Cullinan indicated that drawings operate in a nonhierarchical manner (Robbins 1994). The medical facility in the Lambeth area of London, which provided community-based welfare services, requested a participatory approach involving residents for the design process. The client had already established an elaborate program, operational policy, and accommodation plan before commissioning Cullinan. Thus, Cullinan's office began working on the plan based on these specifications. Cullinan was aware that visual expressions presented in drawings would help the client make decisions during the project.

According to Cullinan's office, the drawings were effective tools for consensus-building during discussions throughout the process from concept building to construction. The point, though, is not that drawings were exchanged between Cullinan and the client; they were also used in discussions among fellow clients. Drawings were used to solve problems between the architect and the client, and they were used for presenting technical and conceptual directions to the client and as a tool for trial-and-error experimentation among clients.

These examples provide a valuable clue to how the framework of "visualized architecture" can be used as a basis for developing critical interpretations between the anthropologist and the others. Nevertheless, we must also remember that this framework entails problems regarding the identities of the narrators of culture, as post-modern anthropology has shown. In the following chapters, this book draws on case studies to consider the processes that occur through the three phases of architectural anthropology.

NOTES

1. For a detailed discussion, see Kikuchi (1958).

2. Aby Warburg conceived the method of iconology. This method was first employed in the "Iconologia" of the Baroque period, which sought to interpret an image (*eikon*) as logic (*logos*). It was subsequently developed into iconology by Warburg.

3. This element generally denotes cultural phenomena that deviate from high culture. However, it transcends both categories of popular and high culture and refers to de-territorialized culture, such as language, religion, values, behavior, and clothing.

4. The functions of the architect are generally defined based on Leon Battista's definition of architecture in Alberti's *De re aedificatoria* (On the Art of Building) (1991); it is considered that the architect occupation came into being during the same period.

5. In novels, see Marguerite Yourcenar's *The Dark Brain of Piranesi* (1984) original text: *Sous bénéfice d'inventaire* (1962).

Chapter 3

Occupation—The
Matter of Dwelling

A CASE STUDY OF READING ARCHITECTURE
IN THE BROAD SENSE: DAANG TUBO

This chapter examines informal settlements within the University of the Philippines via a case study of reading architecture in the broad sense. The spatial features of thcsc informal settlements are extreme narrowness, crowdedness, and adjacency. Further, as these features are forced upon the inhabitants, they deprive residents of normal life functions and engender new places of communal living.

There are 19 informal settlements at the University of the Philippines. The University's development plans have influenced these settlements. Further, university authorities have sought to grasp their conditions and rethink the illegal occupation form of dwelling. Thus, focusing on one of the settlements, Daang Tubo, this section examines narrow-space dwellings from the perspective of the house, surveying five houses. Moreover, regarding relations among the residents, the study analyzes the emergent space relationships between adjacent houses, the cooperative relationships that exist when houses are constructed, and the relationships in shared spaces.

Accordingly, the study conducted an anthropological field survey via participant observation and an architectural measurement survey to grasp the spatial structure of the community and physical aspects, such as house-building methods. Detailed surveys examined internal spaces and spatial structures of five houses. Notably, the survey team partnered with Urban Poor Associates, Inc. (UPA), which frequently works in the informal settlements on the university grounds.

OVERVIEW OF DAANG TUBO

First, the survey examined the current conditions around the field site, the informal settlements at the Diliman Campus of the University of the Philippines (hereafter "UP Diliman"). The University of the Philippines is the only national university in the Philippines, with approximately 50,000 students. There are seven constituent universities located on 12 campuses nationwide; UP Diliman is the University's flagship campus.

UP Diliman is located in the center of Quezon City across an expansive 493.3-hectare site. Per the 1994 Comprehensive Land Use Plan, the primary land uses in the campus were as follows: classrooms and research buildings, 103 hectares (21%); survey facilities and technology centers, 74 hectares (15%); accommodation facilities and staff-faculty buildings, 103 hectares (21%); and open spaces and development sites, 173 hectares (35%). Most of the informal settlers within the university grounds illegally occupy the open spaces and undeveloped areas of development sites, accounting for 35% of the area where they conduct their lives and form unique communities.

During the field survey in 2004 (UPA 2004), there were 19,234 households of informal settlers in UP Diliman, 161% higher than in 2001. The rate of increase was highest in the Old Capitol (1,410%), followed by Pael Compound (615%) and Area 11 (267%). Despite the increasing trend, densely populated and saturated areas have seen little increase (Pook Dagohoy, Pook Ricarte, and Daang Tubo). Thus, residents have begun occupying new open spaces.

The substantial population increase during the three years after 2001 was because of the demolition of informal settlements adjacent to the campus by Quezon City authorities, after which most of the evicted residents moved to vacant sites close to the university. The university site is maintained and managed by a management team at the university, making it possible for residents to avoid any municipal government policies. Metro Manila also has a history of frequent large-scale slum clearances. Every time a slum is cleared, informal settlers leave the area, but instead of establishing new homes in the suburban residential areas provided by the local government, the settlers immediately return to Metro Manila and create new slums. As this process repeats itself, the settlers choose to occupy land with disputable and unclear ownership rights, cliffy sites, and other areas unfit for land development, or areas where it is challenging for owners to request for their removal (De Soto 2000). In 2004, three parties (i.e., UPA, the UP Diliman authorities, and Quezon City) discussed the idea of granting certain occupation rights to informal settlers living on the university grounds. Informal settlers who no longer had a place to go after being removed got wind of the discussion from residents living at UP Diliman and proceeded to secure living spaces on the university campus, which had ample open space. The main reason for the inflow of settlers was the fact the UP Diliman land was stable and outside the scope of influence of Quezon City policy.

The total area of land occupied by the informal settlements at UP Diliman is 51.5 hectares, 10.4% of the total area of the campus. The informal settlements are spread across 19 areas; one area in 1996 (UPA) was dismantled as part of the university development plan and absorbed by the other communities. In 1996, nine sites occupied 10.9 hectares (Daang Tubo, Sitio Lambak and Sitio Kabute, Villages A, B, and C, C. P. Garcia, Old Capitol Site, Ba-Ex/BAI, and Peal Compound). At the time of the 2004 survey, this area increased by approximately 16.14 hectares as the occupied sites swelled by approximately 148% over eight years. Of the eight areas where physical expansion was restricted due to inadequate land,[1] population density increased due to the reason highlighted above. Thus, since Old Capitol Site and Sitio Kabute provided large, open spaces, they became attractive targets.

Regarding the location of the informal settlements within UP Diliman, 10 areas (Pook Ricarte, Pook Palaris, Pook Dagohoy, Sitio Lambak, Sitio Kabute, Barangay Botoncan, Sitio Libis, Villages A, B, and C, and Areas 14 and 17) are located in spaces surrounding a site of around 21 hectares, where the University staff live; and nine areas (Sitio Mabilog, Arboretum, Pael Compound, Ba-Ex/BAI, Old Capitol Site, Barangay San Vicente, C. P. Garcia, Daang Tubo, and Area 11) are located on undeveloped sites occupying 35 hectares. The largest informal settlements are Pael Compound and Ba-Ex/BAI at 12.4 hectares, and the smallest are Areas 14 and 17 at 0.7 hectares each. Most of the informal settlements are located within university premises or on the borders between university and municipal or private land. We can see that only Villages A, B, and C and Areas 14 and 17 are enclosed within the university grounds. Villages A, B, and C were on the west side across the road from the current site; however, given the need to open up the site under the university development plan, the informal settlement was reconstructed in an area adjacent to the residential area for university staff.

Although the university recognizes settlers' right to reside on the land, it does not recognize their land-ownership rights. At UP Diliman, an alliance called *Nagkakaisang Lakas ng Maralita sa UP* (a gradual union of informal settlement residents, hereafter "NALAMA"), aimed at securing land tenure, was established with help from UPA. Of the 19 informal settlements, 12 settlements (Pook Palaris, Pook Ricarte, Pook Dagohoy, Area 11, Daang Tubo, Barangay Botocan, Sitio Libis, Villages A, B, and C, Areas 14 and 17, C. P. Garcia, and Arboretum) pursued land ownership rights, containing 6,274 households built on 28.19 hectares of land at a density of 223 households per hectare.

In two of the areas not included in NALAMA (Pael Compound and San Vicente BLISS), residents pursue extensive individual land-ownership rights. Moreover, the other five areas (Sitio Lambak, Sitio Kabute, Old Capitol Site, Ba-Ex/BAI, and Sitio Mabilog) wish to maintain the status quo (residence rights only). The seven areas not participating in NALAMA contain approximately 12,960 households occupying 23.29 hectares, with an average concentration of 556 households per hectare, approximately double that seen in the NALAMA areas.

DEVELOPMENT PLANS FOR UNIVERSITY FACILITIES

Ten of the informal settlements are affected by the UP Diliman Comprehensive Land Use Plan. Thus, to develop the university, eight hectares of additional land is required, and residents in six of the 10 areas (Villages A, B, and C, the extended portion of C. P. Garcia, Areas 14 and 17, Area 11, and part of Daang Tubo) are required to evacuate under the university development plan. The north of the campus, where there are large areas of unoccupied land, will cater to developments for commercial activities. The south, in the area bordering C. P. Garcia Avenue, will accommodate the expansion of academic facilities; the land will be used for the Advanced Science and Technology Center and the College of Engineering. Further south, a new road (DPWH) is expected to be built, and the land will be used to expand residential facilities (staff dormitories), and similar community service facilities already provided in the north will be constructed in the south. The specific changes are as follows:

- Pook Ricarte, Pook Dagohoy, and Pook Palaris will be affected by the expansion of C-5 (Katipunan Avenue) in the extension of Circumferential Road 5.
- Villages A, B, and C and C. P. Garcia will be affected by the expansion of the accommodation facilities in the south.
- Areas 14 and 17 will be affected by the future expansion of the College of Engineering, including classrooms and research buildings.
- Area 11 will be affected by the commercial development along C-5 (Katipunan Avenue).
- Daang Tubo will be affected by the construction of the Advanced Science and Technology Center and DPWH, which will connect C-5 (Katipunan Avenue) to Kamias Road.

STAKEHOLDERS IN UP DILIMAN

UP Diliman comprises students, teachers, staff, official small-scale storeowners, and informal vendors. Each group shares mutual benefits, experiences, and values at the niversity and occasionally conflicts with other groups that threaten its affiliation or physical place. Moreover, each group is subdivided into smaller groups based on differences in values and degrees of trust.

However, for each group to continue functioning within and benefiting from the UP Diliman community, the various groups must build trust, share common experiences and values, and move in a direction that can satisfy the needs and maximize the benefits of each group. Responding to the needs and improving the benefits of each group does not mean placing the beliefs and values of certain groups above others. There must be a common recognition of the value of cooperation over confrontation—a basic belief that "all of the different groups should be respected equally to develop the UP Diliman community." The respective UP Diliman stakeholders are as follows.

- Students: Students are the largest group in UP Diliman. The student–faculty ratio is 30:1, equal to or higher than large, private universities in Japan. As of 2006, there were about 50,000 students at UP Diliman. Students are central to the University of the Philippines; they primarily aim to (1) receive a high-quality education at an affordable price and (2) use suitable facilities while pursuing a high standard of learning. Maximizing such student's benefits is the basic tenet in the University's policymaking.
- University Staff: As of 1995, there were 5,061 staff members at UP Diliman. This number included 1,358 professors and associate professors; 523 research, open course, and specialized staff members;   2,342 administrative employees; and 838 others. Approximately 1,000 live in informal settlements within the university grounds. The prime concern for the university staff members are the benefits provided in exchange for their labor; that is, their salary, residency rights, housing guarantee, and social security.
- Small-Scale Store Owners and Service Providers: Both formal and informal small-scale stores and service providers operate in UP Diliman to facilitate the smooth functioning of campus activities. Many stores are family run, and despite their small scale, each business provides services to students, professors, and staff members at an affordable price. There are photocopiers, mobile stationery vendors, laundry service providers, electrical repairs specialists, internet providers, and restaurant owners.

They primarily aim to generate sustainable profit by providing services to students and staff members, the largest groups at UP Diliman.

- Informal Settlers: As of 2004, there were 19,234 households of informal settlers at the university. There are 19 communities within the university grounds, also home to official and unofficial service providers. Informal settlers evidently host students in need of an affordable place to stay that is close to the university. Since certain residency rights are recognized despite the informal settlements, the prime concern of the settlers is to gain the advantage in ongoing activities for securing land-ownership rights and secure sustainable economic benefits.

- UP Diliman Management: As the national university of the Philippines, the University of the Philippines and its constituent institution UP Diliman are responsible for providing the highest standard of education as a core facility for education in Southeast Asia. Accordingly, the university primarily formulates suitable development plans for its educational facilities, roads, research buildings, and staff facilities and advances these plans at the university. The number of informal settlers within the university grounds increased rapidly during the eight years from 1996 to 2004. Thus, with numbers expected to increase unless measures were taken, the university, as the landowner, actively addressed these informal settlement issues. However, the university was in no position to solve this problem alone. UP Diliman is an academic institution responsible for providing education; it did not have sufficient experience or a legal framework for tackling illegal settlement on its grounds.

- Quezon City: Respecting the autonomy of UP Diliman, Quezon City left the task of managing informal settlers on the campus to the university. However, as the number of settlers increased, there was a growing sense that it was not just a problem for the university but a serious societal issue. It prompted city authorities to take a keen interest in developments at UP Diliman. By involving Quezon City, the university can use existing development programs led by the municipal government to address problems related to informal settlements. Moreover, the university saw these development projects as a socially sensitive way of educating students. It is also possible to use such experiences in development schemes at the other campuses.

UP Diliman stakeholders go beyond students and university staff. Thus, to maximize the benefits and minimize the disadvantages of these stakeholders in addressing informal settlement problems, it is important to give due consideration to their interests. Due consideration should also be given to the fact that approximately 5% of the total population of informal settlements   (961 households) are university employees affiliated with the institution formulating the plans.

THE PROPOSAL FOR HOUSING IN
THE INFORMAL SETTLEMENTS

On January 18, 2003, a three-party meeting of NALAMA was realized with support from the Mayor of Quezon City, Feliciano R. Belmonte Jr., President of the University of the Philippines, Francisco Nemenzo, and UPA. As noted, NALAMA was established in UP Diliman to secure land tenure, and 12 of the 19 of the informal communities joined this alliance.

During this meeting, an on-site development plan for one of the settlements, Daang Tubo, was presented, formulated in collaboration with NALAMA (Tao Pilipinas, Inc.), a group of local architects and urban planners, for land inside UP Diliman where the development plan for the Advanced Science and Technology Center was underway. Consultations with the university management resulted in a decision to consider a comprehensive housing proposal for Daang Tubo. The university management proposed the view that the housing plan must be comprehensive, encompassing all settlements, to connect the initiative with efforts to solve problems of informal settlements in UP Diliman. A partnership was formed among NALAMA to secure residence rights and desirable forms of urban living on the university premises, UP Diliman, and Quezon City as the university emphasized the need to move forward under a joint project.

PLANNING WORKSHOPS

In 2004, before the housing proposal was formulated, planning workshops involving informal settlers were held in Daang Tubo, Pook Ricarte, Pook Palaris, Pook Dagohoy, Area 17, and Baragay Botocan. The goal was to field requests from settlers regarding housing and the future of their communities and organize feedback as socioeconomic and physical indicators. The workshop results were expected to be used to develop important options to solve the housing problems of the respective communities, where there was a wide range of interests.

Accordingly, residents' responses to various questions and discussions raised in the workshops were influenced by individual circumstances. For example, in a survey conducted in preparation for the workshops, residents from 11 settlements (Ricarte, Palaris, Dagohoy, Daang Tubo, Botocan, Area 11, Areas 14 and 17, Village A, Villages B and C, C. P. Garcia, and

Arboretum) indicated that they were willing to pay a small rent sum to remain on the university premises. However, many participants disapproved of this idea for economic reasons. The workshops revisited the fundamental question: "What is necessary to help the communities develop?" It confirmed the socioeconomic and physical indicators for measuring the basic needs for developing informal settlements. Interestingly, different results were obtained for the indicators per participants' basic community knowledge and house development for residents. Specifically, while there were significant differences in the amount of floor space desired by residents, between 18 and   72 square meters, this decision was influenced by participants' basic knowledge of which housing option—single detached, duplex, or row houses in socialized housing—was suitable for community development.

The basic demands of the informal settlement communities can be grasped through socioeconomic and physical indicators. Settlers primarily want to establish a developed community complete with community facilities, tenure security, social development programs, and happy citizens. The top three socioeconomic indicators were unity (32%), tenure security (13%), and cooperation (12%). These aspects are recognized as minimum requirements for living securely in a community, with a common awareness that unless these indicators can be achieved, it is impossible to achieve anything else. The top-ranking physical indicators were water supply (15%), power supply (15%), houses (13%), and complete amenities/facilities (10%). However, securing basic livelihood needs remains inadequate: residents want livelihood infrastructure to access safely, cheaply, and quickly.

Compared with socioeconomic indicators, physical indicators showed greater variation, suggesting variable individual needs. When asked how much floor space the residents desired, the most common responses were   22 square meters (27%), the current floor space (19%), and 32 square meters (14%). Compared with the results of a survey of Daang Tubo residents in 2004 and 2005, about 80% of floor spaces were less than 20 square meters, and about half the residents wished to either maintain the current size of the house or increase it by approximately 10 square meters. The residents were fully aware of the limitations on the amount of space that could be used and the cost needed to build a house and living standards, which was reflected in the survey results.

ON-SITE DEVELOPMENT FOR THE
DENSELY POPULATED AREAS

Houses constructed along with the improvements to informal settlements in the Philippines are categorized as social housing and governed by the housing law for low-income earners, BP 220 (Batas Pambansa 220), and IRR BP 220 (the Implementing Rules and Regulations for Batas Pambansa 220).

As of 2004, 19,234 households occupied approximately 51.5 hectares of land, giving an average population density of 373.5 households per hectare. Moreover, when the occupied area is simply divided by the number of households, the average occupancy area per household is 26.77 square meters. According to the open space agreements[2] (Presidential Decree No. 1216) between regular houses, at least 30% of the site area must be open space. Thus, suppose approximately 70% of the area currently occupied is buildable, the average floor space of each household would be 18.74 square meters. Per IRR BP 220, however, the smallest site area[3] for a single dwelling in socialized housing is 32 square meters or 218 houses per hectare. Supposing the houses developed are row houses, the area needed for the current number of households (19,234) would be 88 hectares, 36.5 hectares more than the on-site hectares currently occupied by the settlers. Given the unlikelihood that the informal settlers could occupy new land to cover this gap, and some occupied land will be returned to the university for construction, it is necessary to consider options other than developing row houses.

There are 11 overcrowded areas, six in the north (Sitio Mabilog, Ba-Ex/BAI, Old Capitol, Pook Ricarte, Palaris, and Dagohoy) and five in the south (Daang Tubo, Sitio Libis, Barangay Botocan, Sitio Lambak, and Sitio Kabute). Considering that housing sites cannot be secured in any other campus areas, the university pursued on-site development that extended the houses upward. Meanwhile, to improve land-use efficiency, it was necessary to consider positioning services and public facilities most effectively. By pursuing an appropriate course of development, improvements in the living standards of inhabitants of the residential areas increase the house value. Finally, it was also necessary to consider the requests of individual residents regarding land-ownership rights in the Pael Compound and San Vicente BLISS settlements.

THE NEED FOR ON-CAMPUS RELOCATION

As noted, the University of the Philippines plans to build more roads and academic facilities to expand its education and research base. Therefore, the university considered on-campus relocation of the informal settlements in portions of Villages A, B, and C, C. P. Garcia, Area 11, Areas 14 and 17, and Daang Tubo. The number of households affected by the university development plan is approximately 2,123, over an area of approximately eight hectares.

HOUSING DEVELOPMENT OPTIONS
PROPOSED BY NALAMA

Hence, UP Diliman proposed two relocation sites: (1) an area in the north adjacent to Mariano Marcos Avenue, and (2) an area in the southwest adjacent to Camp Karinga, already containing medium-rise housing. The proposal would have affected Old Capitol in the north and the five areas in the south (Daang Tubo, Sitio Libis, Barangay Botocan, Sitio Lambak, and Sitio Kubute).

Regarding population density, Old Capitol has 578 households per hectare while the five areas in the south average 403 households per hectare. If the proposal had been accepted, there would be an average of 246 households per hectare in Old Capitol and 662 households per hectare in the five southern areas. Population density would be much lower in Old Capitol but higher in the south. Two of the communities involved in the proposal, Sitio Lambak and Sitio Kabute, had not been involved in NALAMA activities. These settlements had not received NALAMA development assistance for supporting the urban poor. Moreover, regarding Sitio Lambak, residents did not participate in NALAMA because they wished to receive land as a part of the development to expand the road in Krus na Ligas. Accordingly, of the households to be relocated to the proposed areas, only 4,767 announced their intention to participate in the proposal.

If houses were irregularly expanded or developed horizontally (sprawl), per the minimum standard house area established based on IRR BP 220 (32 square meters), the highest possible population density would be 218 households per hectare. Thus, if 7,154 households were to be accommodated at a suitable density, 11.9 hectares of land—an extra 7.3 hectares—would be required.

NALAMA proposed two options: (1) housing development to accommodate informal settlers and (2) development of row houses, which would require additional land. The premise of the development options was to accommodate the settlers while evicting settlers, since some informal settlement areas must be returned to the university.

The proposal did not consider financial support from UP Diliman. Moreover, considering the poorest group of residents, a monthly rent of 100 Philippine pesos per house was proposed.[4] The NALAMA communities would be required to assume undivided responsibility for the financial management of the monthly rent, maintenance of peace and order in the community, and real estate management. Further, the proposal clarified the need for residence rights to be guaranteed via the agreement with the Quezon City authorities and the university.

Given the areas of the proposed relocations for the new informal settlements, it is not possible to fit the households by building single-story houses. Accordingly, Option 2 was considered unrealistic, since it conflicted with the basic principle of the development: to return the land to the University of the Philippines.

PROPOSALS FOR NEW HOUSING IN DAANG TUBO

Daang Tubo is located in the southeast corner of the University of the Philippines premises. The site area is about 4.09 hectares and contains 786 households (585 living in houses, 154 in rented houses, and 36 in joint houses). Note that the circumstances of 11 of the households are unknown. The population density is 197 households per hectare. If 30% of the site is open space, the average land area per household is about 52 square meters. NALAMA submitted three housing proposals elaborated below. It aimed to return approximately 1.5 hectares of land to the university for constructing the Advanced Science and Technology Center and rehabilitate the settlers on the remaining 2.5 hectares of land.

- Proposal 1: Row houses: This proposal offers the lowest dwelling density by accommodating each household in separate houses. Consequently, the proposal is unrealistic because it is impossible to accommodate all the residents on the site.
- Proposal 2: Two-family dwellings: This proposal aims to increase the dwelling density to accommodate more households by housing two families in a three-story house. The construction of houses in Proposal 2 depends on the residents building the houses (self-building).
- Proposal 3: Medium-rise housing: This proposal aims to increase the dwelling density further to accommodate even more households by constructing four-story houses. Due to the increased dwelling density, Proposal 3 also allows for the construction of shared facilities, including a basketball ground, church, and community hall. However, it would be difficult for residents to build the four-story houses, creating a need for university or Quezon City assistance.

Most informal settlers in Daang Tubo strongly hoped for Proposal 1 (separate houses and plots for each household). However, since it was impossible to accommodate all residents, Proposal 2 was chosen. In this case, the residents strongly demanded to live on the upper floors during the allocation of spaces based on kinship relations. However, given the challenge for residents to build their houses due to a shortage of funds, Proposal 3 was excluded.

BASIC LIVELIHOOD INFRASTRUCTURE AND INCOME

This section examines aspects of the socioeconomic environment, such as livelihood infrastructure and income, in the UP Diliman informal settlements. The discussion focuses on nine settlements, including Daang Tubo.

Livelihood Infrastructure, Public Services, and Utilities

Approximately half of the residents in the nine settlements (50.1%) use water provided by Manila Water Company, Inc. (MWSS). The remaining residents obtain water from private or shared wells, buy water from neighbors, or use water delivered in bottles. Fixed telephone communications are more difficult to access than water and electricity, and only 6.4% of residents have telephone lines (local calls and the Philippine Long-Distance Telephone Company: PLDT); the rate of ownership of mobile phones was 11.4% at the time of the survey. The rest of the residents do not own communication devices and use communal telephone facilities or borrow from neighbors as needed. In such cases, they pay for the call time in cash or with food or luxury items (e.g., cigarettes). Regarding electricity, except for C. P. Garcia, where only 7.7% of residents use an electricity supply, approximately half of the residents (46.5%) use electricity supplied by Meralco. Meralco is the largest electricity distributor in the Philippines and supplies around two-thirds of the country's electricity, including Metro Manila. Meralco's Depressed Area Electrification Project[5] (DAEP) was a yen loan project organized in collaboration with the Philippine and Japanese governments. The electricity supply rate in Daang Tubo, the survey site, was extremely high at 96.0%. The remaining residents without electricity use candles and kerosene lamps. Although housing materials and structure are discussed in the next section, it is useful to note that the houses are mainly constructed with wood and concrete blocks, with 31.5% built from a mixture of wood and concrete blocks, 15% from concrete blocks, and 21.2% from wood. That is, the houses are built from materials that are easy to obtain. Drainage facilities have not yet been developed in the informal settlements, and in some parts of the communities, wastewater is discharged into university drains. The majority of the residents generally discharge water into rivers and gutters running through the communities, creating major public health problems.

Income, Expenditure, and Savings

Regarding income, 27.3% of residents earn between 3,001 and 6,000 pesos per month; 18.0%, 6,001 and 9,000 pesos; and 11.5%, 9,001 and   12,000 pesos. The Philippines' National Statistics Coordination Bureau Research Team[6] defines poverty as the "minimum per-capital yearly income necessary to buy food and cover other basic needs" (NSCB 2005). It sets the minimum threshold at the purchase price of the food needed for an intake of about   2,000 kilocalories per day. Thus, the poverty line for monthly household income for the standard household (five members) in Metro Manila is 7,858 pesos. Accordingly, more than half of the residents included in the survey live below the poverty line. The proportion of residents earning less than 6,000 pesos per month on average was 54% in Villages B and C, 40% in Daang Tubo, 37% in Sitio Libis and Arboretum, 34% in C. P. Garcia, and 33% in Village A, bringing the average daily income to 200–230 pesos per day. These figures constitute the revenue range for peddlers, laundry service providers, tricycle drivers, and inexperienced builders. At least 100 pesos of this small income is used to buy food for the household; transportation expenses are around 30–50 pesos; therefore, the amount left for utilities, medicine, and education is tiny.

It is challenging for these residents to save money. Negative savings, where debt exceeds savings, were observed in Pook Ricarte (46%), Pook Dagohoy (32%), Sitio Libis (23%), Arboretum (19%), Village A (18%), Pael Compound (14%), Villages B and C (13%), and C. P. Garcia (12%). The informal settlement residents long to secure a regular income, even if the amount is small. With the frequent students and staff back and forth, the university is a strategically important place in settlers' search for economic stability. Therefore, the residents have expressed a clear intent to remain at UP Diliman.

Sari-Sari Stores

A sari-sari store (*tindahang bayan* in Tagalog) is a convenience store selling foodstuffs, such as rice, bread, vegetables, fruit, canned items, and confectionery; drinks; condiments and seasonings; cigarettes and other luxury items; medicine; water; and daily necessities, such as toilet paper. Such stores also rent out CDs, cassettes, and DVDs. The stores sell goods down to the smallest unit, including individual cigarettes, catering to the residents of Manila's poorest areas. In Daang Tubo, more than 40 sari-sari stores serve a community of 786 households.

Shopkeepers can expect to earn a relatively stable, albeit small, income. Setting up a sari-sari store involves an initial cost, and having good relationships with others in the community is important. The stores sell goods and provide microcredit to the informal settlers with limited cash income, as well as emergency food and medications, such as painkillers and gastrointestinal agents. From the residents' perspective, maintaining a good relationship with the sari-sari storeowners also provides insurance.

THE HOUSE CONSTRUCTION PROCESS

In the informal settlements, residents do not build first and move in later: they begin by occupying and living on the land. Houses are self-built using whatever materials are available, and houses are gradually improved after moving in. Despite the challenge to define clearly the house construction process along a time axis, the initial period involves constructing a basic house that is just strong enough to provide shelter from the wind and rain. After that, the basic shelter is upgraded into a house made of wood, concrete blocks, or a wood-concrete mix depending on factors such as the duration of residence, available income, building skills, and the house-building assistance policies of NALAMA, the municipal authorities, and the government of the Philippines.

EMPLOYING LABORERS

Although residents construct the houses in the informal settlements, it is not possible to build a house singlehandedly; settlers seek help from others. Usually, in the case of self-built houses, relatives provide the most dependable source of labor. Moreover, when neighbors are enlisted to help, cooperating fully in the construction helps residents build a large circle of acquaintances. In anthropology, such labor transactions have been explained as a traditional behavior pattern displayed by Filipino people. In the informal settlements, most people do not have a regular job, and many day laborers find work on sites where houses and roads are being built. Thus, some community members possess certain housing construction skills (e.g., laying concrete foundations, building walls from concrete blocks, and building roofs). In some cases, residents pay small sums of money to employ engineers, and this system of mutual aid supports the self-building process.

BUILDING MATERIALS

In the initial house construction stage, builders obtain various materials to build the house (e.g., waste wood and roofing material) from destroyed or dismantled houses. Where necessary, parts such as doors, window frames, and glass are bought from private operators that supply self-build materials. Some of the building materials are produced jointly within the community.[7] In particular, producing the concrete blocks and bricks that form the backbone of the houses is divided up and performed collectively with fellow residents. Freedom to Build, Inc. is a pioneering private operator providing architectural materials in suburbs of Metro Manila where settlers rebuild houses, thereby supporting the self-build process. In the 1980s, Freedom to Build, Inc. also established the De La Cost Housing Project aimed at low- to medium-income earners, which has developed houses under the self-build system and sites with suitable living environments at low costs.

TYPES OF HOUSES

Basic Houses (Shelters)

As the name suggests, shelters (see Figure 3.1) provide basic protection against the wind and rain. Most shelters are made of wood and have highly vulnerable structures, cobbled together from whatever materials are available. There is a high risk of collapse due to strong wind or rain. Roofs are often made of discarded corrugated iron laid across beams, with materials such as

Figure 3.1 Basic Shelters in Daang Tubo. ©2021 Fuyuki Makino.

rocks, tires, and concrete blocks functioning as weights. Walls are made from easily obtainable materials, such as fabrics, corrugated iron, plywood, and plastic. The shelter can also be protected from flooding by raising the floor above the ground.

Wooden Houses

Shelter houses are upgraded over time to accommodate more people, protect against floods, or improve the living environment by, for example, extending the bedroom area. During the initial stage, the shelter is transformed into a wooden structure with a certain degree of space and durability. The house, typically built from wood, plywood, and corrugated iron, is still similar to a shelter. However, there can be more durable houses using building materials from private operators. Parts of the house are fastened together by applying joint metal around the wooden framework. Roofs are not uniform but depend on the materials; styles include flat roofs, single-flow roofs, and gable roofs.

Concrete Block Houses

The next stage involves using concrete blocks for certain parts of the house. The concrete blocks are purchased or produced collectively by the community, helping to lower the cost. The house structure is strengthened with concrete blocks for the walls, making it easy to add a second floor. Informal settlers strongly feel that houses made from concrete blocks are superior to wooden houses. In this stage, inhabitants form attachments to the house through the self-upgrading process, and the house acquires its unique image.

CHARACTERISTICS OF HOUSE SPACES

Further, to grasp the spatial structures of the informal settlement, five houses were examined via a measurement survey. The results indicated a spatial structure with various functions, resembling those found in traditional Japanese dwellings.

Nodes

Nodes function to connect the inside and outside of a house and segment its functions. Houses that also serve as sari-sari stores have nodes connecting the store to the living room, ntryways beyond the door that serves as boundaries between the space opened to others and the private space within. Unlike in Japan, for example, no custom of taking shoes off when entering the house exists in the Philippines. People enter the house wearing their shoes; they might change into sandals or slippers or go barefoot. Residents who shop at the sari-sari store are usually acquainted with the operators; they are often seen entering the living room with shoes on after completing their shopping.

In many cases, nodes are demarcated by a portrait of Jesus or a statue of Saint Maria (see Figure 3.2). More than 80% of Filipinos are Roman Catholics.[8] Regarding annual events, Holy Week[9] and Christmas (*Pasko*) are particularly important. During these religious events, the unique characteristics of "folk Catholicism" (Kawada 2003), a fusion of Catholicism and

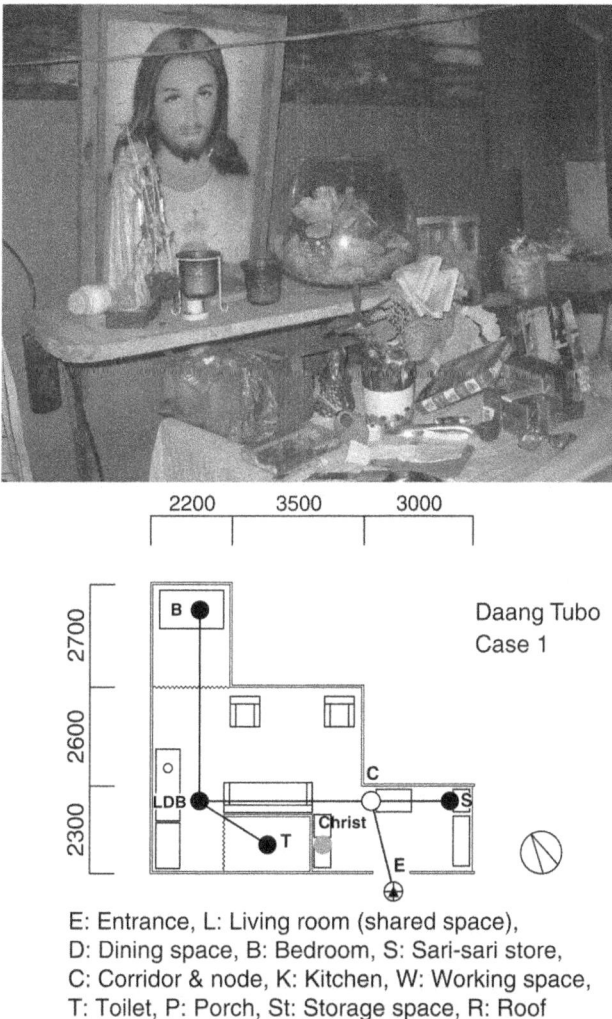

E: Entrance, L: Living room (shared space),
D: Dining space, B: Bedroom, S: Sari-sari store,
C: Corridor & node, K: Kitchen, W: Working space,
T: Toilet, P: Porch, St: Storage space, R: Roof

Figure 3.2 Floor Plan Case 1 and Portrait of Jesus. ©2021 Fuyuki Makino.

native animism, can be observed. In the Philippines, worship of Our Lady of Fátima[10] (the Virgin Mary) and the Baby Jesus (Santo Niño) is prevalent, and impoverished households often have statues of such objects of worship. Worship of Santo Niño came to the Philippines when Magellan gave a statue of the holy child to the wife of the local chief. The beliefs of Catholicism then merged with native religious beliefs. In many modern impoverished areas with young children, worship of Santo Niño and Our Lady of Fátima have educational significance when warning children to avoid evil actions. Thus, in addition to their practical functions in the house, nodes are used as switchover points to the spiritual dimension.

Living Room Space

The living room occupies the space adjacent to the sari-sari store on the other side of the node. While providing a shared space for residents, it is also frequented by other community members; the room leads to the toilet and bedroom(s) located deeper within the house. It is common for the living room to double as a bedroom at night, and it often has both shared and private functions.

Bedroom Spaces

Bedrooms are the only private spaces inside the small houses. In Daang Tubo, the study often observed the pattern where private space is created by obstructing sight with an opaque partition (see Figures 3.3 and 3.4). Most of the bedrooms were located on the far side of the living room, away from the entrance. Whereas other community members often visited living rooms, bedrooms were restricted to functions of storing personal belongings and sleeping. However, since the partitions used to divide the house areas were made from basic materials such as plywood, almost all noises could be heard in the next room. Thus, private space is the conscious division created by obstructing the view of the bedroom.

Dining Spaces and Kitchens

The symbolism of spaces where people handle fire and kitchens containing stoves is a common theme in anthropology.[11] In Daang Tubo, separate stoves were often being used by individual households within the same house (see Figure 3.5). In one such case, the eldest son lived with his parents after marrying and having four children, yet the house contained separate bedrooms and kitchens. Although meals were eaten together with parents in the common living room space, the cooking spaces were separate. A word that frequently

Figure 3.3 Floor Plan Case 3 and Bedroom. ©2021 Fuyuki Makino.

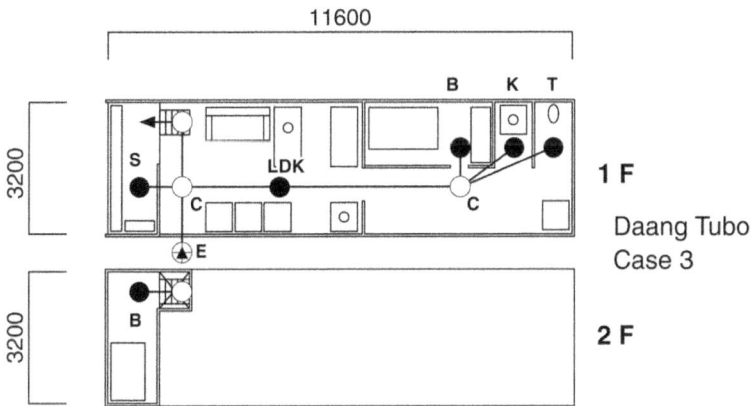

E: Entrance, L: Living room (shared space),
D: Dining space, B: Bedroom, S: Sari-sari store,
C: Corridor & node, K: Kitchen, W: Working space,
T: Toilet, P: Porch, St: Storage space, R: Roof

came up in conversations with the residents was "*pagsasarili*," or "independence." Thus, achieving independence, mainly financial, is a traditional value in the Philippines. The Philippines has a long history of subordination to foreign powers,[12] and there is a strong degree of resistance to coercion by rulers. The residents used the word "*pagsasarili*" to explain the existence of

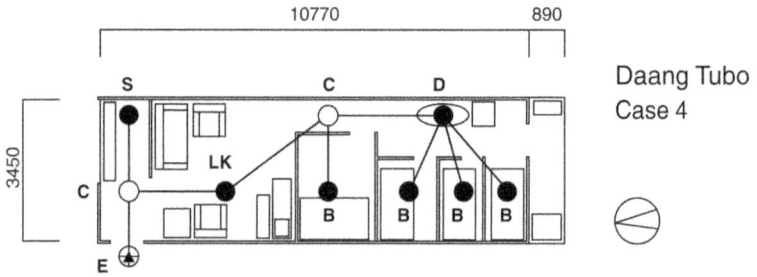

E: Entrance, L: Living room (shared space),
D: Dining space, B: Bedroom, S: Sari-sari store,
C: Corridor & node, K: Kitchen, W: Working space,
T: Toilet, P: Porch, St: Storage space, R: Roof

Figure 3.4 Floor Plan Case 4 and Plywood Partition. ©2021 Fuyuki Makino.

independent kitchens, displaying a strong desire to escape from the poverty in which they lived.

A DAY IN THE LIFE OF A FAMILY

This final section describes a day in the life of a family living in Daang Tubo. Family S has four members (all names are pseudonyms): the father (Samuél, 28), the mother (Nenita, 29), the older daughter (Carla, 9), and the

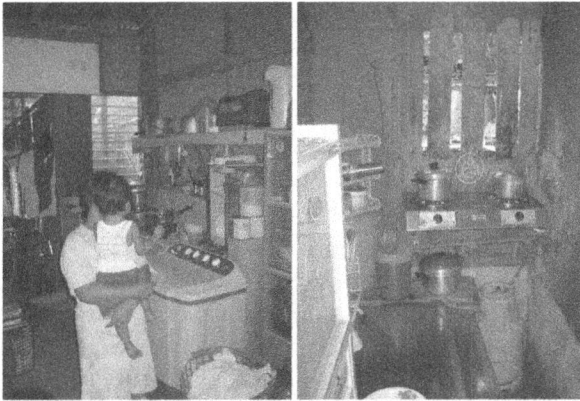

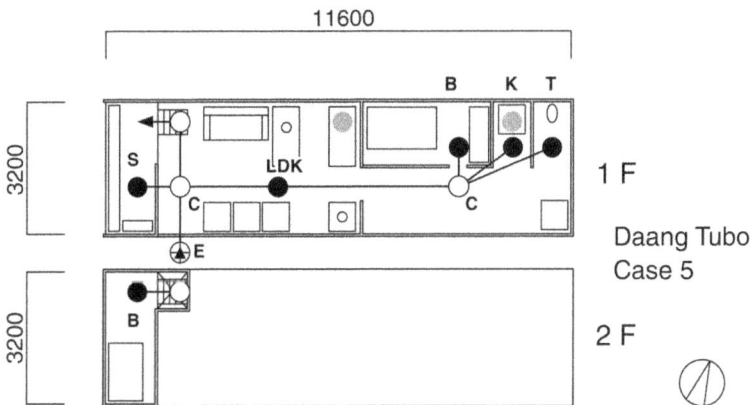

E: Entrance, L: Living room (shared space),
D: Dining space, B: Bedroom, S: Sari-sari store,
C: Corridor & node, K: Kitchen, W: Working space,
T: Toilet, P: Porch, St: Storage space, R: Roof

Figure 3.5 Floor Plan Case 5 and Kitchen. ©2021 Fuyuki Makino.

younger daughter (Juliette, 2). The family's day begins at dawn. Samuél and Nenita wake up at six a.m. Many houses do not have running water; residents fetch water from a communal supply. Family S does not need to fetch water because their house has a water supply. When they have money to spare, they buy tanks of drinking water.

Nenita prepares breakfast. Samuél is smoking cigarettes outside. He usually buys cigarettes at a sari-sari store near the house. He buys them individually, smoking a few each day, not by the pack.[13] For breakfast, they have rice, instant coffee, and the small fried fish left over from the night before. There are two electrical appliances in the house, a radio and a television. In Daang

Tubo, music can be heard spilling out from various places in the community. Samuél delivers building materials. He sets off for work shortly after seven a.m. He generally labors by the day and sometimes works as a construction worker. He also helps out at Nenita's sari-sari store.

After taking Carla to elementary school, Nenita washes the dishes and clothes in the sink. She discharges the water into a nearby ditch. Before lunch, she heads to the house of her mother-in-law (Elma) with Juliette. Lunch is normally eaten at Elma's house and comprises leftovers from breakfast brought by relatives. Nenita then buys sweets for Juliette at a sari-sari store and engages friends gathered there. Although Nenita runs a sari-sari store, she buys items from other stores. The children play on vacant land close to the store, and community friends watch the children together to make sure they do not stray too far. Nenita returns to her sari-sari store and starts work. In the morning, her joint operator Nena is in charge of the store. Nena and Nenita are also good friends.

At three p.m., Carla returns from school. According to Nenita, with assistance from NALAMA, many community children attend school. Nenita wants to keep her children in school, at least up to the secondary (high school) level.[14] She wants them to acquire skills through secondary education and escape from life in the informal settlement. Carla takes Juliette and heads to the plaza. There is a basketball court. While providing a place for children to play, it also serves as the location for the Catholic Sunday service and a community space where residents gather. At five p.m., Samuél returns to the community. He then exchanges information with a friend at the sari-sari store, eats dinner with the family, and heads out to a friend's house. During the evening, there are frequent power outages, leaving the whole community in darkness. After putting the children to sleep, Nenita visits her friend, where they interact, watch television, and listen to the radio. She returns home at   10 p.m. and retires to bed.

IMPROVISED PRACTICES

The term *bricolage* means to tinker or assemble items in a DIY fashion. In France, a person who engages in bricolage is a *bricoleur*, a craftsman who, without establishing an overall plan in advance (or even if there is a plan and that plan changes), can appropriately incorporate pre-gathered fragments to create various works while adapting to changes and new circumstances. In *The Savage Mind*, Lévi-Strauss (1969) introduced the method of using debris and remains to make tools that address immediate necessities unrelated to items' original purposes. Regarding bricolage, Lévi-Strauss likened "savage thought" (*la pensée sauvage*), a knowledge system possessed by humans since ancient times, to bricolage craftsmanship, contrasted it with scientific thought created in the modern period, and considered the question of what constitutes a universal knowledge system.

He considered that myths and their structural patterns are formed through bricolage. Though assembling various social remnants in a certain place produces a heterogeneous repertoire, by uncovering structures among these miscellaneous items through "savage thought," connections are formed with existing social relations, and elements fit into place as if they belonged there all along.

Since the relationships between the whole and its parts are ambiguous in bricolage, these relationships change per their circumstances. When such changes occur, parts that entered the assemblage later may take on greater significance, fundamentally transforming the state of the whole. In impoverished areas, dynamic changes in living spaces, values, or social organization via improvised practices appropriated for a certain time and place, occur within a short time, producing various temporary relations that quickly expire. In follow-up surveys several months later, houses often disappear completely. The exercise of reading architecture in the broad sense in the context of Daang Tubo was also an attempt to grasp these various bricolage practices adopted by community members.

NOTES

1. In Villages A, B, & C and C. P. Garcia, the degree of expansion of the informal settlements is less than 4%.

2. See Presidential Decree No. 1216 and 957 for details of the regulations.

3. See HLURB Resolution No. 579 for details of the regulations.

4. At the time of the survey (2004–2005), 1 peso was worth about 2 cents.

5. Kikuchi and Makino measured social influences from an anthropological perspective in the Metro Manila Depressed Area Electrification Project conducted by the OECF (currently JBIC: Japan Bank for International Cooperation) in September 1998 (Kikuchi and Makino 1999).

6. The National Statistical Coordination Board (NSCB) was established in 1987 under the Ramos administration. It is a government agency involved in formulating and adjusting statistical policy.

7. The materials used to make concrete blocks are cement, sand, and gravel, materials with which builders and laborers in the community were accustomed to working. Workers made sand shifters to produce gravel of uniform size and purchased cement cheaply from construction sites.

8. According to statistics published by the National Statistics Office of the Philippines (NSO), Roman Catholics constitute the overwhelming majority at 82.9%,

followed by Protestants at 5.4% and Muslims at 4.6%. Buddhists represent 0.1% of the population.

9. Holy Week is a one-week period before Easter.

10. Our Lady of Fátima is a title of the Virgin Mary based on a Marian apparition. In 1917, the Virgin Mary is reported to have appeared in a small village in central Portugal, bestowing a message on three shepherd children (Lúcia, Francisco, and Jacinta).

11. Regarding beliefs about stoves, no anthropological discussion would be complete without mention of Zao Jun, the Chinese stove god. Concerning kitchens, "fire" is often discussed in conjunction with the Indian god Agni and the ancient Roman god Vesta (Iijima 1986).

12. The Philippines endured a long period of colonial rule, under Spain (1565–1898), the United States (1898–1946), and Japan during World War II. She gained independence in 1946.

13. One cigarette costs two pesos. A box of 20 cigarettes can be purchased at the supermarket for around 25 pesos.

14. During the study, education in the Philippines comprised six years of elementary education and four years of high school education (the six-four system). The second stage corresponds to junior and senior high school education in Japan and the total period is two years shorter than Japan's six-three-three system and similar systems in other countries.

Chapter 4

Improvement—Self-Build

A CASE STUDY OF READING ARCHITECTURE IN THE BROAD SENSE: THE COMMUNITY MORTGAGE PROGRAM

In Metro Manila, impoverished urban areas occupied by innumerable informal settlers have developed on a wide scale. The number of informal settlers increases every year. Landownership rights are crucial in considering the houses and dwelling styles of the urban poor. Slum-upgradation projects do not function effectively without considering landownership (De Soto 2000). Conversely, there are also many cases where addressing landownership rights has induced residents' interest in improving their houses, leading to successful projects. In the Philippines, the Community Mortgage Program (hereafter CMP)[1] is an effective method of addressing landownership rights while improving people's houses and lives.

This chapter examines several upgrading projects conducted in impoverished areas, where self-build practices were incorporated under the CMP method, resulting in substantial environmental improvements in informal settlements. The discussion focuses on three areas in Metro Manila suburbs: the San Agustin homeowners' association (hereafter HOA), Samarima HOA, and Macoda HOA.

OVERVIEW OF THE CMP

After the People Power Revolution (EDSA I) the CMP, as part of an enabling strategy[2] by the Philippines' Aquino administration,[3] was established in 1988 to upgrade and develop slums and other blighted areas. The program was prescribed in the Urban Development and Housing Act (Republic Act

71

Number 7279) of 1992 and later substantiated in a set of implementation guidelines[4] released in 1996. Then, in 2004, the Social Housing Finance Corporation (SHFC) was established through Executive Order No. 272, and the CMP was placed under its control, along with other housing aid policies. SHFC works with local government units (LGUs) to implement the CMP. LGUs are obliged to provide housing services to residents under the Urban Development and Housing Act of 1992.

Since the 1990s, families in poorer areas have been able to obtain loans to fund housing construction. At that time, 30,000 pesos were provided to build a house on undeveloped land; developed land was financed at 45,000 pesos and a landed home was financed at 80,000 pesos. In the case of undeveloped land, the inhabitants would complete the house through a self-help construction process; then, additional loans would be made if necessary. In contrast, since apartments built on developed land and landed homes are already complete, so loan amounts are set higher. Loans are provided according to the financial situation of the residents; they have a maximum repayment plan of 25 years with 6% interest. From the start of the CMP project to 2001, a total of 854 communities were established and 106,273 households were supported (Mitlin and Satterthwaite 2004); by 2020, more than 300,000 households had received support. Amid the COVID-19 pandemic, from January to November 2020, SHFC provided more than 922.5 million pesos through the CMP. Overall, SHFC has helped more than 11,700 households through 32 projects (Del Rosario 2021).

CMP is a financing system for residents of informal settlements, which transfers landownership rights to settlers where the owner of the occupied lots wishes to sell the land. In target areas, as the land is acquired, plots are rearranged, and infrastructure is established, including water supplies, electricity, and drainage facilities. At the heart of the policy approach is an expectation that, by stabilizing landownership rights, the program reforms residents' awareness of life improvement, promoting improvements to the living environment and house-building initiated by residents.

The CMP comprises three stages.

- Stage 1: Acquisition of land and allocation of landownership rights to beneficiaries
- Stage 2: Development of the area and allocation of land
- Stage 3: Construction and upgrading of houses by residents

Stage 1 involves the most complex procedure for acquiring landownership rights. It involves (a) submitting a provisional land purchase contract (agreement with the landowner); (b) evaluating the land purchase price; (c) submitting the CMP loan application, including plans for infrastructure development; (d) screening application documents and approval; (e) evaluating the mortgaged property; (f) issue of warranty; (g) transfer of landownership rights to the Community Association; and (h) loan and payment to the landowner. This procedure may take several years to complete. Landownership rights in Metro Manila are an extremely complicated matter, muddled by Spanish colonial rule, the confusion before and after World War II, and changes in the political system. Many cases exhibit problems even during the procedure of determining the landowner to begin step (a). Stages 2 and 3 involve the house construction and community development by residents, which is also a long-term process.

The three main stakeholders in the CMP are eligible residents, the NALAMA program operator, referred to as the "Originator," and the Community Association receiving the loan.

Eligible Residents

The area must have been occupied since 1986 or earlier and have been recognized by a government agency to be eligible for the CMP (National Home Mortgage Finance Corporation 1998). Moreover, residents must have lived in the informal settlement for at least two years. Therefore, not all residents living in the informal settlement are eligible for the program.

The Originator

The Originator is a government-approved certified organization responsible for coordinating the overall CMP process from establishing the Community Association to house-building and community development. The Originator is essential to the project, particularly in the first stage, screening beneficiary residents involved in forming the Community Association and preparing and negotiating documents to be submitted to the government in collaboration with the residents.

After stage 1 is complete, the procedures concerning residents' payment of mortgages to the government are handled by the National Home Mortgage Finance Corporation (NHMFC); however, the Originator conducts support activities, liaising between the residents and the NHMFC. Penalties are determined for delayed mortgage payments, and mortgages that are three months in arrears are frozen. Where residents are in arrears for extended periods or evade co-payments, the Originator replaces the debtor.

The Community Association

Under the CMP, residents must form a Community Association with the Originator's support. This Community Association can also be an incorporated organization—a cooperative, HOA, or condominium corporation. The areas included in the present survey established an HOA. The conclusion of a contract of sale between the HOA and the landowner is a condition for receiving the loan. Once both parties have agreed to the purchase, the HOA acquires the designated land by completing the application procedure while receiving a low-interest loan from the NHMFC with the land as collateral. The residents use this loan to make payments to the landowner. The HOA collects the monthly repayments from the residents and pays the NHMFC. With a maximum loan period of 25 years, the HOA has a crucial role in the process.

DIVERSIFIED CMP PROJECTS

The challenge of providing socialized shelters for low-income households is becoming more complex. That is why SHFC launched a new modality in 2019 to accommodate this rapidly evolving field (Social Housing Finance Corporation 2019). It enables the construction of shelters to be carried out quickly and to meet the demand for safe, resilient, and sustainable housing. Some of them have already achieved great results.

Vertical CMP

In November 2019, SHFC handed over Ciudad de Strike 2 in Bacoor City. This project was for 1,500 families who lived in the waterways and dangerous areas of Las Piñas and Paranaque cities. This is a large-scale vertical CMP project with 20 three-story buildings. The amount of financial assistance is 648 million pesos. SHFC also funded the Sulangon Heights Homeowners Association project in Dapitan City. This is Mindanao's first vertical CMP initiative and will benefit more than 600 households.

Post-Disaster Recovery and Rehabilitation CMP

Another new modality is the post-disaster recovery and rehabilitation CMP. SHFC supports community housing rebuilding projects in the event of a large-scale natural disaster. The Guadalupe Homeowners Association, launched in December 2019, received its first support. It helped about 150 families affected by Typhoon Yolanda.

On-site and Site Upgrade/Development CMP

This modality is similar to the traditional basic CMP but is for organized communities that already live in the area without the consent of the land-owner, namely informal settler families (ISFs). It may also be initiated and funded by a government agency or private sector entity in conjunction with migration policy.

Turnkey CMP

Through the development of turnkey-based housing projects, SHFC aims to provide a large supply of socialized housing. A turnkey project is a collective undertaking that allows the finished product to be sold to any purchaser. The turnkey CMP thus aims to sell the finished home to any buyer. Housing project developers are required to comply with a balanced housing development program by participating in this Turnkey CMP.

Other CMP Modalities

Other modalities include: LGU CMP, Sectoral CMP, Culturally Sensitive CMP, Farm Lot CMP, Industrial Workers CMP, Mixed-Use CMP, and Housing for Peace Process and Nation Building CMP.

The basis of these new CMPs is to aim for community development under the initiative of residents. The new CMP has evolved to be accessible and appropriate for beneficiaries.

OVERVIEW OF THE THREE CMP AREAS

The following sections overview the three field sites and examine aspects such as house arrangement in each area. The three areas were selected from the Foundation for the Development of the Urban Poor[5] (FDUP) project, which has achieved the best results under the CMP. The San Agustin and Samarima HOAs were off-site projects, whereas the Macoda HOA was an on-site project. The Samarima HOA was in the second stage (the documentation stage is complete), and the fieldwork was conducted in the informal settlement before the residents moved to the new site. The San Agustin and Macoda HOAs were in the third and final stage.

San Agustin HOA

The San Agustin HOA was formed by residents affected by the infrastructure development of the Simona HOA in Taytay, Rizal Province. An off-site CMP project is currently underway. In December 2003, residents began moving to the relocation site. Funds for acquiring the land were acquired through a CMP loan and microcredit by the NHMFC. Payment to the former landowner was also complete, and the project was in stage three. During the survey, 71 housing units had been constructed (10 units remained under construction), and approximately 60 households had moved into the new homes.

The San Agustin HOA is located in a hilly area on an alluvial fan, with several flatlands along its slope. Blocks 1 and 12 face a wide street, of which three crescent-shaped roads have been built. Residents built their houses along these roads.

Samarima HOA

The Samarima HOA was formed by residents affected by infrastructure development in two areas of Marilao (by PNR Property and Moldex Property). An off-site CMP project is currently underway. The FDUP proceeded to screen residents eligible for relocation, and families that had completed the screening process had already begun moving into the new homes. During the survey, the project was in the initial stage: residents dug a communal well, as the house plots and roads were being prepared. Residents with landownership rights expected house construction on plots via the self-build method, shared-space development, and community development. Though the new environment was better than in the former since the new site was in the Metro Manila suburbs, residents must find work in a nearby town. Thus, they worried about their economic situation.

Macoda HOA

Unlike the other two areas, the Macoda HOA was an on-site CMP project. The area is located between an existing residential area and a tract of farmland. Moreover, residents accessed livelihood infrastructure, such as electricity and wastewater facilities, illegally from the residential area by occupying the adjacent land. The Macoda HOA acquired complete ownership of the illegally occupied land through the CMP, and the land was reallocated to eligible residents.

During the survey, Meralco constructed electricity facilities; the possibility of building roads remained under discussion. Where houses already occupied the reallocated land, the new houses could not be constructed until the existing houses were completely demolished. The house-upgrade effort was not progressing as planned, as old and new houses shared space.

In the Macoda HOA, the drainage facilities were terrible, and urgent measures were required to address flooding during the rainy season. The houses were built with concrete blocks, with many mortared or painted walls. Residents' intentions to construct permanent dwellings were reflected in the housing construction as land-ownership rights are acquired.

THE HOUSE CONSTRUCTION PROCESS

In the informal settlements, houses were built by residents. In areas where CMP projects were implemented, houses were often built using the "core housing" method, where contractors are responsible for constructing the core part of the house, and the residents finish off the interior parts. This method provides a certain degree of structural stability at a manageable cost and generates advantages for both the assistance provider and the beneficiaries.

Next, the study makes an overview of the core housing approach. Core housing is a house-building method used in areas where the development of livelihood infrastructures, such as roads, water supplies, and electricity, is scheduled and set to take place. Partly built houses, typically constructed up to the wall level, are provided to residents, who then complete them by installing a roof and arranging the interior. In practice, the level to which the houses are built varies per project, with some houses having kitchen and house walls and some, roofs. The houses built in the CMP areas are typical of the core housing method. Although the core parts are identical, the houses vary greatly upon completion, depending on finances and the approach of residents.

These days, "core housing" is more than a building method: the term is now used to refer to housing construction projects aimed at low- to medium-income earners. Among the first private developers to implement core housing projects in the Philippines was Freedom to Build, Inc., implementing its first project in the Manila suburb of Dasmarinas in 1974. The company set up an office to supply a wide range of construction materials (e.g., building materials, window frames, and glass) to residents and informal settlers in the target areas. Further, it provides extensive support with construction, including advice from construction engineering staff, helps transports materials, and helps establish building organizations. Moreover, adopting the slogan "Housing by People," the company advanced house-building activities centered on resident participation. Since the 1980s, as a developer of housing for low- to medium-income earners, it has purchased

cheap land in the suburbs of the city, developing infrastructure and implementing projects to provide core housing in the form of row houses and
two-story houses.

Building Materials

In the CMP areas, most houses are built with concrete blocks. In the San
Agustin HOA, before residents move in, houses are constructed by community members from concrete blocks up to the height of the window frames
(approximately 2.0 m). After moving in, residents self-build the portion
above the window frames. Additional parts, temporarily constructed using
wood once the residents have moved in, are gradually replaced by concrete
blocks, and the walls of the house are finished with mortar.

In the CMP areas, individual differences in attitudes toward life improvement were clearly reflected in the houses. Furthermore, the production of
concrete blocks was handled within each community. In the San Agustin
HOA, since all of the houses were constructed using the core housing
method, a facility dedicated to producing concrete blocks was established for
communal use by residents.

Housing Plans

In the San Agustin HOA, the housing plots developed through the CMP were
35 square meters (30 square meters for the house and 5 square meters of open
space). Although Macoda and Samarima HOA plots were of similar size,
since no distinction was made between the house area and the open space,
houses were often built across the plot. In the San Agustin HOA, the basic
plan involved building an almost square room, measuring five by 5.2 meters,
with an attached toilet protruding two meters from the house. The plan has a
bedroom, dining room, living room, and kitchen, demonstrating the attempts
to fulfill various living room functions in one square room.

EXTENDING THE SPACE

Residents expanded the confined houses built in the CMP areas. Vertical
expansion is the most characteristic form of spatial expansion. Since landownership rights are clear, there has been very little horizontal expansion
involving the occupation of adjacent land owned by others.

In the CMP areas, the one-room spaces constructed by the core housing
method were used for various purposes (e.g., individual rooms, kitchens,
bedrooms, closets, and drying areas). Moreover, since concrete blocks were

Figure 4.1 Extending the Space in the Raised-Floor Style. ©2021 Fuyuki Makino.

used for the house structure, a degree of durability was achieved, making it possible to extend the houses for various purposes relatively freely. In the Macoda HOA, since much of the community is inundated during the rainy season, many houses were expanded vertically in the raised-floor style (see Figure 4.1).

Since the houses were small, residents who had acquired their own land through the CMP often transferred their living rooms and dining areas to spaces outside the house. For households with many children, the interior functioned only as a bedroom, and other living functions were transferred to spaces outside the house, increasing the amount of shared space in the community.

The San Agustin HOA observed cases of house extensions. The land was excavated behind a house to make way for an extension. The family planned to pour concrete into this hole, extending the existing house by building a wall from concrete blocks. However, this attempt to expand the land was met with dissatisfaction by other residents. Thus, the construction was terminated per the opinion of the community leader, who was concerned about neighbor-hood relations.

Further, by moving living functions outside the house, certain individual functions can be secured through shared recreational spaces (e.g., pool tables) and community plazas. The indefinite boundaries between personal and shared-use are reflected conceptually and in real space. Residents inhabiting these spaces, where notions of private use and shared use overlap, have a broader view of what constitutes a dwelling. Thus, the community is per-ceived as a single dwelling.

USE OF SPACE

Mirroring the findings of the previous chapter, characteristic uses of space in the CMP areas include the creation of private rooms and the use of separate kitchens. The main reason for creating private spaces was to secure bed space, and several similarities were observed regarding the methods used to achieve this purpose. Two methods were used to separate rooms: "semitransparent partitions" and "opaque partitions." The semitransparent partitions were made from semi-see-through materials, such as curtains, to create private rooms without creating a feeling of oppression. Moreover, by introducing different levels within the room and changing the view position, steps were taken to create a sense of moderate partitioning even though the room was not physically divided. These steps allow residents to dwell in the confined space without feeling oppressed (see Figure 4.2, 4.3, 4.4, 4.5, and 4.6).

The opaque partitions were made from non-see-through materials, such as plywood, to divide the room into private areas. Moreover, many residents secured bed space by creating closed spaces, using lofts and split floors. Even private spaces divided by opaque partitions were largely ineffective in terms of sound insulation.

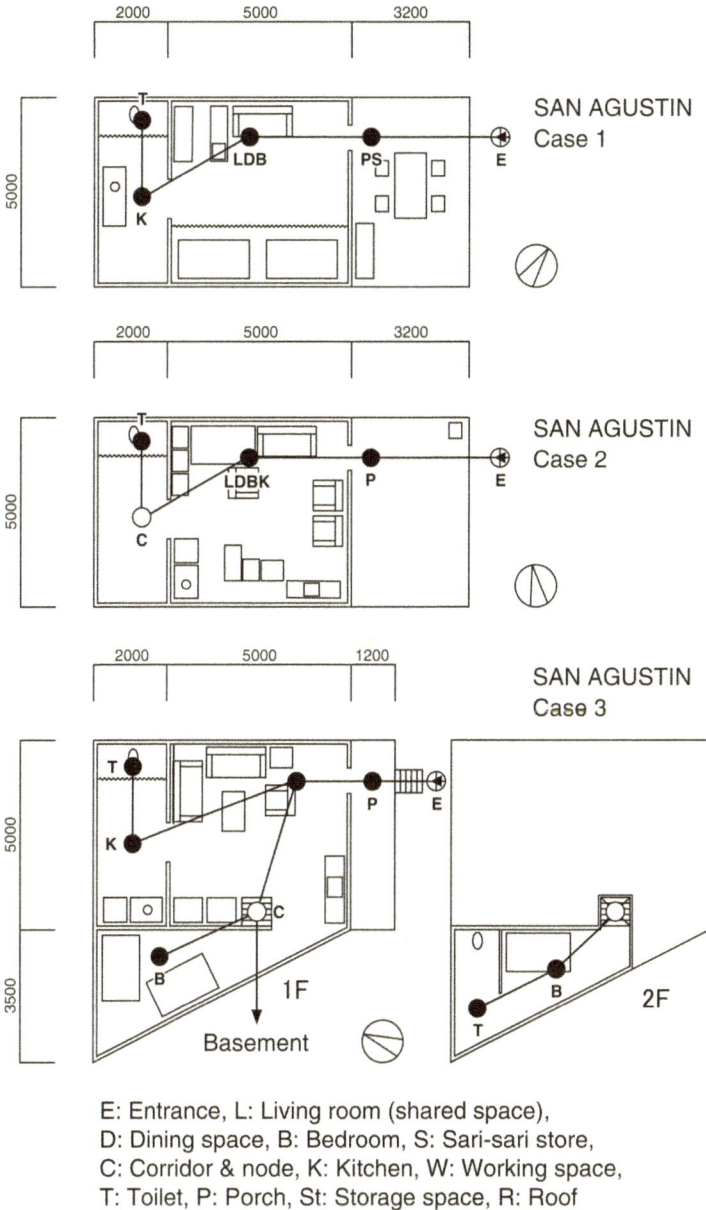

Figure 4.2 Floor Plan in San Agustin HOA Case 1–3. ©2021 Fuyuki Makino.

E: Entrance, L: Living room (shared space),
D: Dining space, B: Bedroom, S: Sari-sari store,
C: Corridor & node, K: Kitchen, W: Working space,
T: Toilet, P: Porch, St: Storage space, R: Roof

When the targets of support under the CMP were selected to screen and approve individual households, the basic system was one household per house. However, multiple families often share a single house. In these cases,

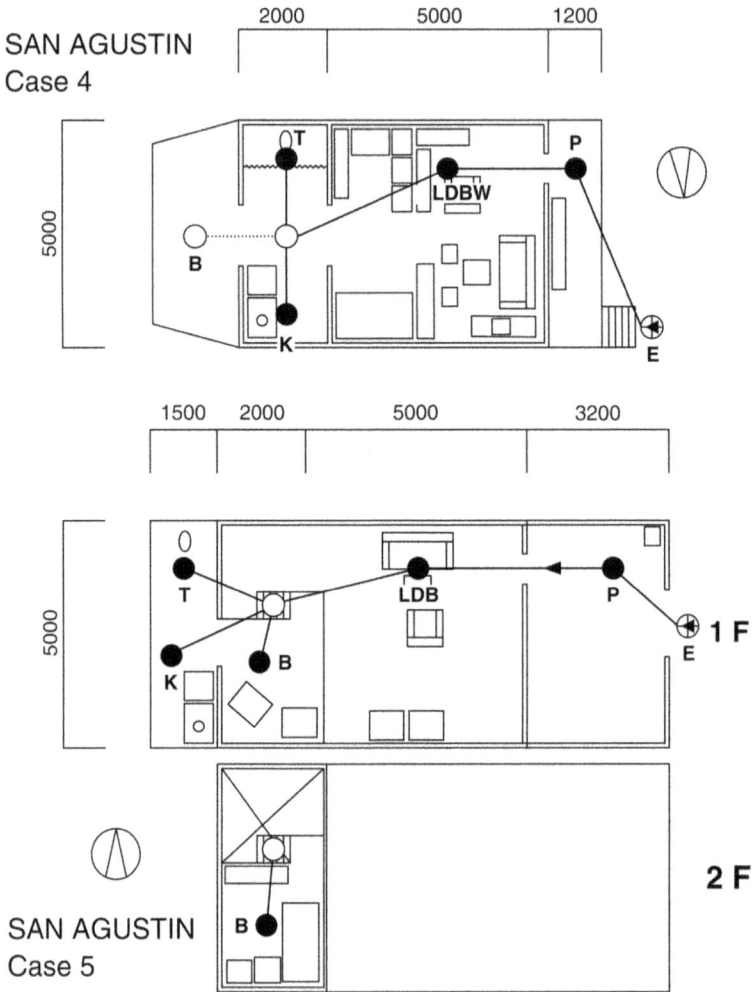

E: Entrance, L: Living room (shared space),
D: Dining space, B: Bedroom, S: Sari-sari store,
C: Corridor & node, K: Kitchen, W: Working space,
T: Toilet, P: Porch, St: Storage space, R: Roof

Figure 4.3 Floor Plan in San Agustin HOA Case 4–5. ©2021 Fuyuki Makino.

separate kitchen spaces are created for each family, and living functions are divided within the house. This use of separate kitchen spaces was also observed in the informal settlements of UP Diliman.

Many houses have workspaces. One similarity among CMP areas is that men often work outside the community, and women raise the children, work in the community, and do the housework.

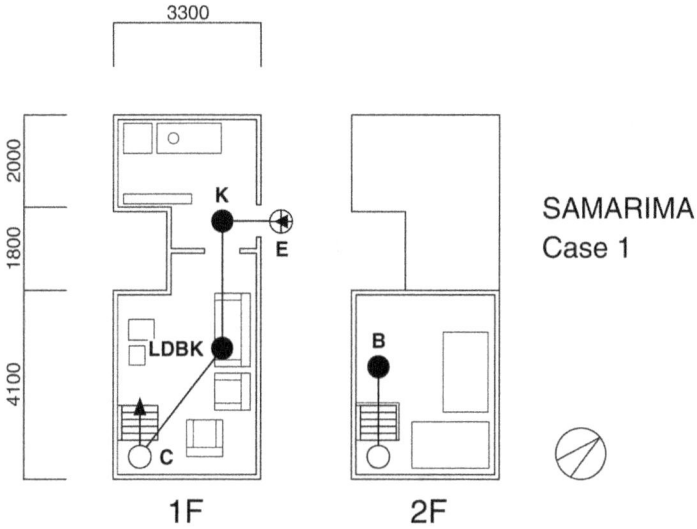

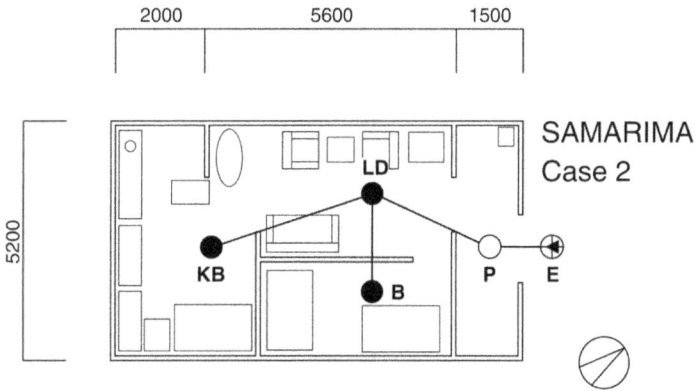

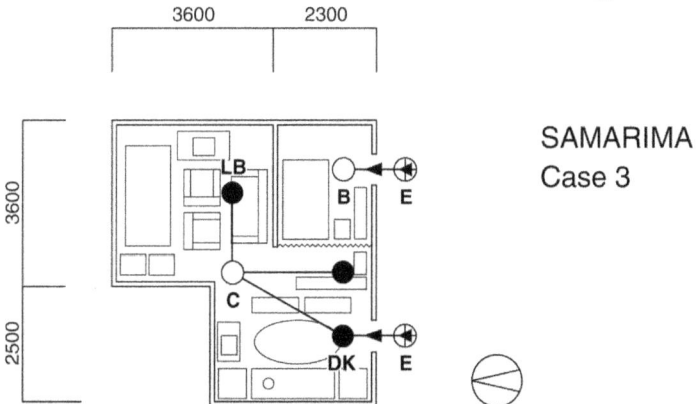

Figure 4.4 Floor Plan in SAMARIMA HOA Case 1–3. ©2021 Fuyuki Makino.

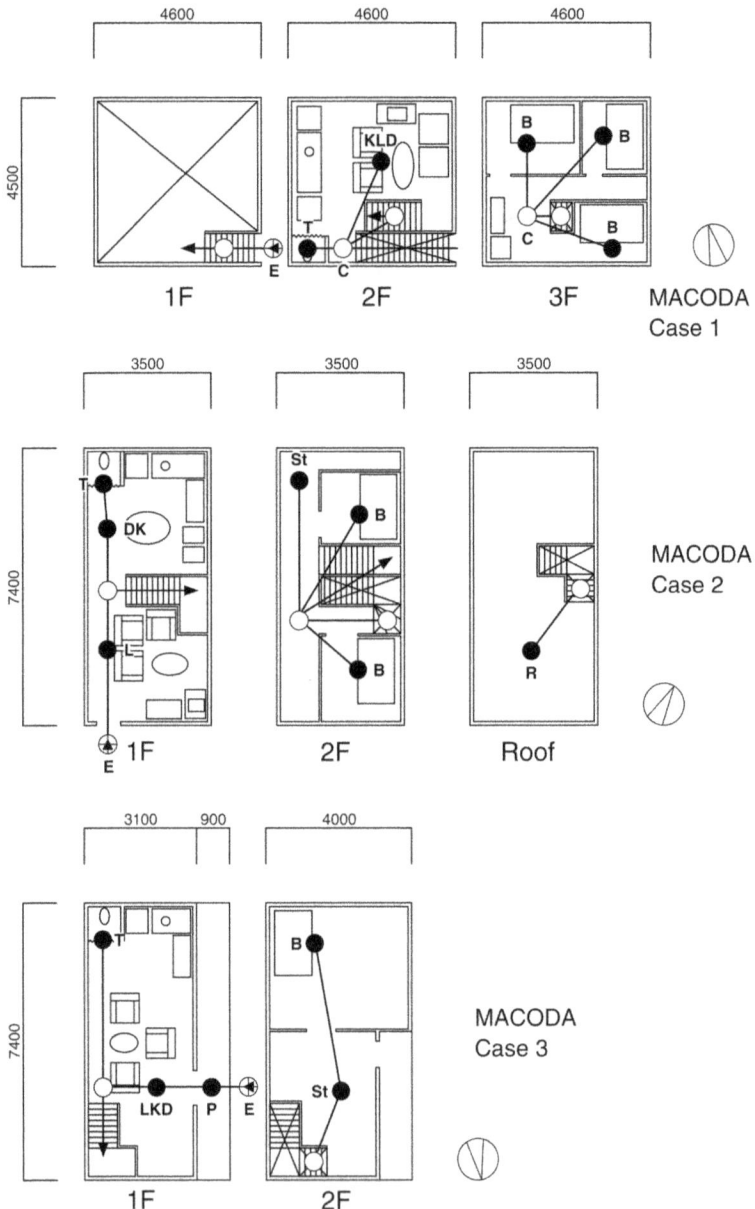

Figure 4.5 Floor Plan in MACODA HOA Case 1–3. ©2021 Fuyuki Makino.

The sari-sari store is a typical example of a workspace inside the house. As is the case at UP Diliman, many sari-sari stores were observed in communities developed under the CMP. Residents also engaged in various other types of

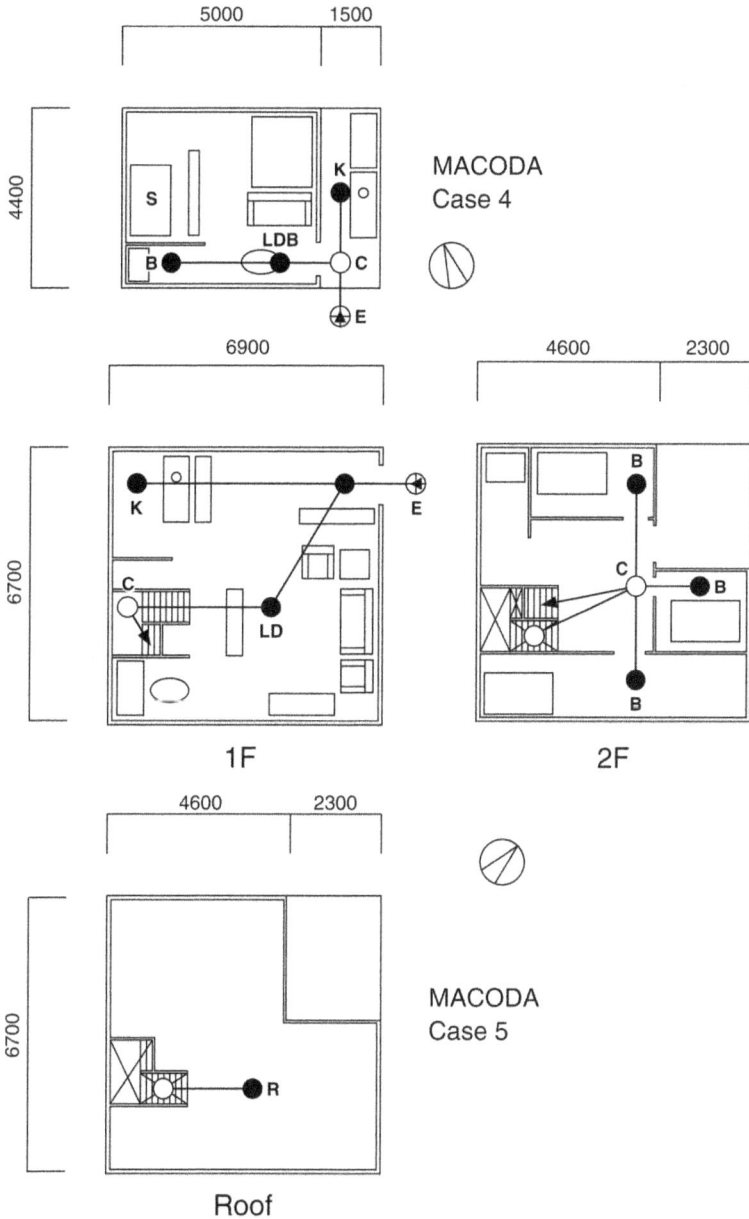

Figure 4.6 Floor Plan in MACODA HOA Case 4–5. ©2021 Fuyuki Makino.

homework, including sewing and operating electrical stores, beauty salons, and eateries.

INDEPENDENT LIVING SPACES

A common characteristic of the three areas of the San Agustin, Macoda, and Samarima HOAs is the desire among married couples living with parents to establish independent living spaces. It reflects the traditional dwelling style where couples establish independent living spaces after marriage (Racelis 1967). However, faced with severe economic conditions, residents cannot build their own houses, which creates a need to improvise with the small house instead. The following section examines common features observed in the survey areas across three cases from the perspective of relations among cohabitants.

Nuclear Family (Separate Rooms as Children Grow Up: San Agustin)

As the children grow up, private space is needed inside the house. In the San Agustin HOA case, the one-room building is divided into two main areas: a living room and a bedroom, moderately partitioned by a thin curtain. The room, lighted by the south-facing window, is sufficiently airy. The children sleep in comfortable bed space. Moreover, the living room, reduced in size, does not give a feeling of oppression given the curtain's moderate partitioning effect. The wife of the eldest son in Survey House No. 1 said: "The room is already small, so we don't want to divide it with a wall. We're family, so we don't need separate rooms. When the children grow up, we want to build a second floor and use that as our bed space."

Extended Family (Separate Rooms for Each Household: Macoda HOA)

For extended families, there are cases where separate rooms are created for each nuclear family. In the Macoda HOA case, seven people live in one house—the father, the mother, the eldest daughter, the eldest daughter's husband, their child, the second daughter, and the mother's younger sister. The bedrooms, which must serve seven people, are located on the second floor; the first floor provides shared space for the family and contains a living-room-cum-kitchen and a toilet. In the second-floor bedrooms, the eldest daughter sleeps with her husband; the second daughter, her mother's younger sister; and the mother and father, their grandchild.

Cohabitation of Multiple Families (Dwelling with Non-Relatives: Samarima HOA)

Cohabitation involving multiple families is rare in the CMP areas. This case was discovered in the community of the Samarima HOA before the residents moved. Two motherless families were living in one house. The owner of the house had four children (two boys and two girls). There were five people in the family because the man's wife had passed away. He worked as an elementary school teacher and lent a room to his friend's family, but he was not receiving rent because his friend was unemployed. Space was divided between the two families using plywood sheets, giving the appearance of two completely separate living areas. The situation benefited both families since the friend looked after the children while the house owner was at work.

> At first, I planned to lend him the room temporarily, but we've been living together now for about six months. It's helpful that he looks after the children while I'm at work, but we're moving soon [because of] the CMP, so I also have to look for work. I think my friend will continue living in this house after we move out. (Father: Survey House No. 7)

RECONSTRUCTION OF RESIDENT RELATIONS

The community associations in the CMP areas (i.e., organizations formed by informal settlers) are united by the common purpose of improving life in the settlements and obtaining landownership rights. Therefore, many of the residents belonging to these organizations have different birthplaces and, sometimes, different languages or religions. Moreover, in the off-site CMP areas, the neighborhood relations that have been maintained among residents were severed in the relocation process, making it necessary to reconstruct resident relations at the relocation site.

For example, the San Agustin HOA is located in Antipolo City, Rizal, about one hour's drive from Manila. Residents began moving to the settlement, containing 106 households, in December 2003. During the survey, approximately 60 households had moved in. Since this was an off-site CMP project, reconstructing neighborhood relations during the relocation was necessary; however, residents already maintained excellent relationships in the early days after moving in.

Resident relations in the San Agustin HOA probably began as residents participated in the project when the HOA was established. Since the procedures for acquiring land under the CMP are complex, residents required weekly workshops with the FDUP, the Originator. They regularly met with fellow CMP participants at the workshops and advanced the project in collaboration with the FDUP. These activities became the foundation for inter-resident relations.

Further, while the San Agustin HOA addresses land issues and maintains peace and order in the community, the Action Group, an organization by residents whose houses have working spaces, aims to improve the economic and social aspects of community life. Moreover, the Food Supply Associates buys joint stocks of affordable food products for community members. Organized by women who conduct settlement life activities, the association is trusted, with strong participation.

Attention has focused on the CMP method, which secures landownership rights while improving settlement life. However, focusing on the community associations that drive the program to success is vital. The incorporated organizations function as community pillars. In the CMP, they were nominated to receive official financing from the government. Thus, while the community associations can be considered economic organizations, they are also "symbols of unity" among residents participating in the CMP, existing as communities in and of themselves.

The neighborhood relations formed among residents began with groups of people from different backgrounds, brought together through the community associations required under the CMP. Subsequently, these relations diversified to include community organizations, created by families transferring life functions previously contained in small houses outside the house, as well as *compadrazgo* and other traditional relationship systems. Thus, to examine the new forms of relationships developing in impoverished urban areas, we must understand the hierarchical relations formed in such living spaces. This subject is discussed in the following chapter.

NOTES

1. Community mortgage programs are not common to the Philippines, unlike other countries in Asia and Latin America experiencing similar problems. In the Kampong Improvement Program in Indonesia, although the issue of landownership rights was not clearly addressed, the act of dwelling in the target areas was indirectly approved, as public funds were invested in infrastructure, such as roads and water and sewage facilities, increasing desire among residents to improve settlement life (Uchida 1993; National Home Mortgage Finance Corporation 1998, 55–85).

2. Under the enabling strategy, the roles of the government and other public organizations in direct housing provision were reduced to those of private housing

development organizations, operating in both informal and formal sectors. Moreover, they were supported and promoted (Fukushima 1992).

3. Corazon Aquino was the 11th President of the Republic of the Philippines (1986–1992). In opposition to her predecessor, Ferdinand Marcos, she promoted agrarian reform and decentralization.

4. The UDHA was enacted in 1992 as the basic law on urban housing development. The CMP is provided in Section 8. The implementation guidelines were prescribed in 1995 by the National Home Mortgage Finance Corporation and approved by the NHMFC in 1996 (National Home Mortgage Finance Corporation 1998).

5. The FDUP was the first CMP Originator, approved by the NHMFC in 1988. It played a pioneering role as an originator and had the greatest achievements under the CMP.

Chapter 5

Interpretation—Spaces, People, and Communities

This chapter discusses the emergence of spaces, relationships, and communities in impoverished urban areas regarding the fieldwork conducted in the informal settlements of the University of the Philippines and the three areas where CMP projects were conducted. The elastic relationships among residents, varying with time and place, are examined through confined houses that are particularly characteristic of impoverished urban areas and through the face-to-face living spheres accompanied by narrowness, crowdedness, and adjacency. The study observes the "Philippine urban type" of interpersonal relations, where others are invited into the private sphere, but people are connected by ambiguous relationships in which differences between individuals are maintained.

FACE-TO-FACE SOCIETIES

According to Lévi-Strauss (1963), anthropology divided society into two types, "authentic society" and "inauthentic society." Oda saw this distinction as "a fundamental distinction between the small-scale 'authentic' societies formed through direct, real-life contact among individuals and the large-scale 'inauthentic' societies formed through print and broadcast media that emerged after modernization" (2009, 249–50). Per this description, the criterion of authenticity (*niveaux d'authenticité*) does not refer to the "authenticity" denied by postmodern thought. It refers to the "difference between rational, indirect communication through 'rules,' 'currencies,' and 'media' and the mutual relationships that occur physically, face-to-face— that is, communication involving irrationality that takes place 'between' concrete individuals" (2009, 248). Thus, it is only natural to project the past onto small-scale societies, where people are connected by face-to-face relationships while associating modernity with indirect communication[1] via the continually expanding real-time communication media. In recent years, however, importance has been placed on face-to-face communication. Modern people living in the modern era have established a foothold in both "authentic" and "inauthentic" societies.

This discussion focuses on living spheres accompanied by narrowness, crowdedness, and adjacency in impoverished urban areas. Per Lévi-Strauss, these are authentic, face-to-face societies. As noted, the criterion of authenticity, the degree of which is "estimated according to the scope and variety of the concrete relations between individuals" (Lévi-Strauss 1963, 369), expresses differences in the level of perceiving others between societies formed through indirect communication developed in the modern period, such as capital, media, information, transportation, and small-scale societies where concrete individualized relations can be perceived face-to-face in daily life. The term "authenticity" here easily evokes images of small-scale, closed communities before societies were influenced by modernization and globalization of societies that preserved their homogeneous traditional culture. However, Lévi-Strauss, who always questioned the notion of universal culture, interpreted society not as a closed community but as a pluralistic and ambiguous network, including individuality and heterogeneity, rejecting the dualism between modern (urban) societies and traditional societies (farming villages). That is, "face-to-face" relationships are constant even in diverse societies with the most advanced communication methods. Lévi-Strauss used the word "authenticity" to express this system of relations, identifying it as vital in examining the state of society.

Given Lévi-Strauss's "authentic societies," individually and at the center of present-day urban life, it should be possible to refocus on the miscellaneous occurrences (individual and heterogeneous) abstracted from the principal discussion of anthropology through globalization and the familiar "face-to-face" relations lost in the process of urbanization.

CHAINS OF IMAGINATION

In *Imagined Communities*, Benedict Anderson (1987) argued that all communities larger than a certain size are "imagined." That is, communities exceeding a certain size have transcended, more or less, face-to-face relations and are no longer "authentic societies." Moreover, explaining communities at the image level, Anderson argued that "communities are to be distinguished, not by their falsity [or] genuineness, but by the style in which they are imagined" (1987, 49). The Javanese village is an example of a community imagined differently than the nation. Anderson said: "Javanese villagers have always known that they are connected to people they have never seen, but these ties were once imagined particularistically—as indefinitely stretchable nets of kinship and clientship. Until quite recently, the Javanese language had no word meaning the abstraction 'society'" (1987, 49).

The communities imagined by these Javanese villagers can be regarded as places where the face-to-face relations of Lévi-Strauss's authentic society have expanded. In these communities, members who never met share images to connect conceived through the formation of individual "face-to-face" relations (e.g., clientship and kinship). Conversely, in the case of the nation or tribal society (ethnic groups), members who never met share "a homogeneous 'national language' and a 'national history' consisting of homogeneous, illusory memories shared through national systems, such as media and education" (Oda 2001, 311). Against this backdrop, the individual and community are directly connected through the indirect communication noted by Lévi-Strauss. Anderson classifies communities regarding differences at the image level (i.e., whether the end form of the shared image is sought in the direct (indirect) experiences of the authentic society (inauthentic society)."

Under this approach, even a single community can be conceived altogether differently depending on the level of the image. Communities also allow for imagination that extends outward from "face-to-face" relations: for example, commenting on an event in a faraway place, a community member might say, "a friend of mine once lived there" or "one of my relatives went there." Such methods allow for the community to be interpreted as a sharable experience.

In other words, by finding sources of commonality in the experiences of "authentic society" (e.g., shared kinship, clientship, customs, and memories), the particularistic network of relations with others can be grasped as a community that is both sharable and inclusive of difference.

ACCEPTING DIFFERENCE

In postcolonial anthropology,[2] the concepts of strategic essentialism and Creolism were formulated as ways of grasping a reality in which the cultural boundaries of the nation are being eroded by accelerated globalization, individual areas have been recognized as culturally diverse, and it is no longer possible to describe people and groups based on singular identities such as ethnicity, class, and gender (Motohashi 2005; Imafuku 1991). Strategic essentialism asserts that the employment of a unified identity by oppressed minorities to opposing oppressors must be regarded as a strategy for resistance, rather than simply criticized from an Orientalist perspective. Creolism supports cultural diversity based on the idea that unified identities, even resistive ones, can only function oppressively. These two very different currents involve problems that are two sides of the same coin.

In strategic essentialism, even though groups are mobilized against the oppressor based on a resistive minority identity, given that a unified essentialist position is sought, it leads to the oppression of the differences and diversity that always exist within the group. However, Matsuda noted that Creolism succumbs to the "trap of foreignization" (Matsuda 1999). In overemphasizing cultural diversity, majorities (the West) and minorities (the colonies) end up being represented in the same light, and by treating them as players in the same game, the structural relations between ruler and ruled that exist between them are concealed. Per *In Praise of Creoleness* (Bernabé, Chamoiseau, and Confiant 1993), Creolism can be defined as a culture created through bricolage, where people with cultural roots in Africa's highly diverse communities "developed native language, to convey thoughts and emotions in 'face-to-face' relationships, from pidgin languages that were somehow created by combining elements that happened to be available at the time, including the native languages and cultures of Africa, the European languages and cultures of the white rulers, and the languages and cultures of the Carib Indians, who slipped into extinction leaving behind only a faint trace of their language" (Oda 2001, 304). It is worth reconfirming that the development of Creolism was closely related to the existence of various communities, a point of overlap with *The Savage Mind* (Lévi-Strauss 1969).

The concept of cultural hybridity, which accepts difference, is not aligned with either strategic essentialism or Creolism; it holds that people deliberately use divergent qualities of both traditional and modern society in life practices. Furuya explained the concept of the problem of a court battle over the restoration of landownership rights to an indigenous tribe from the Amazon Basin in Brazil (Furuya 1996, 277).

Per his idea, what made the Kayapo strategy original and effective was its hybrid nature—its lack of coherence and inconsistencies (e.g., its self-presentation as "traditionally aggressive Indians" and use of video technology, its cash receipts from tree felling and gold mining, and its self-presentation as ecological). These hybrid strategies are effective because modernity demands consistency and imposes binary choices "between x and y" based on dualistic categories. However, the Kayapo initiatives example was incoherent through the modernity lens—the game rules had reversed. The very classifications, hierarchies, and orders upon which modernity is based served to deconstruct the duality of tradition and modernity, essentialism, and anti-essentialism.

Furuya indicated that what is necessary is to recognize that people who are oppressed and discriminated against, while practicing hybrid strategies, can also employ essentialism (1996, 276). Furuya sees the Kayapo, who inconsistently employ both typical essentialist strategies of indigenous tribes and modern strategies to recover their lands, as inhabiting both worlds, on each side of the tradition—modernity and essentialism—Creolism divides. In an essay titled "*'Ba' ni yotte Musubitsuku Hitobito*" (People Connected by "Place"), Yoshioka pointed out that inhabitants in the Raga area of northern Vanuatu distinguish the world of traditional customs from the modern world of school—a world shaped by Western Christianity—and conduct their lives in both cultural worlds (Yoshioka 1994). In short, the people of Raga incorporated the two worlds of modernity and tradition in their lives. Matsuda's *Teiko-suru Toshi* (A City of Resistance) adopted a similar view (Matsuda 1999).

As highlighted, it is essential to grasp the real-life practices of a given society through face-to-face relationships when interpreting residents' life practices. Thus, the relationships among residents would seem to have established a modernity-tradition bridge rather than drawing a border between them. By focusing on the perspective of accepting the differences of others, it is possible to grasp the substance of bricolage within actual life practices, which constitutes neither assimilation into modernity nor reversion to tradition.

Accordingly, the following sections examine residents' living situations around the theme of private and public space per the fieldwork in the informal settlements and CMP areas before considering the formation of values for accepting difference. Moreover, the elastic human relations among residents, expanding and contracting with time and place, are discussed with reference to a survey into the adjacency and human relations of house spaces.

INTERSECTION OF PRIVATE AND PUBLIC SPACE

First, consider the intersection of private and public spaces and the externalization of living functions in the informal settlements and CMP areas where the fieldwork was conducted. Spaces characterized by narrowness, crowdedness, and adjacency were typical of the UP Diliman and CMP areas. The externalization of living functions by these conditions can be viewed as a way for residents in small houses to secure more living space, compensate for space lost to beds, and restore the spatial functions needed to live. This phenomenon served to blur the boundaries between private and public space and resulted in the enlargement of the "face-to-face" living sphere.

EXTERNALIZED LIVING FUNCTIONS AND
TRANSFORMATION OF PRIVATE SPACE

The externalization of living functions prompted by the narrowness, crowd-edness, and adjacency of the informal settlements and CMP areas involved transferring various living functions that could not be accommodated inside the house—living rooms, dining spaces, kitchens, toilets, and workspaces—to spaces outside the house.

For example, San Agustin HOA residents ate most of their meals at breakfast, lunch, and dinner outside the house and on the street, borrowing adjacent houses during the rainy season or evening rains (see Figure 5.1). Moreover, the externalization of dining spaces increased the movement of residents within the community, promoting the use of "face-to-face" semipublic spaces.

Residents without spare income shared dining spaces with neighbors, taking dishes to each other's houses; the externalization of living room spaces saw neighbors entering spaces typically shared by families, increasing opportunities for residents to share time and place. The dining and living room space function externalization required residents to maintain close face-to-face relations with their neighbors. Thus, it was possible to observe residents' intentions to maintain good relations within the community. The

Figure 5.1 Externalized Living Functions in San Agustin HOA. ©2021 Fuyuki Makino.

externalization of living functions involved the physical transfer of space and led to the provision of new places and opportunities for communication among neighbors.

PRIVATE USE OF PUBLIC SPACES

From a different perspective, the externalization of living functions means using public places for private purposes. Since landownership in the CMP areas is clear, the boundaries between community land and private land are defined in a cadastre. However, in informal settlements, such as those at UP Diliman, all land is occupied without ownership rights, and such public-private distinctions simply do not exist. However, among residents inhabiting informal settlements, vaguely defined boundaries exist between privately occupied land and land used by community members.

The shared areas of informal settlement serve several purposes; the streets and roads, the flow lines of daily life, are occupied privately in certain circumstances. In many impoverished areas, part of the land borders roads, which form part of the area, and these roads inside the community are appropriated for private use by residents. The unsurfaced roads, arranged in mazelike patterns, impose highly intricate, disorderly structures across whole areas. Although surfaced roads exist in some parts of the CMP areas, other than residents, people rarely use them. These roads, used as plazas, eating spaces, and mobile shop spaces, go beyond their original transportation function.

The private use of roads includes small-scale occupation within communities; the same practices can be observed in places all over Metro Manila. The sidewalk spaces adjoining Manila's highways and main roads provide a startling window into the diversity of people's everyday practices. This private use of public roads occurs in various patterns, ranging from temporary use to continuous use at certain times or on certain days. Public roads were constructed to convey traffic; thus, occupying them for private use is illegal. Even so, residents who illegally occupy public roads can be seen to be engaging in everyday practices that transform transportation spaces into places where people maintain direct relations. Hence, road spaces must be regarded, in Rosaldo's terms, as "busy intersections," (1989, 17) where people create culture as they come and go. In informal settlement communities, some road spaces are even used as agricultural land; unless these activities are forcibly dismantled, they easily develop into semipermanent occupations.

Two major uses of the shared portions of the informal settlement are plazas and churches. Since the Philippines endured centuries of Spanish rule, the spatial structures of major cities retain a strong Spanish influence. In colonial cities of Cebu, Panay, Manila, and Vigan, square blocks developed around plazas accommodate churches, government facilities, and houses of the ruling class. In the Intramuros section of Manila, one of these areas has been restored to its original state.

In the informal settlements, plazas, churches, and, in some cases, shared facilities are used in sets by residents as common land. Such practices constitute a plaza culture that does not exist in Japan. For example, in Daang Tubo, an informal settlement at UP Diliman, the plaza and church were situated together as a set. This plaza is used as a public space: a basketball court during the day, a place for worship, or a place for holding Sunday meetings. However, residents occupying land adjacent to these areas have transferred some of their living functions outside their houses to this shared space, using it as a temporary private space to hang their laundry or eat meals.

THE SARI-SARI STORE AS A COMMUNICATION HUB

Sari-sari stores feature prominently in the cramped settlements (see Figure 5.2). As we have already noted, sari-sari stores are small retail outlets that sell goods, by piece or volume, to the residents of impoverished neighborhoods. Some stores also allow payment in weekly and monthly installments.

Figure 5.2 The Sari-Sari Store in Daang Tubo. ©2021 Fuyuki Makino.

Moreover, the sari-sari stores provide essential services to the urban poor, occasionally providing microcredit to residents. In Daang Tubo, more than 40 sari-sari stores serve a community of 786 households. Given the many stores in these small communities, the nature of the sari-sari stores cannot be captured simply by treating them as mere retail outlets or profit-seeking service providers. Despite the aim to sell goods and services, individual stores cannot secure enough profit because of the competitive saturation. Thus, it is worth examining the raison d'être of the sari-sari store regarding its role as a hub of "face-to-face" communication in the community.

It is apparent from observing customers from inside the sari-sari store that the same residents use the store several times per day. As they buy cheap goods, such as cigarettes and drinks, residents converse about various matters inside and outside the sari-sari store. Within the web of relations that develop in the impoverished neighborhoods, where confined houses are physically adjacent, and residents are in constant "face-to-face" contact with one another, it is essential to build and maintain smooth relationships. Moreover, as living functions are externalized, residents' basic living functions, including business transactions, take various forms. A typical example is purchasing daily portions of items such as foods, condiments and seasonings, daily necessities, and medicine. Labor is also actively exchanged in the domains of childcare, housekeeping, and retail. Such systems support the routine practices of informal settlers, who live a hand-to-mouth existence. By using the space of the sari-sari store to provide a service in the form of a place where residents can share information, a wide array of information is exchanged, and smooth relations among residents are maintained.

> When you take the road into the community, there's a sari-sari store right there. Even if we don't need to buy anything, we always gather there. It's a good place to communicate with others. You can take your friends and get to know people from other communities as well. It doesn't have to be the sari-sari store, but that's the perfect place to get together. (Resident of San Agustin HOA)

Another resident of Daang Tubo stated "I go to the sari-sari store to buy a cigarette every morning. If you collect plastic or metal and take it to the store, they'll exchange it for money. They also do credit. People often gather there, and you can hear all kinds of information." Purchases of goods at the sari-sari store are made in exchange for the provision of a place for sharing information. Various types of information are exchanged when residents make purchases, which helps maintain "face-to-face" relations in the community through neighborliness. The store operators can increase their profits by selling goods while obtaining information from various residents because their store is a center of information exchange. Thus, the sari-sari stores go beyond the goal of securing profit to function as hubs of communication and information sharing, where "face-to-face" relations are expanded.

"FACE-TO-FACE" RELATIONS AND VALUE FORMATION FOR ACCEPTING DIFFERENCE

In the impoverished urban areas, where residents with different places of origin live in small houses in close proximity, harmony is vital in community life. Although native languages vary based on where residents were born and raised, Tagalog and English are prevalent in Metro Manila.

Traditional Filipino values expressed in Tagalog include *pakikisama*, *utang na loob*, *galang*, *delikadesa*, and *hiya*, and many words denote interpersonal-social relations, such as the *suki/bata* and *lakad* systems (Kikuchi 1980, 48). Underlying these terms is the common view of maintaining smooth human relations. Residents in informal settlements share these traditional values within their "face-to-face" relationships while strategically dismantling and partly applying them to real life.

Pakikisama

When community spaces are diverted to other uses, as private and public spaces overlap, residents must maintain stable interpersonal relations by adhering to certain rules. This attitude among residents can be expressed as *pakikisama*. A traditional Filipino value system, pakikisama functions as a principle of partnerships, modulating concessions to certain collective views and cooperation within the group.

For example, when providing products or a certain amount of labor within the community, group members must take an equal share. It does not mean things are always distributed equally—one's portion varies per the degree of involvement—but it is necessary to maintain such awareness when sharing. This value system is an essential basic principle for suppressing selfish behavior and living together in the community.

Utang Na Loob

When houses that comprise living spaces are extended in impoverished neighborhoods, work is normally undertaken by residents. However, it is impossible to complete the entire process alone, and some help is required from family members, relatives, or neighbors. In the Program C areas, enlisting collaborators is crucial since so many houses are constructed from concrete blocks. Family members provide materials and funding, and neighboring residents supply manpower. Neighbors expect others to come to their aid in times of necessity during house construction or extension.

During the survey, there were no cases where money was paid in exchange for labor provided by neighboring residents. This system of relationships, "utang na loob," operates based on debts of gratitude. Reciprocal relations where debts incurred by individuals are repaid to others exist at a basic level in any society. However, the hallmark of reciprocity in Filipino society is its inclusion of internal debts; where people fail to display acceptable behavior, they are stigmatized as "walang hiya ka" (without shame); since this can lead to isolation in the community, it creates a social mechanism of extreme fear. Per the utang na loob rules, operating in the background when community members work together, people exchange labor without payment in impoverished neighborhoods.

The *Suki/Bata* System

Hygiene in impoverished urban neighborhoods is terrible, and the infant mortality rate for under-one-year-old children is seven times or more than that in Japan. Even when people fall ill, they can rarely afford to visit the hospital; thus, health problems weigh heavily on residents. When residents need money during an emergency, they borrow it from relatives in the community, sari-sari stores, and small-scale creditors (microcredit), or rely on suki relations. In Tagalog, suki means "regular customer" or "patron." A "suki relationship" then denotes a relationship with a protégé or close friend. Notably, the concept includes certain relationships of mutual aid reminiscent of kinship.

For example, in Daang Tubo, when a child falls ill, the family first buys several days' worth of medicine at a sari-sari store or pharmacy that dispenses medicine by piece. In urgent cases, the child is taken to a public hospital close to the informal settlement. At this time, if the family is close to the sari-sari store operator, it might be possible to pay on credit, holding off payment until the end of the month, for example. Where this is not possible, however, the family might borrow money from a person with whom they have a suki relationship. Of the three important factors in Filipino behavior patterns (social acceptance, social possibilities, and cooperative relations of economic protection) (Kikuchi 1980, 147), in the informal settlements where most residents are extremely impoverished, relations of economic protection are the most important.

THE COMPADRAZGO SYSTEM

Consider the compadrazgo system in the Philippines. The Philippines was under Spanish colonial rule for about 370 years (1521–1898). Thus, a ritual co-parenthood system, "compadrazgo," spread throughout the country along with Christianity (Roman Catholicism). The original compadrazgo system comprised spiritual relationships between godchildren and godparents formed at a baptism ceremony. There are actually three godparents: two formal sponsors recognized by the church and one cosponsor. As spiritual relationships are formed with formal sponsors, similar relationships develop between the cosponsor and the godchild and the real parents of the godchild. As in actual blood relations, spiritual relationships help maintain powerful ties among residents.

However, in more recent years, compadrazgo has taken on a new form particular to the Philippines; the system's original religious functions have all but disappeared. The core element of the compadrazgo system is the relationship between a child's godparents and biological parents. In traditional Philippine society, which emphasizes kinship, constructing relationships is vital, and compadrazgo is the principal social system for integrating others in kinship. A child's godparents and biological parents call each other "*pare*" and "*mare*," and these spiritual relationships even extend as far as other relatives of both families. These relationships help establish mutual aid relations, not so much between the godparent and child but between the godparent and the child's biological parents.

In the impoverished urban areas, compadrazgo relationships are formed either with residents in the same areas or friends from the same hometown. Where both families had children, compadrazgo relationships are extended in both directions. Further, there are cases where residents have not maintained mutual aid relationships, given that life in the settlement in destitute economically and emotionally, even though mutual social and economic aid, which are the core of compadrazgo in the Philippines.

The original compadrazgo system was constructed and maintained through lifelong "face-to-face" relations. However, this attitude has changed considerably among residents of poor urban neighborhoods. Residents were forced to sever relationships they had hitherto maintained in their urban neighborhoods as they repeatedly moved from their settlements under the national and municipal government policy. These experiences have convinced them that the compadrazgo relationships in new settlements are not long-lasting. However, the practice of forming new compadrazgo relationships involves a solemn awareness of reality: to survive in poor urban neighborhoods, one must first expand one's network as widely as possible, maintaining an extensive network of mutual aid relationships. Moreover, the practice of broadening one's network by forming new compadrazgo relationships helps people situate themselves in society and construct their identity. Thus, in impoverished urban areas, compadrazgo relationships have economic dimensions (they are necessary for city life) and traditional dimensions (facilitating identity by expanding self-referential relations).

By establishing dissimilar others as "godchildren" while maintaining these dissimilarities, the compadrazgo system nests godparents and biological parents within mutually protective relationships. This practice also represents the "acceptance of difference" systematized through baptism rituals. However, the relationships in impoverished urban neighborhoods are looser than the ritual relationships typical to the Philippines and emerge as ambiguous connections when applied to real life.

JOINT AWARENESS OF "PLACE" AND "NEIGHBORHOOD"

Filipino social structure is based on bilateral descent, and individuals must find people with whom they can form the mutual aid relationships needed to survive life in their generation. Accordingly, individuals identify kindred (on both maternal and paternal sides) as objects oriented on the ego and establish complementary mutual aid relations via compadrazgo relationships with non-relatives.

Per Kikuchi, the principles of personal gain or loss connecting individuals and private structure are the foundation of interpersonal relations under the bilateral descent system, making person-to-person relationships primary (1994, 559). Thus, people in non-kinship relations become objects of jealousy, and it is challenging to establish the joint awareness by which autonomy as a group is maintained. Societies that lack this group coherence are "uncrystalized societies" (Kikuchi 1991). However, Kikuchi (1980) and Muratake (1984) use the terms "group domicile" and "group-oriented kin concept" to describe communities that develop in bilateral societies, as opposed to "membership" in unilineal societies where rights and obligations are clear. They noted that communities exist as groups bound by a loose sense of solidarity in the Filipino bilateral descent society and clarified the existence of community leaders resembling caretakers.

Community awareness connected by loose networks, and the emergence of leadership, were also observed in the Daang Tubo settlement at UP Diliman. These leaders were expected to promote the upgrading project by the UPA, which had been experiencing delays.

Community leaders were caretakers connecting the UPA and Daang Tubo, who were required to collaborate with social workers in gathering various information items and finding ways to improve the informal settlements at UP Diliman in the future. For example, Resident C understood the UPA improvement project and participated in NGO activities. During the field-work, Resident C, a caretaker in the community, and a UPA staff came along on a visit to each house. Resident C was a man (aged 59) who ran a sari-sari store in a community adjacent to C.P. Garcia Avenue; he was among the longest-standing members of the Daang Tubo community. Since his sari-sari store was situated at the community entrance, it was frequented by residents; thus, he was well known. Since he also issued microloans, he was well-respected in Daang Tubo. The UPA expected C to assume the role of a leader for the whole community.

Since Daang Tubo is an informal settlement, there are no community boundaries. Moreover, the movement of people is highly fluid, as many new informal settlers arrive and move on. Accordingly, residents draw on "face-to-face" relationships and traditional relationships as they root their livelihoods. Inhabitants of the informal settlements hail from various places and have different social backgrounds, traditions, and languages. However, a sense of solidarity has emerged from the "face-to-face" relationships imposed by close-quarter living. In these communities, we can observe the "supra-familial" relational system (Kikuchi 1980, 165), where people live in shared spaces (with a sense of place and neighborhood). Moreover, since chronic economic hardship is also shared, the importance of relationships among residents increases, feeding this sense of solidarity. In the Daang Tubo community, this solidarity is underpinned by "face-to-face" relationships, an extension of which is a joint awareness that the residents are "sharing a par-ticular place or neighborhood."

As their place of living, informal settlers have a keen interest in the future of Daang Tubo. Residents were fully aware that, as inhabitants of the same land, their solidarity would profoundly shape any future projects to upgrade the settlement.

THE SHARING OF SEQUENCES

Using the word "nostalgia," Rosaldo (1989) encouraged us to reflect on modern anthropology. He criticized the yearning for cultures and societies that imperialism agents[3] had destroyed and their mourning of the extinc-tion of these forms of life as "imperialist nostalgia." Rosaldo's subsequent attempt to reconstruct social analysis asserted the need to dismiss cultures and communities rendered nostalgically as ideal societies as fictions and further abandon the autonomous position of the researcher, where anthropologists can conduct objective analysis and interpretation. Per Rosaldo, anthropologists must not detach the workings of oppressed people from the self but aim for an empathic understanding, actively employing emotions and ethnical perspectives.

In the informal settlements, where people live in cramped houses and close proximity, a relational system can be identified in which traditional conventions are at play. However, this does not mean settlers live nostalgic lives, embracing traditions passed down from farming villages and hometowns. In "face-to-face" living spaces, traditional relationships are employed to survive the present, as settlers weave their distinct narratives. Traditional relationships deployed in these living spheres should not be regarded as original forms, which might impose all-out communality, but as devices adapted to modernity for building loose interpersonal networks that function to subsume others and differences with others.

We have seen how shared spaces, such as sari-sari stores, plazas, churches, and roads, help expand sites of "face-to-face" contact and facilitate various information sharing among community members. Another important aspect in examining elements shared by residents with diverse backgrounds, such as the subjects of this book, is the "momentary sequences" that occur in places of living shaped by narrowness, crowdedness, and adjacency. These sequences reveal the transitory strategies pursued by residents as they confront their present challenges.

THE EYE OF THE OTHER

At all Metro Manila corners, one can observe the informal occupation of land and house construction for informal settlers. Approximately 710,000 households of informal settlers in Metro Manila account for approximately 40% of the population (NHA 2000), and an enormous number of settlers have occupied land at UP Diliman, with 19,234 households. Tolerance of public places is a reason for such an escalation. The degree of tolerance toward informal occupation, observed in interviews with UP Diliman students, often stems from the pragmatic view that the settlements should not be regarded as a problem unless a nuisance is caused to the students since settlers will only be replaced by others if they are removed from the land. Moreover, many students do not view informal settlers at UP Diliman as a problem because many settlers provide convenient services for students, such as affordable accommodation and jeepney rides around campus.

The intervention of the university authorities and politicians from Quezon City is also an important factor. In particular, university authorities are aware that approximately 20% of the university staff reside in informal settlements and constitute approximately 5% of the total population of the settlements. For the staff, the settlements are convenient, inexpensive, and close to the university. For the university, expenditure can be reduced, in areas such as residency rights, housing guarantee, and social security, by overlooking this living situation. Politicians are also unlikely to act since 19,234 households would provide more than enough people for a grassroots expansion movement. In an interview with a university employee, the interviewee reported that although she was not living in an informal settlement on campus, she did know several UPA staff members who were. Per this interviewee, although staff members know informal occupation is illegal, the affordability of the houses and their proximity to the workplace is a strong pull factor. Rent is paid to informal settlers who supply the living space; however, several intermediaries are involved in the housing rental process, and there is a significant intermediary margin.

CREATING NEW AWARENESS IN THE COMMUNITY

The informal settlers are vulnerable to slum clearances conducted during public works, such as road expansions and commercial development. Government agencies of Metro Manila adopted a range of measures to tackle the problem of increasing numbers of informal settlements. According to the National Housing Association (NHA), in the 20 years from 1982, approximately 76,000 households were forced to move (NHA 2002). Although some of the evicted settlers were rehabilitated elsewhere, many of them returned to occupy new land in Metro Manila. Thus, the process of mandatory migration policy and illegal occupation was repeated several times.

The CMP, discussed in the previous chapter, provides a notable method for ameliorating the informal settlement problem. Landownership rights are acquired via a long-term, low-interest loan from a public institution, with land as collateral, issued on the condition that a land transfer agreement is concluded between informal settlers and the landowner. The concrete goal of securing landownership rights is important in enhancing residents' awareness of life improvement, drawing out their self-support capacity.

One prominent characteristic of the CMP is the involvement of the HOA-incorporated organizations. When initiating a CMP project, residents must form an HOA. The HOA is the incorporated organization that concludes the land transfer agreement with the landowner and receives the long-term, low-cost loan; land transfer agreements cannot be concluded with individual settlers. Even after the land has been acquired, the HOA continues to function as a community body, managing residents' monthly loan repayments and dealing with non-payers.

The CMP involves a highly complex set of procedures related to the land agreement, and a period of several years or more, from initiation of the project to completion, is required. The requirement is partially due to the distinctive multilayered nature of landownership rights in Metro Manila. Due to the Philippines' long colonial history, war, and changes to the political system and land policy, there are instances where multiple landowners exist or where delays occur in the confirmation process due to a lack of database coverage. Even after a finalized agreement between the HOA and the landowner, much time is required from receiving the government loan to paying the landowner. Therefore, the land is sometimes resold to a third party during this period. The CMP process also includes a wide range of other issues, including illegal syndicates, which approach the HOAs masquerading as landowners.

The CMP loan system, called the Housing Unit Loan Program, has a maximum 25-year term of payment. The HOA is essential in the loan process since the loans are repaid continually over a long period. When problems occur during this process, the HOA is required to advance appropriate solutions. Residents belonging to the HOA undertake the complex, long-term CMP procedures from a base of mutual cooperation. Therefore, residents who share the HOA experience and succeed in acquiring landownership rights develop a strong sense of belonging to the HOA.

HOA LEADERSHIP

Since HOAs are formed by residents who happen to be living in the same informal settlement, they can be regarded as groups that subsume others who may be different. The most important attribute when selecting the HOA leaders is the ability to coordinate relationships among HOA residents to maintain strong ties. Leaders are also required to address various problems in the HOA appropriately and, therefore, accomplish tasks to solve problems.

Regarding the ability to coordinate relationships, leaders must exercise Filipino social norms; however, they must also consider religion. Appropriately dealing with Protestants, Muslims, and Buddhists separately from the Catholic majority is crucial in engineering friendly relations in the community. Regarding problem-solving and providing a direct window for FDUP consultation, leaders are required to engage in various external negotiations and maintain networks among organizations while occupying a position between the HOA and organizations (e.g., when negotiating an agreement with landowners and conducting loan procedures of the Housing Unit Loan Program).

In the three CMP communities, HOA leaders were determined based on recommendations by the FDUP, the CMP originator. Since residents are fully aware that the keys to success in CMP projects are appropriate HOA management and the activities of its leaders, even if FDUP intentions impact the selection of HOA leaders significantly, it is not considered problematic. A resident in the Macoda HOA said that "the first HOA community leader was Resident D's son, who had already lived here for many years. He could speak Tagalog, Ilocano, and English, so he was the right man for the position connecting the Originator and the CMP site."

The Macoda HOA's next leader was selected via an election by third parties recommended by residents involved in the CMP. Resident B (female; aged 46) was selected for this position. Below is an examination of the circumstances surrounding her selection.

Resident B shared a house with her husband (aged 46), their eldest daughter (aged 22), eldest daughter's husband (aged 22), grandchild (aged 0), second eldest daughter (aged 20), and Resident B's younger sister (aged 40). Since Macoda HOA is an on-site project, many residents have lived there for many years. Resident B had lived in the area for 27 years. She did not live in the same place for the whole period; she moved to live in a nearby area for some time.

She was born in Mindanao, and after completing elementary education, she studied at high school for one year before dropping out and moving to Manila. As the eldest daughter of five children, the goal of her relocation was to remit money to her family. She worked various jobs introduced to her by a resident from the same hometown, including work as cleanup staff (picking up garbage), a sari-sari store assistant, and an ice cream and drink peddler. Resident B's turning point was when she participated in some NGO workshops on microfinance. Microfinance is the smallest form of the loan system to provide small loans to people in impoverished areas without collateral or a guarantor. Residents may be required to form small borrowing groups. In the microfinance activities conducted by a nonprofit organization (NPO), Resident B was responsible for assisting the formation of borrowing groups and handling procedures to consolidate residents' mutual guarantees. It marked the beginning of her political activities. Resident B gradually won the NPO's trust as groups and individuals she assisted rarely defaulted on their repayments. Since residents also behaved in a way that maintained her trust, both of these relationships deepened.

The fact that Resident B hailed from Mindanao and had a good understanding of Muslims was also significant. The basic notions of Islamic finance dictate that when microfinance is provided to Muslims, no interest, however small, should be accrued. Therefore, a problem arose due to differences with the loan conditions established for other residents. Resident B proposed a new system that would keep Muslim residents on the same level as others in terms of loan conditions as follows: "In accordance with the basic rules of Islamic finance, instead of fixing interest on loans, how about donating a certain amount to the NPO or paying interest in kind through joint goods or foods for the community when repayments are proceeding as planned?" Through these activities, Resident B gradually earned goodwill among the residents and within the NPO as a trustworthy person with well-balanced negotiating ability. Furthermore, one resident commented that she could participate in the NPO workshops because her husband, an electrician, received a fixed income.

Resident B was selected as a leader of the Macoda HOA in CMP from among the residents because of her ability to coordinate relationships and accomplish tasks. The HOAs formed through the CMP projects are managed jointly by residents and transcend any blood relations or territorial bonds. As the leader, Resident B sought to strengthen residents' awareness of mutual ties by foregrounding the acquisition of landownership rights as a common goal.

AMBIGUOUS AWARENESS ABOUT LANDOWNERSHIP

Landownership rights acquired in the CMP projects may be held collectively by the HOA or divided among individual residents. Many residents hope landownership is divided among individuals. In the three CMP areas, shared portions, such as plazas, roads, and community facilities, are owned by the HOA; the rest is divided among individuals. Residents discussed the use of shared portions of land acquired through the CMP project at the beginning. Thus, consider the Samarima HOA residents' views on landownership rights.

The residents perceive spaces such as plazas, roads, and community facilities through an ambiguous awareness that these spaces are public and private. Residents are aware they pay for a home lot area and their share of open space when land is purchased. The phenomena observed in the CMP areas, where public space was used for private purposes and private space was transferred outside the house, have affected the ambiguous private–public meanings attached to shared spaces.

It is challenging to get a real sense of this ambiguous awareness surrounding landownership from life in modern Japan, where funds are raised by taxation and indirectly distributed as public goods. This sense may be closer to a European, as opposed to Asian, "citizenry," where the city is perceived as common property.

COMPADRAZGO AS STRATEGY

Given that CMP participation is based at the family level, blood relations can be scattered across different areas. Moreover, cases in which the relationships residents built and maintained are destroyed due to the forced evictions via local government policy can often observed in the impoverished neighborhoods. CMP HOAs do not comprise relationships that developed through the traditional formation process, where community members share the same land over the long term. In the HOAs, resident participants of the CMP projects sought to acquire landownership rights and escape poverty, which cannot be achieved by relying on traditional kinship relations. Accordingly, the common economic benefit is a more important component of the HOAs than traditional, kin-based relationships. Hence, the HOA communality and economics seem to be incompatible with more traditional interpersonal relationships.

As noted, some residents strengthen their relations with neighbors by forming compadrazgo relationships. This situation could be a reversion to the traditional style of interpersonal relationships, thus securing landownership and settlement rights. Residents at field sites established compadrazgo direct and indirect relationships with their community leaders and neighbors. They must perform procedures under a modern system (agreement, negotiation, loan, debt, and repayment) to secure land, even forming communities. However, the Philippines' bilateral descent system lacks a base for establishing communities since groups form via kinship-based mutual aid relations among individuals. Accordingly, the group membership expands, and its scale increases by integrating others into kinship relations via compadrazgo. Strong ties are unnecessary for ritual relationships in impoverished urban neighborhoods. Only the traditional framework is retained as ritual relationships are incorporated into the community of others embodied as the HOA. Residents must adapt to modern land acquisition systems. However, to accept the establishment of the community of others, one must follow Filipino values and social structures, such as compadrazgo. At the field sites, the religious significance of compadrazgo relationships has waned to a mere formality necessary to establishing networks with others in economic organizations. Arguably, the compadrazgo essence is lost and replaced with tradition as a strategy for building and maintaining economic relationships.

This chapter has interpreted "face-to-face" living spheres fraught with the features of narrowness, crowdedness, and adjacency characteristic of impoverished urban areas as a domain of "authentic society." The discussion considered that aspects shared by inhabitants of these urban communities, which accommodate the two systems of modernity, are situated in their "face-to-face" life practices. Moreover, by reinterpreting the traditional compadrazgo system as a ritual modified along urban lines to formalize the inclusion of such difference, it is possible to regard the relational systems observed in the impoverished urban neighborhoods as constituting loose, ambiguous networks with footholds in both tradition and modernity.

NOTES

1. For today's society, internet-based communication methods (e.g., email, blogs, SMS, and messaging applications) should also be included.

2. The former colonies successively gained independence from the late twentieth century; however, various problems remained between the former colonies and suzerain states. Edward W. Said's *Orientalism* was among the background theories of post-colonialism, the trend in cultural research that began as an attempt to understand these problems.

3. In addition to state officials and constabulary officers, Rosaldo saw missionaries and anthropologists as agents of colonialism.

Chapter 6

Design—Making Social Architecture

This chapter aims to obtain useful knowledge for housing improvement in poor areas by considering examples of housing improvement efforts in architecture. The housing improvements architects work on have mainly addressed various social problems in developed countries since modern times. From the latter half of the nineteenth century to the first half of the twentieth century, there were major changes in economic activities and social systems due to the industrial revolution in Western countries. Many of the social problems that arose during the rapid industrialization overlap with the items needed to improve housing in poor areas in developing countries today. Modern architects have tried to answer these social problems using architectural design. Therefore, this chapter mainly deals with important architectural efforts and residential construction from the beginning of the twentieth century. Today, technological progress is rapid, but it is based on the efforts of this early social architect. Here, the following items are considered essential for designing social architecture:

- Hygiene improvement (overcoming epidemics)
- Environmental improvement (harmony with nature)
- Economic improvement (reduction of construction costs by introducing mass production)
- Functional improvement (improvement of the standard of living)
- Understanding of social structure

The above items describe the particularly important efforts of modern architecture. There is no need to rely on modern, highly complex construction techniques or state-of-the-art materials to improve poor areas based on self-building. Rather, knowing the early architectural endeavors of modern times is important in considering prototypes of homes to be built in poor areas.

For example, attempts at functional natural ventilation rather than mechanical ventilation are better suited to the realization of social architecture.

Moreover, this chapter discusses the urban improvement efforts that are developed by architects. From the beginning of the twentieth century to the post–World War II period, the industrialization of urban areas progressed rapidly, and it was necessary to have a city plan that responded to population concentration. Here emerged some important urban planning attempts. Large-scale plans do not directly help improve slums, but those concepts and ideological efforts are important for the improvement of slums. They incorporate effective use of public space. Therefore, they can be useful for fostering the concept of community development that creates collaboration among slum dwellers. They also explain social capital, which is essential for the improvement of slums. Social capital constitutes consciously shared norms, values, and trust, built by people's relationships. The connections between individuals and social networks created by fostering social capital lead to reciprocity and credibility. People's involvement in social interactions—between individuals and in small groups, organizations, etc.—leads to participation in local government and ultimately to trust in higher-level government agencies and international organizations. Building social capital is paramount in the process of architectural anthropology and social architecture design and inevitably adds cultural elements to architectural items. Consideration of cultural factors unique to each region is important for continuous community and housing improvement. Building relationships with residents and deepening mutual understanding can also connect the elements of modern architecture to social architecture. Finally, as a case study, I will explain the Disaster Recovery Program in the province of Camarines Sur, the Philippines. The architectural methods addressed so far provide valuable clues for housing improvement in poor areas.

FOR SOCIAL ARCHITECTURE DESIGN
1: HYGIENE IMPROVEMENT

Sanitation in many impoverished areas is extremely poor. This situation was once common in urban areas of Europe and the United States. In Europe in the late nineteenth and early twentieth centuries, after the industrial revolution, the urban concentration of factories forced workers to live in cramped homes. Due to air pollution in factories and poor water and sewage systems, unsanitary living environments became a major social problem in cities. Moreover, many middle-class people in cities lived in brick apartments, with heavy walls, small windows, and problems with daylight and ventilation. Interiors were adorned with expensive ornaments such as upholstered furniture, carpets, and long drape curtains. Thus, dust tended to collect in the complicated detail work in the fittings. The rooms were not well lit or ventilated, the humidity was high, and the accumulated dust was moldy. The unsanitary city environment resulted in the spread of epidemic diseases to both lower and middle classes, resulting in many deaths. The Spanish flu, which prevailed from 1918 to 1920, caused many deaths worldwide, starting in Europe.

Tuberculosis was one of the leading causes of death in Europe. Moreover, tuberculosis was highly infectious, necessitating patient isolation. Medical technology at that time could not adequately treat tuberculosis. Therefore, tuberculosis patients were required to rest, eat a healthy diet, and live a healthy life in the sunlight and fresh air. Under such circumstances, many wealthy patients used a tuberculosis rest facility called a sanatorium. The Adirondack Cottage Sanatorium (Coulter 1885), one of the earliest tuberculosis treatment facilities, was founded by Dr. Edward Livingston Trudeau and built in Saranak Lake, New York. The sanatorium was designed in the Late Victorian style by architect W. L. Coulter. Livingston Trudeau aimed to regain his health in an open and lush environment. Initially, the sanatorium was an enormous cottage. However, as the number of tuberculosis patients increased, it became a medical treatment facility with hospital functions. Specialized buildings for tuberculosis treatment were designed to help patients recover and prevent the transmission of the disease (Donaldson 1921).

Against this background, modernist architecture played a part in improving the living environment. Modernist architecture arguably increased its social recognition by creating medical facilities. The keywords for improving hygiene are sun, air, and outdoors (Hobday 2009), which overlap with modernist architecture keywords.

Alvar Aalto designed a sanatorium in Paimio, Finland, in 1932. Its design emphasized horizontal surfaces by eliminating decoration. The finished surface of the building was painted white, giving a clean impression. It featured a wide glass window surface. Each floor and patient bedroom had a sunbathing balcony. Patients could pull their bed out to the balcony and sunbathe outdoors. Further, a sundeck was built on the top floor of the building. Patients with tuberculosis spent several years in a sanatorium, requiring a communal life with medical staff to assist in the treatment. Thus, the sanatorium facility was equipped with conference rooms, chapels, staff housing, and promenades (Schildt 1984). Hence, a community was formed among tuberculosis patients and staff. Aalto called the entire building a "medical instrument" and designed the sanatorium to contribute to treating tuberculosis (Pallasmaa 1998). "The main purpose of the building is to function as a medical instrument [. . .] One of the basic prerequisites for healing is to provide complete peace (Aalto, in Reed 1998, 29)."

Le Corbusier presented the following five principles that comprise a "new architecture" instead of traditional Western masonry architecture (Le Corbusier 1931). He designed Villa Savoye (1929) to incorporate the "Five Principles of Modern Architecture." These principles accord with the aspect of improving hygiene.

- Pilotis: Free architecture from the ground up to accommodate traffic, plants, and exercise.
- Roof garden: Free the roof and sky for sunbathing, exercising, and gardening. Protect your home with a damp layer.
- Free ground plan: Free the shape and layout of the room from the structural walls. You can free the layout with a partition wall.
- Horizontal windows: You can make large windows to brighten the inside of the building uniformly.
- Free façade: You can freely design, like painting a picture.

Villa Savoye has a washroom at the entrance. Its structure circulates air from the courtyard, a roof garden, and continuous horizontal windows, making it a very hygienic dwelling. Moreover, the modern design eases house maintenance and reflects a hospital building design. Modern architecture, born in the early twentieth century, contributed significantly to improving hygiene to prevent infectious diseases (Campbell 2005). Notably, the design of modern architecture created an indispensable significance to existence in the social situation at that time.

FOR SOCIAL ARCHITECTURE DESIGN 2: ENVIRONMENTAL IMPROVEMENT

The UN Environment Program (UNEP) was founded in 1973 and has led international collaborative activities on the environment. UNEP has also developed most of the many international environmental laws currently in use. There are three important documents for considering international environmental issues.

- Rio Declaration on Environment and Development: The Rio Declaration is based on the Declaration of the United Nations Conference of the Human Environment, which was adopted in Stockholm in 1972. At the Stockholm Conference, a global intergovernmental environmental conference, it was stated that long-term economic development needs to be linked to environmental protection.

- Agenda 21: Established at the Rio Summit. A 40-chapter blueprint for action that addresses specific issues regarding sustainable development. Agenda 21 also said that population, consumption, and technology are the main causes of environmental change.
- Brundtland Report (*Our Common Future*): Established the principle of environmental protection. This groundbreaking report emphasizes that if humans do not change the way they live and do business, they will face intolerable human and environmental damage.

Building an environmentally friendly and sustainable society is a universal issue. Today, various efforts are being actively made to realize a sustainable society. However, efforts so far have not been sufficiently successful. The seriousness of problems such as global warming continues to increase. There is an urgent need to realize a low-carbon society, a sound-material-cycle society, and a society that coexists with nature.

Frederick John Kiesler is one of the people who pointed out the environmental problems that characterize the present situation from the architectural and ideological points of view in the early twentieth century. Kiesler was an architect who presented an important environmental idea by fusing nature and architecture in modern architecture. Kiesler was an "unbuilt architect," and very few of his ideas were realized in his lifetime, one exception being the Temple of the Book (1965) in Israel. An important architectural work that reflects Kiesler's ideas is the Endless House (1950). The house has a unique shape, like an organic cave. Kiesler introduced the ideas of biology and evolution that developed in the early twentieth century into architecture. The unique organic form of the Endless House references cellular life. The building interior is protected from the outside environment; it is connected to and separated from the outside environment through a film or membrane. Kiesler created a relationship similar to the functional cell boundaries of an organism regarding the boundaries between the inside and outside of the dwelling. It was not a strong boundary in traditional architecture, nor was it a weak boundary that immediately connected to the outside world. Traditional strong boundaries are masonry walls while a weak wall is a highly transparent boundary such as glass. The new boundary Kiesler considered was one that keeps the inside and outside in equilibrium. He aimed for an environmentally friendly equilibrium that combined natural convection and mechanical equipment. For Kiesler, architecture was a device to create a mutual human– environment equilibrium (i.e., health).

The unique form and concept of the Endless House equilibrium are influenced by Kiesler's *Correalism and Biotechniques* (1939). Correalism shows Kiesler's unique way of thinking about human beings and the environment. He stated that when the boundary is removed, life is exposed to the outside and dies. From here, he believes that architecture must be the boundary between humans and nature. In endless houses, cell shape is used as a metaphor to symbolize the dynamic equilibrium of cell membranes, rather than explicitly indicating the presence or absence of boundaries with architectural elements such as walls.

FOR SOCIAL ARCHITECTURE DESIGN 3: ECONOMIC IMPROVEMENT

In chapter 4, we introduced the CMP initiative in the Philippines. This is an important measure for sustainable housing improvement in impoverished areas. The discussion showed that economic improvement is not enough to make housing cheaper; projects linked to employment and monetary policy are also required. On the other hand, in the actual construction of houses in impoverished areas, it is possible to combine mass-produced industrial products with self-building. Long-life standard products also facilitate maintenance. Attempts to build industrialized homes began in the early twentieth century, aimed at allowing many to have a comfortable living space. In this section, I will discuss important architectural endeavors undertaken in this regard, with the keywords mass production, industrialization, and low cost.

Dymaxion House (1928)

Buckminster Fuller (1928) presented the idea that many people should have a comfortable living space. Thus, in 1928, he devised the Dymaxion House (1928), where many people get a comfortable living space by mass production. Dymaxion is a compound of the words "dynamic," "maximum," and "tension" (Sieden 2000). The Dymaxion House is the first mobile house designed for mass production in the twentieth century. Its shape is very distinctive. It is circular and has a pillar in the center; the floor and roof are hung by a tensile material stretched from the top. Buckminster Fuller aimed to create a new building as an industrial product that can be supplied at low cost by improving its compatibility with various terrains due to its structure of lightweight aluminum. In 1945, he codeveloped a mass-produced Dymaxion residential machine commonly known as the Wichita House. However, it was difficult to commercialize due to financial problems.

Tropical House (1949)

Jean Prouvé (1949) designed a tropical house in 1949 as a prototype of an inexpensive, easy-to-transport, and easy-to-assemble house for French colonies in Africa. He worked with architects such as Robert Mallet-Stevens and Le Corbusier to design industrialized homes. The tropical house is built on a simple one-meter grid system (Prouvé 2011). All parts except for the building's main structural elements are made of aluminum and can be constructed by two people. Thus, parts larger than 13 feet and heavier than 220 pounds are not used. Prouvé employs aluminum for durability and ease of assembly. Further, the Blaze Soleil, which blocks direct sunlight, is separated from the sliding door and the insulating skin inside the fixed panel. The floor is stilted to control humidity, and warm air under the floor is sucked up by the central (natural) ventilation chimney. Prouvé tried to design a comfortable living environment, considering the tropical climate. The ease of conveyance and assembly are significant factors in housing assistance.

PREMOS (1946–1951)

Kunio Maekawa (1946–1951), along with Dr. Kaoru Ono, a professor at the University of Tokyo's Second Engineering Department, designed PREMOS as a prefabricated house with wooden panels. It as an early mass-produced house in Japan after World War II. Maekawa was consulted on how to use the machine by Sanin Kogyo Co., Ltd., which was defunct after the war. Sanin Kogyo was originally a company that manufactured large gliders during World War II. Since Maekawa was involved in the construction of the Sanin Kogyo factory, he contributed to the manufacture of PREMOS. The housing shortage in Japan after World War II, short of 4 million units, was severe. About 1,000 prefabricated houses were built, and architects were crucially involved in the early days of prefabricated houses in Japan. However, most were houses for coal mine workers in Hokkaido and Kyushu rather than ordinary houses because the sales system that enables mass-produced housing was insufficiently developed. PREMOS was designed for people requiring housing; however, it was a failure. Further, PREMOS was linked with the domino system explored by Le Corbusier, Maekawa's master, and the subsequent architectural issues leading to the minimum housing in Japan (Van Sande 2020). Maekawa tried to make up for the shortage of housing materials after the war with industrialized housing.

Case Study Houses

The Case Study Houses project was launched in January 1945 by the California magazine *Arts & Architecture* as a response to the housing shortage in the United States caused by World War II. Case Study Houses aimed to investigate how prefabricated homes could help mass-produce homes and meet postwar needs (Smith et al. 2009). Eight modernist architects designed the case study house. The work revolutionized the way Californians view housing and the environment. Since then, the project has expanded to more than 23 units. However, many of the case study project designs did not use prefabricated parts and were criticized for not being suitable for mass production.

Case Study House No. 8/Eames House

Charles and Ray Eames (1949) designed Case Study House No. 8 in 1949. During the war, Eames pursued the potential of molded plywood as a furniture design and was interested in low-cost, high-quality, mass-produced prefabricated materials. This idea is reflected in the furniture and design of the case study house. Eames House is a work in which all the basic parts are made of prefabricated parts. It comprises an elongated rectangle of 175 inches long and 20 inches wide. The entire rectangle is divided into bays of 7.5 feet wide, 20 feet deep, and 17 feet high, created by a steel structure. The structural frame employs 4-inch H-columns, 12-inch open web joints, and glass.

Case Study House No. 22/Stahl House

Pierre Koenig learned how to build a steel-framed house from an architect named Rafael Soriano who worked at Richard Neutra's office. Rafael Soriano is known for his pioneering use of standard ready-made steel and aluminum in homes and stores. Koenig began designing independently in California in his twenties. Case Study House No. 22 Stahl House (Koenig 1960) is a steel-based building made of ready-made materials (Steele 2002). The characteristic of the Stahl House is the large opening of the steel sash. Koenig seeks to find the most economical way to skip a steel column. He also seeks the cheapest way to make roofs with deck plates. In this case study house, the standard of allocation employs standard parts such as sashes sold as they are. These points are very different from Buckminster Fuller, which lacks the pursuit of economic efficiency in his search for architectural design aimed at mass production. However, after World War II, he considered its affordability, intending to propose housing for the general public. This situation is expressed by the term industrialized vernacular. Pursuing this economic efficiency is among the most important matters when considering the development of poor areas.

Moreover, the Stahl House of Case Study House No. 22 did not aim for the same architecture to be sold to the masses. It employed industrialized building materials for on-site bricolage, a style in which industrial products are adapted and shaped per location. This style of combining ready-made materials on-site is also important when considering housing assistance in impoverished areas.

Kings Road House (1921)

The Kings Road House was designed by Rudolph M. Schindler, who adopted the construction method of tilt-up concrete slabs, in which concrete, clear glass, or frosted glass are poured into a mold, and after hardening, is raised on-site to make a wall. Tilt-up concrete slabs are act as protective walls for the Kings Road House. Schindler significantly reduced costs by leveraging sliding glass panels and tilt-up concrete slabs.

Kings Road House is also related to the environmental improvement in the previous section. The overall plan connects two L-shaped apartments. The innovative use of this industrial material, the open floor plan, integrates the external environment into the home and sets a precedent for modern California architecture. It is also related to the functional improvements in the next section. The two apartments are connected by a utility room. The utility room has kitchen, laundry, sewing room and storage functions. At Kings Road House, everyone had to get together in the communal kitchen to do the housework. There is no traditional living room, dining room, or bedroom as you would find in a traditional home. The dwelling was designed as a communal dwelling and workplace for two young families. In this sense, it is closely related to the improvement of functions considered in the next section.

FOR SOCIAL ARCHITECTURE DESIGN4: FUNCTIONAL IMPROVEMENTS

Since the industrial revolution, the focus of production activities has shifted from agriculture to industry, and social life has changed significantly. Industrialization produced a large number of wage-earning workers as a labor force, but they left rural areas and flowed into cities. As a result, the urban population has increased rapidly, and new industrial cities have emerged. This has changed people's lifestyles drastically and created new social problems, such as the occurrence of air pollution in cities and the increase of the urban poor. Naturally, new urban planning and architecture were needed to suit new lifestyles and work styles. Agriculture requires a home that integrates work and housing, but since modern times, more people will go to work in factories, so housing and workplaces will be separated. The separation of living functions was compatible with the idea of modernism, which pursues rationality by eliminating unnecessary decoration. In short, changes in the times, driven by changes in technology, have revolutionized the functionality needed in homes. The Bauhaus was a school that provided comprehensive education on art and architecture, aiming for rationalistic and functionalist architecture. Around the same time, the Great Kanto Earthquake (1923) occurred in Japan. The earthquake caused enormous damage to Tokyo, with an estimated 105,000 dead or missing. The town of Edo, which had existed since the Middle Ages and made up the core of the metropolis, was burned down, and urban planning and housing corresponding to the new lifestyle emerging under Japanese modernization were required. The Dojunkai project created a place to realize a modern life. Here, I will give an overview of the history of the Bauhaus and explain the housing projects of the Dojunkai.

Bauhaus

The Bauhaus was founded in 1919 in Weimar, Germany, to provide comprehensive education on art and architecture. Bauhaus' ideas can be traced back to the Arts and Crafts movement in England at the end of the nineteenth century. The Arts and Crafts movement challenged the mass production of inferior industrial products under the industrial revolution and emphasized the importance of handicrafts. British poet, thinker, and designer William Morris led the Arts and Crafts movement (Thompson 1955). Under its influence, the Deutscher Werkbund (German Association of Craftsmen) was established by architects and craftsmen in Germany. Therefore, they promoted standardization to improve the quality of products, aiming at the fusion of art and industry. Hermann Muthesius, Henry van de Velde, Joseph Maria Olbrich, Peter Behrens, Walter Gropius, Bruno Taut, and Josef Hoffmann participated in the Deutscher Werkbund, as did the architects of the Vienna Secession and the Jugendstil. One of the most important events in the history of modern architecture is the 1927 housing exhibition sponsored by the Deutscher Werkbund. A series of experimental houses (Weissenhofsiedlung) were built in Weissenhof, a Stuttgart suburb. Seventeen architects, mainly from Germany, participated, making the area into a place to practice modernist architecture. Ludvig Mies van der Rohe created the plan and built houses designed by Le Corbusier, Gropius, Hans Scharoun, and others.

The Bauhaus moved to Dessau in 1925. Gropius designed the school building in Dessau; it was imitated in various countries, including the United States and Japan, as a masterpiece of modernist architecture; other Bauhaus buildings were also influential internationally. By eliminating unnecessary decoration and pursuing rationalism, the Bauhaus established a framework for modern design. Gropius resigned as principal in 1928 and was succeeded by Hannes Meyer. Meyer championed standardization and quantification and emphasized economic efficiency and scientificity. In 1932, the Dessau school closed and moved to Berlin, becoming a private school. Mies van der Rohe was appointed principal and inherited Meyer's policy. During the 14 years leading up to the closing of the school in 1933, Bauhaus created the prototype of modernist architecture using the cutting-edge materials of the time, iron and glass, and had a major impact on contemporary art and architecture. The Bauhaus design was extremely rational and simple, making it suitable for mechanical mass production. Therefore, with the rise of modernist architecture, Bauhaus design methods spread across countries.

Natural Disaster Reconstruction Projects and Slum Improvement

Japan is also a country that suffers from such large-scale natural disasters. After the Great Kanto Earthquake of 1923, which caused great damage to Tokyo, large-scale redevelopment and slum improvement were carried out. In addition, new houses were proposed with the aim of breaking away from the old way of living in this era. The devastated slums in Tokyo were similar to the areas in Manila. Introducing architectural reconstruction cases in Japan can therefore be useful for understanding ideas of reconstruction and slum improvement in the Philippines.

The epicenter of the 1923 Great Kanto Earthquake was in Tokyo Bay and caused severe damage to the urban areas of Tokyo and Yokohama. The damage was particularly bad in downtown Tokyo, which was densely populated with wooden houses and block development had been delayed. Even before the earthquake, the need for noncombustible apartments had been recognized in downtown Tokyo. However, the damage was worsened due to an insufficient supply of reinforced concrete housing.

The Dojunkai was established in 1924 by the Ministry of Home Affairs of Japan. The government funded the project due to the earthquake and the need to both ensure the creating of new replacement housing and anticipate possible future disasters. First, temporary wooden barracks houses were built in Tokyo and Yokohama. Beginning in August 1925, the Nakanosato apartment, the first reinforced concrete apartment building of the Dojunkai, was constructed. The Nakanosato apartment was designed by Yoshikazu Uchida's laboratory in the Department of Architecture, University of Tokyo; it was completed in August 1926. Thereafter, the Dojunkai Design Department led the construction of Dojunkai apartments (16 locations) in Tokyo and Yokohama. The Dojunkai supplied high-quality housing mainly to the city's middle class and conducted slum area improvement projects. The Dojunkai reconstruction project is often used as a reference for slum improvement plans. In particular, Minowa and Sumitoshi apartments were model projects for slum clearance. The project also incorporated vocational training and medical facilities. It was recognized that these efforts were important for slum clearance (Bourdier 1992).

At the Dojunkai apartments, a reinforced concrete structure, rare at that time, was adopted. Here, a new lifestyle with gas, water, and flush toilets was proposed. In 10 years, about 2,800 units were built in 16 locations in Tokyo and Yokohama. Moreover, each house was carefully designed per its surrounding area.

Nakanosato Apartments

The Nakanosato Apartments was the first building to start construction as part of the Dojunkai. The north side faces the Hikifune River, and the two buildings along the river are lined with stores on the first floor. An assembly hall was set up in the courtyard. The meeting place was a temple-style wooden structure and became the center of the community of residents. Here, ceremonial occasions of residents were held, and it was a place where children gathered. It was popular because it was a reinforced concrete apartment building, rare at that time. Such housing construction is also popular in the slums of the Philippines.

- Completion: 1926
- Number of Buildings: three stories and six buildings
- Total Number of Units: 102

Minowa Apartments

The Minowa Apartments were small apartments in which the Dojunkai was involved, with 52 units in two four-story buildings. Before the Great Kanto Earthquake, the Minowa area was a slum saturated with illegal settlements. The construction of the Minowa Apartments was a model project for improving housing for impoverished people. The reconstruction land plot project conducted as part of the Dojunkai significantly changed the cityscape of the area. There were family-friendly units on the first to third floors of the building and single corridor-type dwelling units on the fourth floor.

- Completion: 1928
- Number of Buildings: four stories and two buildings
- Total Number of Units: 52

Sumitoshi Apartments

The Sumitoshi Apartments were also a model project for slum clearance. Zenrinkan, a social welfare facility, was built adjacent to the Sumitoshi Apartments, and a factory for vocational training was set up in the courtyard.

Here, both community welfare and financial independence were planned along with housing construction. Further, the slum clearance, conducted under the Dojunkai, was an improvement project for the living environment, including the establishment of a health center and a vocational training center.

- Completion: 1927–1930
- Number of Buildings: three stories and eighteen buildings
- Total number of units: 294

FOR SOCIAL ARCHITECTURE DESIGN 5: UNDERSTANDING OF SOCIAL STRUCTURE

New developments in industrialization and capitalism had created great divisions in society beginning in the nineteenth century. Many conflicts had arisen, especially between capitalists and workers. Gender discrimination and racial discrimination also remained rampant. In the early twentieth century, labor movements and women's suffrage movements took place throughout North America and Europe. A large-scale demonstration was held in New York on March 8, 1904, demanding women's suffrage and improved working conditions. The first strike in Japan was initiated in 1886 by female workers at the Amemiya Silk Mill in the city of Kofu, Yamanashi Prefecture. However, the Japanese labor movement was totally suppressed and did not develop sufficiently.

After World War II, the Japanese labor movement revived and developed amid democratization under the United States occupation. The United States recognized the existence of trade unions as one of the major forces of democratization and actively supported them. As a result, trade unions became a major force in shaping Japanese society. In this history of social improvements, architectural movements occurred in response to social change.

Kitchen Improvement Campaign

In Japan, from the 1920s, lifestyle improvement movements touched various areas, including housing and clothing. Thus, lifestyle changed from traditional Japan to a Western-influenced style due to Western influence, the introduction and establishment of scientific knowledge, urbanization, and industrialization. Government affiliates and offices conducted government-made movements to improve people's lives and repeatedly urged them to improve their lives. Such attempts comprised the lifestyle improvement movements, such as the kitchen improvement movement (Watari 2010).

In modern Japan, modernization progressed rapidly in urban planning and social systems. In the free society of a Taisho Democracy, discussions were held on improving women's status; a kitchen improvement movement began to improve women's working environment. At that time, the kitchen comprised an on-floor and a dirt floor (*doma*); it was common to use a *tsukubai*-style sink on the solid floor and a *kamado* in the dirt floor. A *kamado* is a traditional Japanese kitchen stove used for cooking grains and groceries. A *tsukubai* is a sink made by hollowing out stones and rocks in the garden and was originally used to cleanse the mind and body before entering the tea room. When cooking three times a day, the movement of crouching and standing each time the women needed to switch from using the traditional Japanese *kamado* and *tsukubai* was a heavy burden for women, particularly older women. At that time, firewood was used in Kamado. During cooking, the women also had to crouch frequently to ignite the firewood and manage the fire while cooking. Also, since the *kamado* is installed in a dirt floor, it was necessary to go back and forth between on the solid floor and dirt floor, stepping up and down between them each time throughout the work; thus, the first step for improving women's situation was to improve the kitchen. Modern water and gas facilities were introduced. Women's improving working environment was shown in the winning proposals for the kitchen design prizes developed by the Housing Improvement Association in 1918. The composition of the kitchen was more organized. The sink, gas table, and cooking table were installed at the same height, greatly improving work efficiency. This new design became the prototype of the modern kitchens that followed, but they were only implemented in some urban areas.

The Gender Element

The relationship between social improvements and housing is not unique to Japan. The Schroeder House (Rietveld 1924) in Utrecht, for example, was designed by the Dutch architect Gerrit Rietveld and Truus Schroeder in 1924. There is a studio, study, kitchen, housework room, and maid's room on the first floor. The second floor has a living room, Schroeder's bedroom, a son's room, and a room for two daughters. The partition between the rooms on the second floor is movable, and when moved, it can be used as one large room. Freeing the room from its fixed function was the idea of Schroeder. As Friedman notes,

> Passionate about art and about each other, both saw the house as an opportunity to create a totally modern environment, free of the repressive traditions and rules—both social and architectural—that kept them from new experiences and the expression of emotions. Their commitment to this partnership was

long-standing: they would continue working together on a number of important domestic and other design projects, particularly during the 1920s and 1930s. (Friedman 1998)

Schroeder incorporated a break from the bourgeois-dominated social system of the time into her home design. Reflecting this break in how living space is designed is necessary for improving housing in the context of social change. For example, she created a new design aimed at women's social bedrooms, citing elements of De Stijl.

Other innovative homes designed by architects in the early twentieth century often had women as clients or saw women taking strong initiatives in home design. These include the Hollyhock House, designed by Frank Lloyd Wright; the Villa Stein-De Monzie, designed by Le Corbusier; and the Farnsworth House, designed by Mies van der Rohe. The architects sought to express social change from an architectural perspective, reflecting the demands of female clients in the design. Even if some of the functions of the house are lost, the architects moved away from traditional customs (such as women tending to their homes and men engaging with society) and adopting the newly advanced lifestyle of the time. Many architectural solutions were attempted in line with such new societies and lifestyles.

URBAN IMPROVEMENT EFFORTS

Urban improvement at the time of the establishment of an industrialized society in the latter half of the nineteenth century and the first half of the twentieth century cannot be equated with pursuing the quality of the modern environment, culture, and living environment. However, the idea of improving the miserable civil life and poor living environment found in overcrowded cities was held in common with the present day. Prior to this, in the late eighteenth and nineteenth centuries, Baroque urban remodeling, in which the private property of feudatory princes and aristocrats, such as gardens and walls, was rendered open to the public, was not conscious of improving the living environment of the common people. The magnificent urban planning that connects the plazas and memorial buildings with wide straight roads can be said to be a spatial device for the rule of the state's powers. On the other hand, the main focus of modern architects' urban planning is to improve the living space of residents. Therefore, it can be said that architects' efforts to improve cities since the modern era should be referred to for the improvement of impoverished areas. Many people who greatly influenced modern urban planning appeared during this period, such as Ebenezer Howard, Tony Garnier, Clarence Arthur Perry, Le Corbusier, and Frank Lloyd Wright.

Howard's Garden City concept (1965) sought an ideal city in the suburbs, where urban and rural areas coexist, rather than improving existing cities. On the other hand, Le Corbusier's La Ville Radieuse (1930) aimed to transform the big city. It was a model in which the land was opened by high-rise buildings and used for open spaces such as green spaces. Perry's Neighborhood Unit was also an architectural solution for planning community formation for urban residents.

This section gives an overview of the history of CIAM, an organization for modern architecture and urban planning ideas, and outlines the Athens Charter as a set of principles of urban planning. It then outlines some important urban planning proposals that have been addressed to improving the living environment.

CIAM: Congrès International d'Architecture Moderne

The Congrès International d'Architecture Moderne (CIAM) is an organization for modern architecture and urban planning thought (Mumford 2000) CIAM was organized in 1928 by Le Corbusier, Sigfried Giedion, and others to pursue modern architecture and urban planning principles. Initially, 28 architects, mainly from Europe, participated. CIAM formalized the rules of modern architecture by consensus. It also sought to use architectural design as an economic and political approach to improve world problems. Hence, CIAM sought to greatly expand the scope of application of architecture as a social improvement method. Thus, it greatly impacted social sciences. Particularly noteworthy is the Athens Charter, established at the fourth conference. It had a notable impact on urban planning worldwide; meanwhile, it was criticized for its functionalism.

At CIAM 4, in 1933, the Athens Charter was adopted as a set of principles for urban planning. It aimed at realizing a functional city in the modern architecture movement and proposed the ideal form of a modern city. CIAM's architects aimed to shape society and cities of the future through functional planning. Meanwhile, air pollution and dense living spaces were problems in cities; it was not possible to fully meet the needs of residents. There was also a common understanding that city authorities and government perpetuated urban flaws. They shared the sense that architects should play a central role in improving the city. CIAM 4 represented the basic concept of typical modernism. It considered the city as an organism based on positivism, realized by engineering and social science, and requiring to be hygienic for all.

Nonetheless, CIAM ideas regarding its methodologies and programs were diverse, with no unified doctrine. At the June 1931 Berlin Extraordinary Conference prior to CIAM 4, the difference in ideological positions is clearly distinct. For example, the Swiss group prioritized materialistic and deductive

methods over idealistic and inductive methods of urban analysis methodologies, and the Polish group prioritized data collection over analysis. There
was also much disagreement on whether cities should be designed based on
a contemporary comparative study or on a diachronic and historical basis.
At the same time, participants recognized that collaborative research with an
academic approach provided better insights into urban issues. They posited
CIAM as a research organization.

At the tenth meeting, Team X, a group of young architects led by Alison
and Peter Smithson, criticized CIAM's functionalist architecture and urban
planning. They also proposed a new direction for advocating dynamic architecture and urban planning. Thus, CIAM was effectively dismantled.

The Athens Charter

The 95-article Athens Charter was established within the CIAM research
organization. In other words, it is a very peculiar position in the sense that it
is a text agreed to by CIAM member architects. The Athens Charter categorized the city into four places: living, working, recreation, and transportation.
By zoning these places appropriately and clearly, it tried to create a new
methodology for urban planning. After World War II, it was actually used as
an urban planning textbook. The most important of the four elements is the
element of living.

The Athens Charter builds high-rise buildings to create better living space
and green open space in limited urban space. It advocates that high-rise
houses should be separated from each other, prohibited from being placed
along the main road, and that cities should secure more open spaces. The
Athens Charter aimed to ensure health, proper population density, and enough
sunshine for all. For workplaces, it minimized the distance from residential
areas and separated factory areas and residential areas using a green zone.
Mass transportation connects the separated cities, and main intersections separate pedestrian roads as multilevel crossings. The trunk road and the roads
in the residential area are also separated, and the trunk road is surrounded by
a green zone, separating the trunk road from the residential area.

The Athens Charter has set out a policy of creating an ideal city to improve
the cities affected by rapid population growth and deterioration of the living environment. Looking at the model of Plan Voisin by Le Corbusier as
described below, it seems that a strictly planned city excludes humans, but it
is nevertheless necessary to confirm a concrete plan. Le Corbusier recognized
the importance of human-centered planning.

87. For the Architect Occupied with the Tasks of Urbanism, the Measuring
Rod will be the Human Scale: After the downfall of the last hundred years,

architecture must once again be placed in the service of man. It must lay sterile pomp aside, concern itself with the individual and create for his happiness the fixtures that will surround him, making all the movements of his life easier. Who can take the measures necessary to the accomplishment of this task if not the architect who possesses a complete awareness of man, who has abandoned illusory designs, and who, judiciously adapting the means to the desired ends, will create an order that bears within it a poetry of its own? (Le Corbusier 1973: 101)

URBAN PLANNING PROPOSALS

The following plans are architectural improvement plans for the urban environment created by architects in response to the problem of deterioration of the living environment due to urbanization at that time.

Modern City and Plan Voisin (Le Corbusier 1922)

Le Corbusier exhibited "Modern City" at the Salon d'Automne, in Paris in 1922. Modern City was conceived as a city model representing basic principles rather than providing a solution to urban problems. He presented "Plan Voisin" in Paris at the 1925 International Decorative Arts Exhibition. Plan Voisin is an application of the principles of modern cities to Paris. It too did not aim to solve Paris's urban problems; instead, it presented a reflection of Paris ordered by basic principles while retaining historic buildings such as the Louvre Palace.

Radiant City (Le Corbusier 1930)

Le Corbusier presented his "Radiant City" at the third CIAM. As a logical consequence of Le Corbusier's urban studies, Radiant City was presented as a universal urban model. Thus, in 1933, *Ville Radieuse* (The Radiant City) was published. This book noted the basic principles of modern urban planning in the Athens Charter, such as the sun, greenery, natural conditions of space, housing, work, and transportation. Radiant City was the theoretical foundation of Le Corbusier's urban planning and greatly influenced modern urban planning. Le Corbusier worked on practical urban planning in Chandigarh, India, in the 1940s and situated lessons he learned in Chandigarh as a practice of Radiant City.

Tokyo Plan 1960 (Tange 1961)

"Tokyo Plan 1960" is a city improvement plan for Tokyo proposed by architect Kenzo Tange in 1961. Tange thought Tokyo's urban structure could not withstand the rapid population growth during this high-growth period. Thus, he discarded the centralized, closed urban structure from the Edo period (that is, the early modern period) and proposed a new urban grid structure that extended from the city center beyond Tokyo Bay to Chiba Prefecture. During the design process, Kisho Kurokawa, who belonged to the Tange laboratory at that time, proposed a "Cycle Transportation System" that enabled mass high-speed transportation by automobiles and monorails. Arata Isozaki designed a vertical shaft with an elevator and equipment piping at each grid connection point, and placed offices between the shafts. Tange's proposals were detailed relative to those of other architects. As an expandable city design to address city growth, this remained a vital ideal.

Tower City (Kikutake 1958) and Marine City (Kikutake 1960)

The Tower City Project and Marine City Project are city plans designed by architect Kiyonori Kikutake and were announced at the World Design Conference in Tokyo in 1960. Kikutake led the Metabolism Group, an architectural movement based on idea that architecture and cities are metabolized as they grow. He thought it was necessary to divide the city's buildings into major structures and accessories so that the equipment could be replaced according to its useful life. The Tower City Project connected tubular spaces to multiple giant concrete shafts that extend vertically; ultimately, the goal was to create a huge skyscraper. The Marine City Project planned to sustainably reclaim the city by creating artificial ground at sea and connecting residential units that were exchangeable.

Brasilia's Pilot Plan (Costa 1956) and the Curitiba Master Plan (Lerner 1968)

Urban planning in Brasilia was started by President Juscelino Kubitschek, who was elected in 1956. The design proposal of architect Lucio Costa was selected for the big project of capital relocation. Lucio Costa's design with a large cross shape hosts the central part (Plano Piloto) of the capital's function. It is said to represent an airplane. Here, various urban planning ideas, such as road design, block design, and land use, are included. In the body part, there is a central avenue (the Monumental Axis) with a lawn in the center, along with administrative districts, industrial districts, hotel districts, and so on. At the starting point of the central avenue, the houses of parliament, the supreme court, and the presidential palace are located. Conversely, the wing part is a residential area, in which apartment houses, shopping streets, churches, schools, etc. are regularly spaced. There is also a clear pattern in the road network that connects these districts: the intersections of the main road and other roads are multilevel crossings, while for other roads, T-type intersections and rotary intersections are adopted, and there are almost no cross intersections. Major buildings such as the houses of parliament and the cathedral were all designed by Oscar Niemeyer, with modernist designs. Many satellite cities are located around Plano Piloto. Since each district of Brasilia is well separated, it was always necessary to move around the city by car. As a result, there were many inconveniences in actual civil life, and Brasilia's urban planning was regularly criticized.

Curitiba is the capital of the State of Paraná in Brazil. Curitiba as a human-scale city is considered an excellent example of urban planning's success. In the 1960s, Curitiba's population increased significantly, reaching around 430,000. In 1964 Mayor Ivo Arzua held a new urban planning competition. The ideas of architect Jaime Lerner were adopted into the Curitiba Master Plan. The main points of the plan are parcel management, traffic control in the city center, conservation of historic buildings in the old town, and construction of a public transportation system. These points are based on criticisms of Brasilia's urban planning. In 1971 Lerner became mayor, and these plans were put into practice. Now Curitiba has an efficient public transportation system used by many residents. In addition, the city of Curitiba has an area of green space that is about three times the standard value required by UNESCO for the city. Curitiba's policy was highly evaluated and was commended at the 1996 Habitat II (the Second United Nations Conference on Human Settlements).

Master Plan for Chandigarh (Le Corbusier 1950)

After India and Pakistan's independence in 1947, a new capital in Punjab became a strategic necessity. The first master plan was by American architect Albert Meyer and Polish codesigner Matthew Novikki. However, Novikki died in an accident, and Le Corbusier took over the plan in 1950. Le Corbusier planned the city per CIAM's urban planning principles. The first plan was to have 150,000 people inhabit the city initially and 500,000 subsequently. Le Corbusier called the divided areas sectors and made provisions for the people of Chandigarh to complete their living, working, and leisure within respective dedicated sectors. The size of each sector was 800 m x 1200 m. Le Corbusier designed symbolic buildings such as the parliament building, the administrative office building, and the high court. Chandigarh has two satellite cities, Punchkler and Moherley.

Like Brasilia, Chandigarh incorporates various urban planning ideas, such as road design, block design, and land use. Le Corbusier categorized the roads into eight categories according to purpose of use and maximum speed and then placed them in appropriate positions. He separated the sidewalks and driveways and planned a road network for pedestrians. He arranged the roads into separate sidewalks and driveways. He also planned a road network for pedestrians. Since Le Corbusier inherited the ideas of Meyer and Novikki, the basic structure of the master plan did not change. However, Le Corbusier changed the plan to divide the rectangle on a mesh.

ABSENCE OF VULNERABLE PEOPLE IN MODERN URBAN PLANNING

The Athens Charter by CIAM greatly influenced the urban planning of Europe, the United States, and Japan, as well as other countries, via a clear theory of urban planning by functionalism, but criticism of it occurred inside CIAM in the 1950s. These criticisms included the complete separation of urban functions, the emphasis on technical feats such as skyscrapers, and the use of strong planning by architects. Jacobs's book, *The Death and Life of Great American Cities* (1961), along with *The Economy of Cities* (1969), is an important book in urban planning research. She opposed non-human centered urban planning and the car-centricity of big American cities. She surveyed the Italian immigrant district in Boston, a redevelopment target from urban planners' point of view. Based on the low crime rate there, she considered conditions for safe streets, specifying the usefulness of having many constant street watchers (eyes on the street). Jacobs also noted the following four conditions for a city to generate exuberant diversity: (Jacobs 1961, 150–51)

- A district and as many of its internal parts as possible must serve more than one primary function (preferably more than two). These elements must ensure that people who go outdoors on different schedules and purposes can use many facilities in common.
- Most blocks must be short; streets and opportunities to turn corners must be frequent.
- The district must have a mix of buildings that vary in age and condition, including a good proportion of old ones, such that they vary in the economic yield they produce. This mixing must be fairly close-grained.
- There must be a sufficiently dense concentration of people for whatever purposes they may have for being at a particular place. It includes a dense concentration in the case of people who are there for residential purposes.

Since the 1960s, such urban planning has been regarded as a bureaucratic, profit-oriented, inhumane practice. However, though the Athens Charter is not used as a concrete urban planning guide, it is considered an effective method of urban analysis.

URBAN PLANNING AND SOCIAL CAPITAL

Social capital has multiple definitions, interpretations, and uses. Robert D. Putnam (1993) posited that social capital promotes mutual support between communities and countries, combating social obstacles in modern society. Here, social capital is built by a social network of people and includes consciously shared norms, values, and trust. Social capital contributes to promoting people's cooperation and joint action, achieving common goals and mutual benefits. Thus, the aim of urban planning should be to build social relations between people in the local community. However, traditional customs and norms are not always effective as social capital. Since tradition is nurtured in regional and societal dynamism and interaction, some practices have an exclusive side and may not be suitable as social capital. For example, social capital's production activities may strengthen and reproduce strict gender roles within a society. Another important piece of social capital is family. However, while strengthening family networks may have an advantage for men, it may hinder the social advancement of women and the construction of external networks. If social capital is sufficient, voluntary, autonomous, and sustainable, then activities will likely proceed smoothly at the local level. But social capital is not formed instantly, and it requires continuous efforts from all parties to nurture it.

Social capital can be categorized into cohesive, bridging, and collaborative types. Cohesive social capital enhances the cohesiveness of members, communities, and groups in society. It encourages cooperation within the organization. Bridging social capital is a network of homogeneous societies, communities, and groups. Collaborative social capital is a network between different societies, communities, and groups. Examples include government–community and NGO-community relationships. Bridging social capital and collaborative social capital strengthen external relationships and increase access to external information and opportunities, strengthening societal, community, and group cohesiveness. Therefore, the three types complement each other. Ensuring openness to the outside improves internal social capital.

TRANSITION OF AMERICAN URBAN
REVITALIZATION AND SOCIAL CAPITAL

As noted, urban redevelopment in the United States was modeled on CIAM's modern urban planning. Thus, slum clearance was frequent until the 1970s. Further, due to the construction of expressways after World War II, the population of city centers decreased, and the hollowing-out phenomenon was common. In the United States, the Housing Act was amended in 1954, but the hollowing out of city centers progressed rapidly. At this time, Jane Jacobs wrote *The Death and Life of Great American Cities.*

In 1965, the US federal government organized the Department of Housing and Urban Development to support the comprehensive redevelopment of cities. In the 1970s, suburban development expanded further. During this period, many large stores opened in the suburbs. *Cities on the Move* (1970) by Arnold Toynbee describes cities during these times.

Thereafter, redevelopment of the city center was conducted in earnest, suppressing suburban development. The federal government enacted the Housing and Community Development Act (1974) and created the Community Development Block Grant (CDBG) system. Accordingly, measures for improving low-income earners' situation in central-city and slum-like living areas were taken. The CDBG system remains effective even today.

Further, the federal government created the Urban Development Action Grant (UDAG) (1974) system to promote urban redevelopment projects; it provided strong financial support until 1989. Hence, large-scale redevelopment buildings were built in major cities. In places such as San Francisco and Boston, restoration-type redevelopment projects using warehouses were implemented, and facilities (cinemas, museums, shopping centers, etc.) with designs that matched each region's unique features, were created. Implementing suburban regulations and aggressive investment in the center creates a city that experiences balanced growth. Boston, Miami, Seattle, and San Francisco are good examples.

In the 1980s, support measures such as the Urban Jobs and Enterprise Zone Act of 1981 were implemented, and efforts to revitalize city centers began. Moreover, a program to preserve and regenerate historic buildings was launched under the leadership of the National Trust. Further, in the 1990s, it became common for residents to participate in urban redevelopment. Development was conducted with an emphasis on the local community. This is the New Urbanism, an effort to restore local communities and maintain and develop the unique environment of each region.

Since the latter half of the 1990s, resident participation has been the main player in regional revitalization. However, cities have seen an increase in gated communities. Moreover, government security measures, such as the efforts in New York City that applied the "broken windows theory" (Kelling and Coles 1995), are effective in curbing crime, but excessive crackdowns limit people's scope of action. Hence, social capital is considered to be declining in the current American society. Thus, it is necessary to build new social capital, incorporating the element of building creative consciousness. Redevelopment projects are not limited to improving the urban environment. A creative environment that constantly revitalizes the city while promoting new ideas is essential. There is currently a need to improve the environment for forming new social capital.

Urban improvement has taken twists and turns in developed countries. Cities should be built for humans, and these forms of social capital are vital factors. Using social capital enhances social stability and common interests without compromising the uniqueness of social groups (Sander, 2002). In particular, cities and village plans in slums are highly contextual; thus, it is necessary to consider history, culture, social structure, and economic inequality and make full use of social capital. Therefore, it is extremely important to study cases of urban development.

Chapter 7

Practice—Sharing Images, Shaping Places

This chapter examines the broad potential of architecture, as connected by critical mutual understanding between the researcher and subjects, based on a case study of collaborative endeavors with residents in the CMP. Sharing anthropological results between residents and anthropologists can provide a foothold to formulating specific architectural ethnography.

IMAGES AND COMMUNITY UNDERSTANDING

The CMP Program comprises a three-stage process. Stage one involves the acquisition of land and allocation of landownership rights to beneficiaries. Stage two involves area development and land allocation. Stage three involves the construction of houses by residents and community improvement. NPO staff and locals participating in the CMP are required to hold frequent workshops at each stage of the process.

Stage one aims to confirm which residents will participate in the CMP and complete the procedures for acquiring landownership rights. The process (confirming and negotiating with existing landowners, acquiring loans from the government agency, and paying landowners) is quite lengthy. It may take several years to complete documentary procedures. Community-wide planning and the construction of individual houses take place in stages two and three. The main activities in this stage are discussions among residents interested in building houses and developing acquired land. This stage also involves negotiations with the municipal government regarding the incorporation of livelihood infrastructure, including water and sewage facilities, gas, and electricity, as well as discussions among residents about road construction in the community. The NPO provides continuous support in these activities, including assistance with technical aspects.

In the workshops on community-wide planning in stages two and three, various discussions were conducted between the residents and the NPO and among the residents, using visual materials such as diagrams, drawings, and models. The FDUP used visual materials to facilitate discussions with residents. The FDUP has been involved in the CMP as an Originator from the beginning, during which time it has accumulated practical knowledge to address various problems that occur during the discussions. It fully understands the effectiveness of using such visual materials as shared tools for promoting mutual understanding among the residents and between the NPO and the residents.

The Macoda HOA is an on-site project in the third stage of the CMP. The FDUP prepared the community site development plan and community-wide prototype model. In this prototype, houses of residents who had formed compadrazgo relationships are situated together following the completion of the community (Macoda HOA) in the CMP project. Compadrazgo relationships are usually established with community leaders or affluent members of the community. However, in the Macoda HOA, compadrazgo relationships are formed between fellow residents experiencing similar economic circumstances, in conjunction with suki relationships.

The community-wide model and the model house were created during the stage two workshops. Noteworthy was not whether the community would follow this model when building houses, but that residents' awareness toward improving their houses was strengthened by visualizing the community-wide image. Moreover, it was used as a starting-point for residents' discussions concerning the community's shared portions. Since the Macoda HOA is an on-site project, residents moved to the newly acquired land as existing houses informally occupying the site were gradually removed. However, problems such as dissatisfaction among residents whose floor space was set to decrease, the order of relocation and rebuilding, and a lack of funding created a situation where progress lagged regarding the community development in stage two although the community had acquired land. Accordingly, the NPO, community leaders, and resident volunteers presented the community-wide model. Subsequently, discussions among residents gradually progressed per the visual materials.

Through this stage, models (visual images) were shared among residents as expressions of the future community direction. However, while these models helped residents form a community image, they imposed uniform images on residents; thus, they were criticized. Nevertheless, the nonhierarchical aspects of the models as visual images enabled the exchange of concrete opinions between the NPO and the residents. Further, the models were vital in providing a common base in discussions between the NPO and residents and among the residents.

THE SHARING OF DRAWINGS

In the fieldwork, various visual materials were used during interviews for the following reasons: (1) Residents already employed visual materials, such as diagrams, drawings, and models, in the CMP workshops. (2) Critical discussions were conducted by residents and the NPO using visual materials. Thus, interviews could be conducted from various angles via visual images. Moreover, to obtain basic materials before the interview survey, a measurement survey was conducted to grasp the state of the houses and dwelling styles. Bakhtin explained the notion of understanding foreign culture as follows:

> Of course, a certain entry as a living being into a foreign culture, the possibility of seeing the world through its eyes, is a necessary part of the process of understanding it; but if this were the only aspect of this understanding, it would merely be duplication and would not entail anything new or enriching. Creative understanding does not renounce itself, its own place in time, its own culture; and it forgets nothing. In order to understand, it is immensely important for the person who understands to be located outside the object of his or her creative understanding—in time, in space, in culture. For one cannot really see one's own exterior and comprehend it as a whole, and no mirrors or photographs can help; our real exterior can be seen and understood only by other people because they are located outside us in space, and because they are others. (1986, 7)

Bakhtin affirmed the externality of the person who seeks understanding. However, anthropology today, having reflected on researchers' position, also requires external subjects to examine the perspective of those seeking to understand them. Developing mutual interpretations of drawings by the others (subjects) and mutually viewing worlds cut out by drawings conceived through the researcher perspective are necessary parts of the survey sharing process.

An interview with a resident who moved from Ifugao Province to Metro Manila revealed the relationship between traditional houses and customs of the Ifugao people per a model found on a house roof during the measurement survey. Further, it was possible to grasp the relationship between concrete-block houses currently being constructed and traditional houses in the Philippines using drawings. In the informal settlements, houses are upgraded from simple shelters to more permanent structures made of wood or a wood-concrete mix. When upgrading from a shelter to a house, building from wood is the most suitable option. Many informal settlers used wood for columns and walls or to extend or strengthen the house. Further, given the Philippines' tropical rain forest, wood is abundant, and temperatures are high. Airy wood and bamboo houses with raised floors had been constructed in various places around informal settlements.

However, many residents wished to build their houses from concrete blocks since heftiness is essential to a good house. Stone-built houses are durable and evoke images of colonial-style dwellings established by the ruling classes during Spanish rule. Residents chose concrete houses for the security they offer in urban living and the high added value. Moreover, since concrete blocks comprise sand, cement, and water, they are highly regarded for house construction in any location. Safety is an essential condition when building houses in informal settlements. The lack of public safety in informal settlements is a major problem among residents. However, improving public safety is not easy. Given that residents must ensure safety, they wished to construct houses from robust concrete blocks.

TOWARD ARCHITECTURAL PRACTICES

The following examines architectural ethnography in impoverished neighborhoods of Metro Manila to apply the anthological study results to architectural planning. The crux of the proposal involves establishing multiple core units in the community and improving the living space through collaboration between providers (anthropologists) and recipients (residents) of assistance with the core units as a base. This section first reviews the field site conditions. Daang Tubo is a settlement within the University of the Philippines premises. It is among 19 such informal settlements and has 786 households. While asserting its landownership rights, the university recognizes the right of the informal settlers to reside on the land. It announced a policy to develop the premises. Since residents inhabit the land, freely building houses, the community assumed a disorderly, mazelike structure. In the rainy season, unsurfaced alleyways resemble rivers, with no streetlamps. At night, public safety rapidly deteriorates in the pitch darkness.

The compadrazgo system is essential in considering interpersonal relationships in the Philippines. Informal settlers employed compadrazgo strategically to fortify neighborhood ties; however, they maintained multiple transitory relations adapted to time and place without full economic assistance. Further, nuclear families account for 78% of households, and extended families typically account for 9%. In informal settlements, there is a strong tendency to seek financial support from relatives. However, it is not directly connected to families living together.

Unable to live in nuclear families or expect financial assistance from relatives, residents sought to maintain communities and reap pragmatic benefits in forming groups that go beyond family. Most houses provide adequate space to sleep, as residents transfer private spaces, such as living rooms and dining rooms, outside the house, dispersing them throughout the community. Conversely, public spaces, such as plazas and roads, are appropriated for private use. Thus, the community fulfills the function of a single dwelling.

Most houses in Daang Tubo are row houses with almost identical building and floor areas. The most common size range for a building area is 10–15 square meters, where 80% of the residents live in houses with less than 20 square meters of space. Only 14% of the houses have more space than the 30 square meters provided to social housing residents; thus, most residents live in immensely cramped living spaces. The externalization of the living sphere helps residents secure more space outside the small house to restore living functions lost to bed space. It encourages space-sharing in the community and blurs the boundaries between private and public space.

BASIC IDEA FOR UPGRADING THE LIVING SPACE

From interviews with residents, the idea arose of integrating certain living functions in small units of five to 10 households and constructing spaces within the units to be shared among several families. Core units must give residents opportunities to create spaces they wish to inhabit. The basic idea is derived from the narrow, self-built houses that define informal settlements and how their living functions are externalized; that is, from living conditions that forced residents to disperse their main living functions (e.g., kitchens, toilets, living rooms, and showers). Another contextual factor that has allowed residents to accept and establish living spaces centered on shared-use is the spiritual relationships formed among neighbors via the compadrazgo system; thus, residents strengthen their interpersonal connections in the community.

Regarding projects, assistance providers (anthropologists) and recipient residents must work together to upgrade settlements. Rather than supplying complete "package" houses, self-building should be encouraged by providing multiple core units for residents to consider the future direction of living spaces in the community. This proposal is a long-term process where providers and recipients of assistance actively explore sustainable modes of living over a given period, and financial support is not necessarily the main concern. During the construction period, residents' lives may change (e.g., children come of age, residents arrive and leave, and kinship relations evolve). Since the optimal solution to house spacing constantly evolves, it is necessary to accept changes and respond flexibly.

ARRANGING THE CORE UNITS

Regarding spatial structure, to upgrade houses per residents' living circumstances, core units must not prescribe a uniform set of spatial functions. Core unit layouts are *penetrating, annexed, apposed*, and *cut-in*. The present spatial conditions necessitate the use of several combinations. For example, if a dwelling is a wooden house, the core housing unit can be embedded in it using the penetrating or cut-in layout. If the house is made from concrete blocks, living functions can be added using the annexed or apposed layouts.

There are several possible patterns for the overall spatial structures developed from core unit layouts (see Figure 7.1). When upgrading existing houses, it is necessary to select the optimal layout and upgrade for each situation. Therefore, an awareness that the house layouts will not always follow these patterns and that actual spatial structures are more flexible and diverse is necessary.

   a. Inner Court Type: This type includes a separate shared space inside the dwelling. As multiple households must share the inner court area, the households surrounding this shared space should have close relationships, including blood and compadrazgo relations.

   b. Multiple Inner Court Type: This type includes multiple shared spaces inside the dwelling. Multiple sets of relatives have access to separate shared spaces. Like the inner court type, households surrounding such shared spaces should have close relationships, including blood and compadrazgo relations.

   c. Open Court Type: This type includes a shared space open to the community. Households surrounding this shared space should have close relationships, including blood and compadrazgo relations. Moreover, part of the court can be shared with other community members.

   d. Multiple Open Court Type: This type is an advanced form of the open court type. It includes multiple open shared spaces. Households surrounding shared space are divided into groups, each of which has access to shared space.

   e. Inner-Open Court Hybrid Type: This type is a hybrid of the inner and open court types. Residents can select a layout with a space exclusively for blood and compadrazgo relatives and a space open to the community.

   f. Separated Type: In this type, households are separate. While households secure a high degree of independence, the space shared by householders is also open to the public. Therefore, residents can share space with new community members and residents.

Private   Shared space

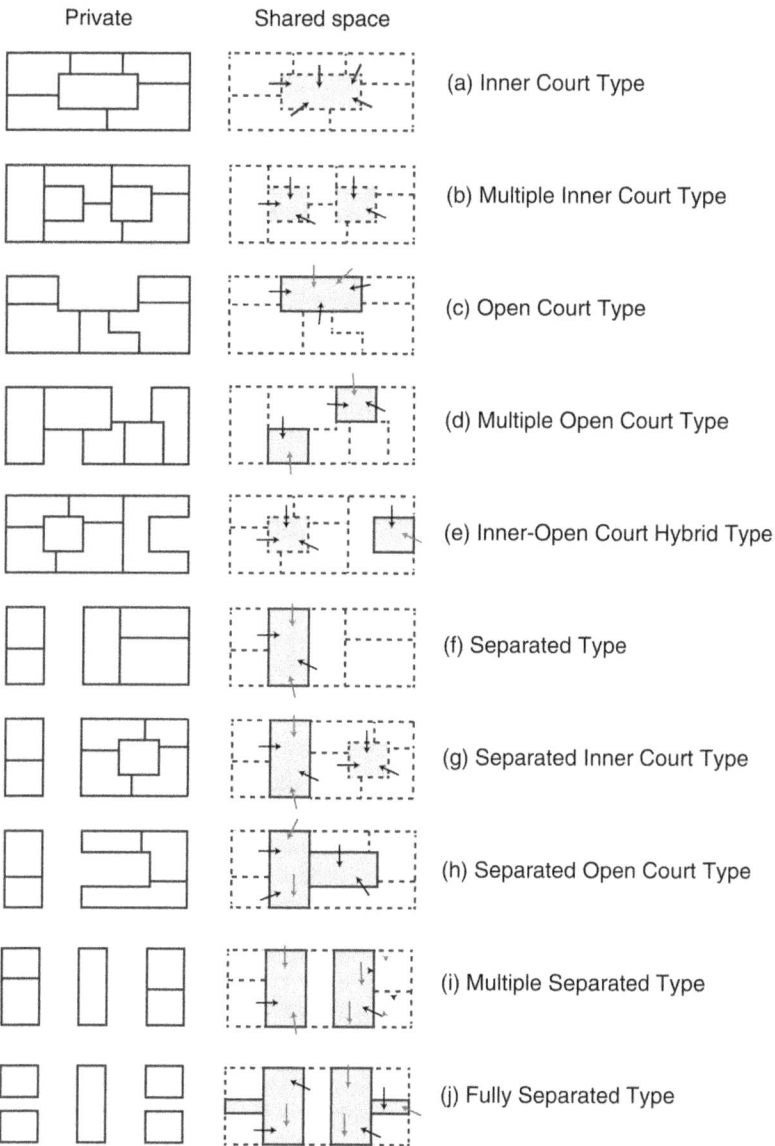

(a) Inner Court Type

(b) Multiple Inner Court Type

(c) Open Court Type

(d) Multiple Open Court Type

(e) Inner-Open Court Hybrid Type

(f) Separated Type

(g) Separated Inner Court Type

(h) Separated Open Court Type

(i) Multiple Separated Type

(j) Fully Separated Type

Figure 7.1 Core Units and Possible Patterns of Spatial Structures. ©2021 Fuyuki Makino.

g. Separated Inner Court Type: This type is a hybrid of the separated type and the inner court type. Because private space is secured, each household is highly independent. Moreover, the public space allows for space to be shared with new residents.

h. Separated Open Court Type: This is a hybrid of the separated and the open court type. The shared space is more public than in the separate inner court type, allowing living space to be shared among (with) adjacent households (new residents).

i. Multiple Separated Type: In this type, multiple separated types are side by side. Thus, mirroring the style of the separated type with public space between two separate households, the multiple separated type divides households into smaller units. Living space can be shared among (with) adjacent households (new residents).

j. Fully Separated Type: In this type, the individual households are fully separated. It also includes patterns where separate rooms are established for individuals, even within the same family. This type is easy for new residents to accept, and the living space is easily shared.

CASE STUDY 1: A GROUP OF HOUSES

Case study 1 was conducted involving a group of houses in the informal settlement of Daang Tubo at UP Diliman.

House and Family

First, house spaces and family circumstances of each household are introduced. The requirements for the layout of the initial core unit are then explained, along with an overview of the core unit and an upgrade simulation.

Family 1

- Length of Residence: 12 years; Number of Household Members: 4; Relatives in the Community: 0
- Father (age 28): electrical maintenance worker; Mother (age 29): sari-sari store operator; Daughter (age 5); Son (age 1)

The sari-sari store takes up approximately one-third of the house space, and the remaining space is divided into three areas, a kitchen, a bedroom, and a loft. The loft can be reached by climbing a ladder from the bedroom. The loft, also used as a living space for the children, contains an electric piano. There is also a window through which light enters the room. Almost all houses nearby are row houses; thus, the window offers a view over the neighbors' roofs. The father is a maintenance worker at the University of the Philippines. The sari-sari store operated by the mother stocks the largest selection of goods in the community. In addition to daily necessities, confectionaries, and medicine, it sells and rents music CDs and film DVDs.

Family 2

- Length of Residence: 27 years; Number of Household Members: 10; Relatives in the Community: 1 family
- Father (age 52): glassblower; Mother (age 54): sari-sari store operator; Son (age 27): photocopier; Eldest son's wife (age 32): housewife; Granddaughter (age 3); Granddaughter (age 2); Grandson (age 1); Grandson (age 0); Daughter (age 17); Mother's elder sister's husband (age 60)

Two households are living in a single space. This house's hallmark is that the room occupied by the eldest son and his wife is partitioned off. There are televisions in the living room and the room occupied by the eldest son and his wife, as well as two sets in the kitchen. When the eldest son married, space was expanded approximately twofold to make a separate room for the eldest son and his wife. While inhabiting the same house, the family has taken steps to secure separate living functions for the two households.

Family 3

- Length of Residence: 13 years; Number of Household Members: 8; Relatives in the Community: 0
- Grandmother (age 59): sari-sari store operator; Father (age 28): tricycle driver; Mother (age 29) sari-sari store operator; Son (age 8): elementary school student; Daughter (age 4); Mother's younger sister's husband (age 29): tricycle driver; Nephew (age 5); Nephew (age 2)

Although the house is divided into three areas (the sari-sari store, a living room/kitchen/bedroom, and another bedroom), no walls separate the rooms, forming a single continuous space. The sari-sari store faces the street, and the room is well lit. However, the living room and bedrooms, located farther inside the house, are dark because there are no windows. A skylight has been installed in the kitchen to allow light to enter through the roof.

Family 4

- Length of Residence: 11 years; Number of Household Members: 4; Relatives in the Community: 1 family

- Father (age 28): delivery worker; Mother (age 29): housewife; Older daughter (age 9): elementary school student (public school); Younger daughter (age 2)

This house is the least spacious of all the houses surveyed. The first floor had a cooking stove, a hammock, a table, chairs, and a television set. One room accommodated the family's living functions. The family uses a toilet and washing facilities at the mother-in-law's house, who lives nearby. This married couple secured a separate room from the parents. The cramped one-room space had a cooking stove, a basic kitchen, and a sink. Though borrowing the mother-in-law's kitchen was possible, the couple wanted to have their own space, however small.

Family 5

- Length of Residence: 21 years; Number of Household Members: 6; Relatives in the Community: 0
- Father (age 45): delivery worker; Mother (age 42): sari-sari store operator; Son (age 23): delivery worker; Son's wife (age 21): housewife; Grandchild (age 3 months); Older daughter (age 22): unemployed; Younger daughter (age 16): private university student

The house has separate rooms partitioned by walls for the parents, the son and his wife, and the older daughter. The walls are made from thin plywood boards. The family hopes to live in a spacious concrete house. Since space was secured for individual family members, the kitchen size was reduced, and the dining space was expanded to an area outside the house.

Requirements for the Layout of the Initial Core Unit

The infrastructure that must be incorporated into living spaces includes items requiring large-scale construction (i.e., gas, water, and sewage facilities) and items relatively easy to install (e.g., electricity). Since core units relate to infrastructure installation work, it is vital to consider gas, water and sewage, electricity, and communications, as requirements for core units.

Gas is primarily supplied to the houses in the form of propane gas. Water for daily use is supplied from wells. It is desirable to purchase drinking water. Since being connected to the sewage system is essential for improving hygiene in the community, this should be considered in the planning process. Some residents steal electricity from the University's power supply, while others officially purchase it from an electricity facility nearby. It is necessary to install electricity meters once development has progressed to a certain degree. Moreover, the popularization of mobile phones means that many residents own prepaid mobile phones.

Gas and Water in the Core Unit

Given the occupant density and site narrowness, the core unit must meet house appropriate minimum space functions. Infrastructure for gas and water plumbing is consolidated in a single space that houses the four functions of the toilet, shower, kitchen, and sink.

Electricity in the Core Unit

Consider developing a core unit as a shared space for various uses (living room, dining rooms, children's study space, and home occupations). While encouraging horizontal expansion, develop a unit with a staircase area to expand onto a second floor. Light the area around the houses with streetlamps to help prevent crime.

Upgrade Simulation

This study presents a simulation of the house upgrading process from the initial layout of the core unit to the layout after 10 years (see Figures 7.2, 7.3, and 7.4).

The products of "face-to-face" living in the informal settlements—spaces with a certain looseness, relationships based on the strategic use of compadrazgo, and relational systems where difference is accepted—can be confirmed, with striking clarity, in the extreme narrowness, crowdedness, and adjacency of the houses. This proposal represents an attempt to share such anthropological results with residents and apply them to a process in which specific forms of architecture (in the broad sense) are created.

CASE STUDY 2: DISASTER RECOVERY PROGRAM

In 2008, an international architectural design contest called the "Millennium School Design Competition" was held as a part of the "Be Better, Build Better Program," sponsored by the Philippines National Disaster Coordinating Council Civil Disaster Office of the Philippines Department of National Defense. It concerned a resident-oriented architectural process.

- Selection for the "Millennium School Design Competition" was sponsored by the government of the Philippines in April 2008.

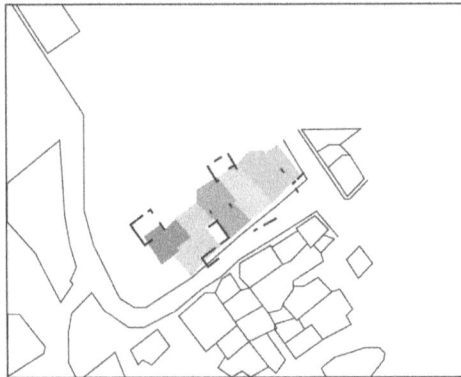

Initial State

(a) Core unit layout

Arrange the initial core units while considering
the infrastructure layout.

Figure 7.2 Simulation—Initial State. ©2021 Fuyuki Makino.

- The "Be Better, Build Better Program" was held by the Philippines
  National Disaster Coordinating Council Civil Disaster Office within the
  Philippines Department of National Defense.

Concept

In 1976, the first United Nations Conference on Human Settlements (Habitat
I) was held in Vancouver, Canada. Meanwhile, the government of the
Philippines sponsored the Manila-Tondo Foreshore International Architectural
Competition (the "Tondo Competition"). The Tondo Competition had a

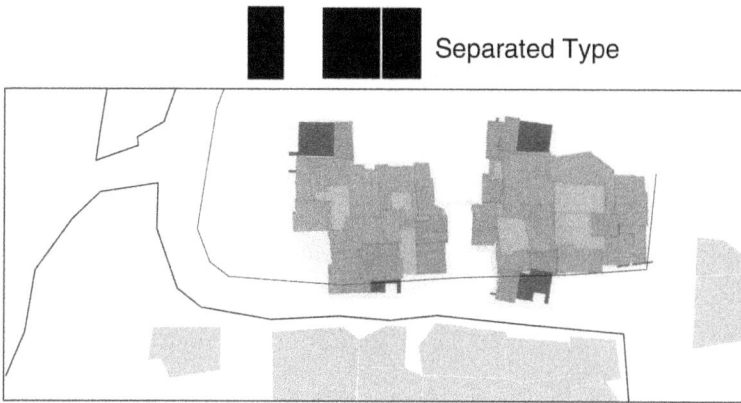

Separated Type

(b) First year
Upgrade to separated type to reflect kinship relations.

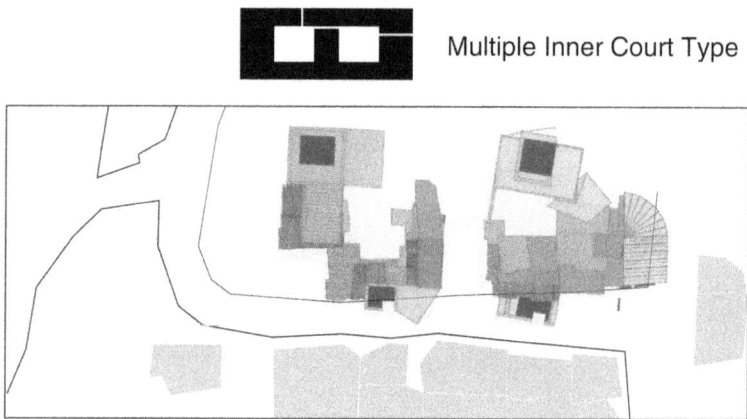

Multiple Inner Court Type

(c) Third year
Upgrade to multiple inner court type to develop shared space
for children and shared living areas.

Figure 7.3 Simulation—First and Third Years. ©2021 Fuyuki Makino.

revolutionary concept, asking people to consider the needs of informal settlers. Thereafter, the United Nations Human Settlements Programme (UN
Habitat) was established to implement the task of improving human settlements, and new approaches regarding these settlements, including housing
plans for the poor, were explored.

The Tondo Competition was an initiative to solve urban environmental
problems affecting many developing countries. It fundamentally aimed to
accomplish a paradigm shift from the development concepts adopted in

Inner Court Type

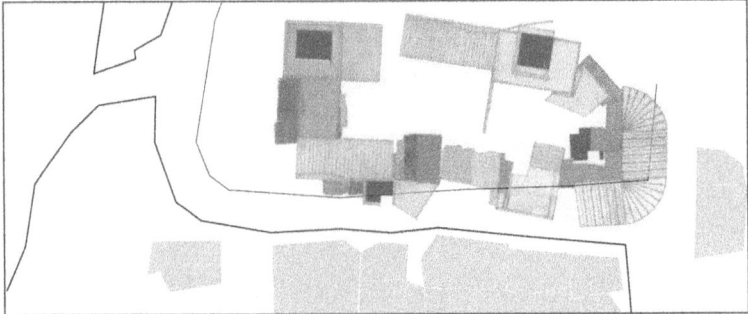

(d) Fifth year

Upgrade to inner court type with closed shape as each of the five families form compadrazgo relationships.

Multiple Open Court Type

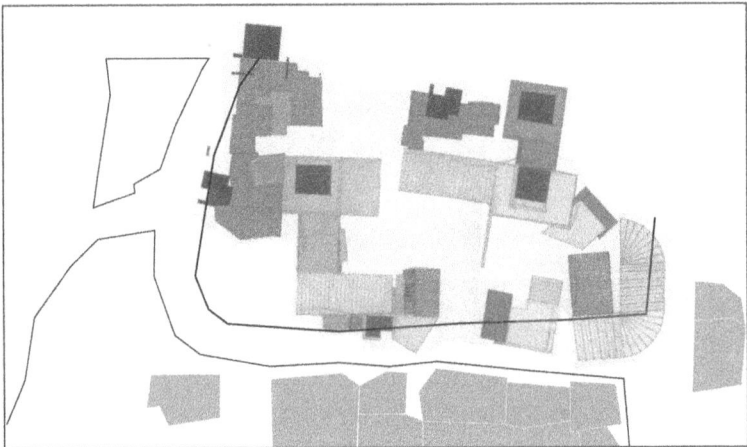

(e) Tenth year

Upgrade to multiple open court type with the arrangement of new core units to accommodate an increase in families.

Figure 7.4 Simulation—Fifth and Tenth Years. ©2021 Fuyuki Makino.

the past, per the understanding that, in the urban environments of rapidly developing countries, such as in Metro Manila, on-site upgrading programs produce better results than mandatory relocation programs. The competition challenged the world to provide new solutions to urban problems involving matters such as the communities, houses, and incomes of low-income-earners. The competition received over 3,000 registrations from 68 countries, resulting in more than 500 applications. The award-winning proposal was developed into a plan to be implemented in Manila.

Building on the Tondo Competition, in 2008, an international architectural design contest called the Millennium School Design Competition was held. This competition represented a new challenge to solving global problems currently facing developing countries, such as population growth, climate change, and poverty. In the competition, participants engaged with present-day global urban problems and explored architectural solutions through revolutionary proposals encompassing aspects including materials, design, and construction methods.

Participants were required to present specific measures and technological solutions against typhoons and earthquakes, characteristic of tropical zones and reflecting school construction concepts in developing countries. Moreover, participants were expected to use sustainable solutions to improve the quality of school construction in developing countries. The new technological proposals for cost-effective and earthquake-resistant sustainable building methods should be converted for use in various areas of developing countries, including the Philippines. The project area was Sagñay in Camarines Sur, the Philippines, a city that suffered significant damage every year due to typhoons.

Organizers and Collaborators

The following seven organizations were involved in the Design Competition:

- National Disaster Coordinating Council (Philippines Department of National Defense)
- Philippine Green Building Council (Government of the Philippines)
- My Shelter Foundation (NPO in the Philippines)
- United Architects of the Philippines (professional organization of architects in the Philippines)
- Disaster Management Network (NPO in the Philippines)
- Redeye (advertising agency in the Philippines)
- Department of Education (Philippines)
- Moreover, three universities participated as sponsor organizations:
- MIT Special Program for Urban and Regional Studies (Massachusetts Institute of Technology)
- Center for Public Leadership, John F. Kennedy School of Government (Harvard University)

- Center for the Study of the Longer-Range Future (Boston University)

At the MIT Center for Urban and Regional Studies, the Millennium School Design Competition winners were announced, after which an exhibition was held at the JFK School of Government.

Proposal: Designing the School of Tomorrow

Whether the results of field surveys can be applied to architectural design and urban planning hinges on the challenges involved in establishing resident-oriented community planning as a development method. In the competition proposal, construction techniques were interpreted not as exclusive to special engineers but as open techniques to be used freely by residents. The proposal aimed to construct relational systems of learning, defining the primordial form of the school as "teacher and students conversing under a tree."

- Concept 1: Reuse of Shipping Containers
  - The project involved a proposal for unit-type architecture in which shipping containers formed the core. The core section of the architecture was made from large, reused containers abandoned around the coast of the Philippines. Containers have sufficient strength to withstand natural disasters such as typhoons and earthquakes. They can also be adapted for various purposes by combining multiple units.
- Concept 2: Resident-Oriented Construction Process
  - The development is based on a resident-oriented construction process, in which residents build parts such as the non-container walls and ceiling sections. The important feature of the project was the process in which residents, students, and teachers considered the ideal state of sustainable school facilities, using container-based spatial construction as a key.
- Concept 3: Integration of External and Internal Space
  - Spaces are provided where external and internal areas can be partitioned freely. The internal and external spaces are connected using raw materials suited to tropical zones. The open (internal) space is used in the dry (rainy) seasons.

Cost-Effectiveness

There are two basic standard sizes for using containers as building materials: 20-foot containers and 40-foot containers. The Philippines imports many goods, such as industrial goods, agricultural materials, and foodstuffs, and many containers are abandoned in areas near the ports. When containers serve as structural units, large containers between transportation lines can be made faster and more simply, providing both time and cost benefits. A container can pack necessary building materials for shipping, thus simplifying and reducing costs. Containers are also easy to stack, saving storage space. The risk of theft and illicit import-export is low, and the containers can eventually be reused as iron.

Flexibility of Use

Even when constructing architecture planned for use as school facilities, it is easy to use containers freely for other purposes by adjusting their arrangement. During typhoons and other disasters, containers can also be used as evacuation shelters, emergency hospitals, and disaster recovery facilities. Hence, they are used by the public alongside sharable plazas, functioning as units that are easy to expand or downsize as necessary.

Sustainable Building

Further, using skylights and high sidelights, natural light is incorporated for indirect lighting. As solar radiation heat rises, the air conditioning load increases, and CO_2 reduction effects decrease. Thus, the temperature is controlled by introducing open space on both sides of the classrooms to allow a natural breeze to enter and circulate inside the classrooms. During severe heat in the dry season, solar radiation heat can be controlled by adjusting the degree to which natural light enters through the skylights and high sidelights. Windbreak forests are planted to reduce damage to houses and cultivated land due to wind. Tall-growing trees with good branch spread are used in areas close to houses, and trees able to withstand salt damage that can grow in shallow soil are used near the coast.

Earthquake Resistance

It is critical to consider the site and conduct rigorous surveys into dangers, such as landslides, avalanches of rocks and earth, tsunamis, floods, and ground subsidence. The foundations on which the containers are installed are not separate foundations but rather a continuous footing made from reinforced concrete that connects the foundations and the ground. Moreover, a wide foundation base is used to increase the soil's bearing capacity and prevent unequal settlement, providing the containers with adequate strength.

Typhoon Resistance

When a typhoon hits, the roof incurs the most damage. In particular, wide shutters are easily damaged, and damaged shutters may also lead to damage to the room interior. The wind pressure controls the opening and closing of shutters.

Construction Technology

The construction process comprises six stages: First, the foundations are laid (Step 1). To prevent inundation due to rain, the foundations are raised above the ground by about 50 centimeters. Next, the first-floor containers are installed (Step 2), followed by the second-floor containers (Step 3). The processes thus far requires heavy machinery operated by engineers and construction workers. The flooring is then laid (Step 4). The ceiling, roof, and sash are installed (Step 5). Stairs are constructed, and the rooftop is greened (Step 6). Residents conduct Steps 4 to 6.

Prototype

The school plan involves combining a container-based assembly method and self-building. Two containers are installed adjacently to form the first floor, and one additional container is installed directly on top to form the second floor.

Since the foundations are given sufficient strength, the first-floor portion can fully withstand strong winds and earthquakes, as well as inundation during typhoons. The stairs to the second floor can be accessed from two directions. The stairs located along the container's length form a plaza, encouraging gathering places for residents via a wide tread surface for the stairs.

The characteristic feature of the sectional plan is the section that connects outside and inside spaces. This area serves as a passageway but can also be used as a classroom. The classroom is not situated in a predetermined space, but forms when people gather in a certain place.

The hallmark of this proposal is the construction process, which is resident oriented and based on fieldwork. Initiatives that apply anthropological results to architectural practices represent a point of departure from previous methods toward establishing an architectural ethnography.

Upgrading impoverished urban neighborhoods involves a long-term process of sustainable development, not mean merely improving spaces. Instead, it addresses all spheres of life, including interpersonal relations, work, child-rearing, and play. This book framed architectural anthropology as the overall process of examining the kinds of places that can be constructed together with residents, developing specific spaces through architectural practices (architectural ethnography), and gradually upgrading the living environment. This process requires sustainable thinking and an ability to establish sustained practices per the cyclical process of "reading, presenting, and making" architecture in the broad sense.

Conclusion

FOR MUTUAL UNDERSTANDING

The first chapter provided an overview of the history of housing research in anthropology and architecture. I considered the methodology of architectural anthropology, which promotes mutual understanding through a common framework, and the understanding of family and social structure through housing. Participant observation will surely be the last academic division left in anthropology as interdisciplinary research increases. The most important points of fieldwork are that researchers leave their homes and that they meet people directly in the field. Anthropology is a discipline based on life in the real world. Architectural anthropology reads scenes and places where memories can be shared, meets people, and shares its findings. In this book, both anthropologists and residents discuss the visual image associated with the studied place and interpret it from multiple perspectives. I examined the issues related to subjects and objects and the possibility of using them as a new tool for mutual understanding.

The case study considered the relationships between living spaces and residents through fieldwork in the illegally occupied areas of the University of the Philippines and the CMP project areas. It was pointed out that a face-to-face place where different memories and experiences can be exchanged and shared is an important factor in establishing new relationships in the city.

As an architectural practice, this study proposed what kind of place can be constructed in the development of an urban poor area, based on the human relations and spatial recognition of the studied area during the field survey. In addition, the last chapter gave an overview of how architecture can serve as a tool for solving social problems. Based on architectural anthropology, the case study proposed a community-centered building process that uses traditional techniques unique to the region.

The idea that the enterprise of architecture as a whole (in the broad sense) could serve as ethnography was conceived during the discovery that living spaces are considered embodied *books* to be read by their inhabitants in anthropological studies. Moreover, architecture is being used in architectural design and management *practices* as a book in which information is shared between architects and benefactors. The idea of using forms of representations other than books as ethnography is not entirely new: in visual ethnography, for example, films, short films, and documentaries have been used as representation methods. However, architectural ethnography in the broad sense is not simply complete when the research output is produced; the spaces it creates, embodied by residents, exist in society as books and are interpreted by each person. The anthropologist rereads the reinterpreted spaces, shares the results gained through this process with residents, and creates new spaces again, forming the basis of architectural anthropology. This book proposes such a recursive process as a possibility for new anthropological practices.

Anthropology, which studies all aspects of human social life, encompasses a wide range of disciplines, including sociology, psychology, philosophy, economics, and political science. Architecture, however, has inherited European composite art from Greco-Roman traditions. In Japan, it has further combined with craftsmanship traditions to constitute an interdisciplinary subject area. The transdisciplinary nature of the two domains straddling multiple fields of study should provide an understructure that supports the new practices of architectural anthropology.

In surveying life in impoverished areas of developing countries and applying this knowledge in sustainable forms to the development of resident-centered approaches configured for each area, many problems can occur when one begins to construct spaces using the survey results in their original form. Projects often fail to progress, unable to circumvent local politics in the target society, which includes challenges such as solving legal issues related to assistance in impoverished neighborhoods; residents' economic problems; introduction of loan systems; the power balances between universities, government, residents, and NGOs; residents' feelings; the mix of religions; and intervention by politicians. Further, technical deficiencies came to bear at the stage where spaces are constructed—the "making" stage of the cyclical process of "reading, presenting, and making." The idea of architectural anthropology while conducting anthropological fieldwork exposed an overwhelming lack of knowledge and skills for the "making" stage. Shaping ideas and constructing them as architectural forms required craftsmanlike expertise that cannot be learned overnight. The first to visually embody the results of the anthropological study emerged after relearning architecture from scratch, acquiring the basic design elements, and qualifying as an architect via architectural design and management practices. It took a much longer time to develop the right side of my brain for architecture relative to the left side for anthropological reasoning.

Despite the hard work, however, the long period may have been the crucial factor that to consolidate the study ideas, which underwent many twists and turns. As noted, architectural anthropology is a long-term, sustainable, cyclical process. Upon arriving at the next cycle, how will the architectural space (the "text" to be read) have been enveloped in the residents' lives? Establishing specific connections from the results of anthropological research to architectural practices presents an ongoing challenge.

In a globalized city, as the number of immigrants increases, many issues, such as those related to the environment, poverty, education, and employment, are intricately intertwined, and efforts from an interdisciplinary perspective are urgently needed. Anthropology and architecture are both disciplines for modern society and humans. I believe that architectural anthropology can help people solve social problems by recognizing their differences and promoting mutual understanding.

Glossary

Architectural anthropology aims to understand the ideas of different cultures and promote mutual understanding through a cycle of reading architecture as text, sharing interpretations, and building. In the process, it is important to understand the way of thinking to understand various phenomena. This glossary summarizes some modern ideas, methodologies aimed at cultural understanding, ideas projected on architecture, and basic terms related to how to read space.

ARCHITECTURE AND THOUGHT

The Enlightenment, coupled with technological innovation in the latter half of the nineteenth century, greatly influenced pioneering architecture (Roberts 2006). Winckelmann's remark about "noble simplicity and quiet grandeur" influenced the field after the mid-eighteenth century (Sime & Mitchell 1911). The Enlightenment became mainstream in Europe from the late seventeenth century to the eighteenth century, thus underpinning subsequent thought. Important philosophical ideas in the latter half of the nineteenth century were utilitarianism (Bentham 2007) and functionalism (Malinowski 1922, Putnam 1975a, 1975b). Phenomenology (Husserl 1970a, 1970b, Heidegger 1996), ontology (Hartmann 1927), hermeneutics (Heidegger 1971, Gadamer 1996), structuralism (Lévi-Strauss 1963), and the Frankfurt School critical theory (Horkheimer and Adorno 2002) made important contributions. Such ideas influenced modern architecture and city planning. Nietzsche's view of nihilism (Crosby 1998) influences abstraction, which is essential in modernist design. Thorough functionalism removed the decoration from the architecture (Loos and Opel 1997). A new construction method that integrates modern thought and technology was developed mainly by Western architects (Frampton 2007). The Deutscher Werkbund and the Bauhaus sought

(Markgraf 2007) to put these modern ideas into practice in design. First, this chapter overviews the relevant modern ideas.

Enlightenment

Enlightenment views were the mainstream ideas in Europe from the seventeenth century to the eighteenth century. French and Scottish thinkers such as Voltaire (2000), Jean-Jacques Rousseau (1997), Francis Hutcheson (2003), David Hume (2011) etc. were especially crucial. It criticizes the Christian worldview and feudal thought and preaches a rational worldview, to liberate humanity. The Enlightenment led to a civil revolution that ended the absolute monarchy. It induced French Revolution ideologically and influenced the new political system (Locke 2013) that replaced the "Divine Right of Kings." A sovereign state was formed in Western Europe in the eighteenth century, each country being under the rule of absolute monarchy. Absolutist nations were struck by territorial struggles linked to colonialism in the New World and Asia. At that time, the industrial revolution was about to begin in England. It was an era when the feudal society collapsed and was replaced with a new modern civil society. The ideas of Voltaire (Pearson 2005), Rousseau (Damrosch 2005), and Diderot (Furbank 1992) eventually led to the French Revolution. The monarch also adopted the Enlightenment view, aiming to rationalize the rule. Enlightened absolutists include Frederick II of Prussia.

In France, in the latter half of the eighteenth century, Neoclassical Architecture emerged against the backdrop of the Enlightenment and the French Revolution. At that time, it was considered a majestic and sublime architectural style, as opposed to the excessive decorativeness and frivolity of Rococo art. It was also associated with the political situation in France during the eighteenth century. During the time of Louis XV, the delicate and soft Rococo architecture (late Baroque architecture) was the mainstream. Subsequently, there was a growing movement to replace the sensual and popular Rococo style, developed in the French court, with a more logical, solemn, and enlightening style. Thus, when the French Republic was established via the French Revolutionary movement, Neoclassical Architecture became mainstream. The United States and other European nations adopted neoclassicism in national buildings, following ancient Greek and republican ancient Roman democracy.

Further, Napoleon's employment of Neoclassical Architecture shaped his political style. The Nazis and Fascist Party adopted neoclassicism as a national monument. Accordingly, Neoclassical Architecture garnered many negative views. However, it was a universal architectural movement because it spread to many European countries and integrated with other ideas, thereby birthing the subsequent modernist architecture.

Modernism

Modernism describes a series of cultural trends from the late nineteenth century to the early twentieth century. It presents the view that traditional forms impede the lifestyles of people who have changed significantly since the industrial revolution (Frampton 2007). Thus, the internal plans and façade of modernist architecture fundamentally simplify or reject traditional practices (Loos and Opel 1997, Mies van der Rohe 1972). Moreover, some architects adopted modern architecture to express a social and political revolution, incorporating socialist ideas. Italian Rationalism is an architectural style under Mussolini's administration. Giuseppe Terragni's Casa del Fascio is a modernist architecture that simplifies the tradition of classicism (Eisenman 2003).

Utilitarianism

Utilitarianism is a concept created by Jeremy Bentham (1789). Bentham argued that doing the right thing against a good policy induces "the greatest happiness for the greatest number" of people. The idea is that the moral value of action is determined solely by its contribution to overall utility. The Panopticon is a facility designed by Bentham, inspired by his younger brother Samuel. Panopticon is a surveillance system in prisons. It is designed such that an inmate's private rooms, arranged in a circle, face the guard tower. The Panopticon did not allow inmates to see each other or the guards; the guards could monitor all inmates from that position. Bentham believed that raising the well-being of criminals and the poor was essential to maximizing societal well-being. Bentham sought to maximize the economics of operation and the welfare of inmates.

Cultural Relativism

Cultural relativism was advocated by Franz Boas (1887). It is the idea that human beliefs and customs should be understood in the terms of the culture to which they belong. That is, the claim is that the values, human beliefs, and customs of one culture should not be evaluated using the norms and values of another culture.

Functionalism

Functionalism in cultural anthropology is the idea that social customs, annual events, institutions, and cultural elements mutually support each other to form a society. However, functionalism in architecture posits that architects must design buildings based on their functions. Architect Louis Sullivan (1896) famously said that "form ever follows function," saying that buildings should be constrained only by their function. "It is the pervading law of all things organic and inorganic, of all things physical and metaphysical, of all things human and all things superhuman, of all true manifestations of the head, of the heart, of the soul, that the life is recognizable in its expression, that form ever follows function" (Sullivan 1896, 408). Moreover, functionalist architects, who said that decoration had no function, criticized the complex decoration in Louis Sullivan's architecture. Le Corbusier (1931) and Mies van der Rohe (1972) championed Sullivan's goal of extremely simplified architecture.

The ideas based on utilitarianism and functionalism ideas which dominated this era were influenced by the Great Depression that began in 1929 and the severe economic conditions of the two World Wars. Since subsequent follow-ers embraced the technical aspects, modernist architecture was regarded as a mere white box; thus, it progressed to postmodernism.

Bauhaus and Functionalism

Invited by William Ernest, Grand Duke of Saxe-Weimar-Eisenach, Henry van de Velde had founded the School of Crafts in 1906. In 1908 he had become the principal of the school. However, as a Belgian, he became an enemy of Germany in World War I, entrusted Walter Gropius with the craft school, and left Germany in 1917. This craft school was the origin of the later Bauhaus (Droste and Gossel 2005).

In 1919, Gropius became the first principal of the Bauhaus. He was influ-enced by De Stijl, in the Netherlands, and began to employ a more rational-istic and functionalist way of thinking.

As early as 1919, through the painter Feininger, de Stijl was already beginning to be known at the Bauhaus-at Weimar. Two years later van Doesburg himself began to divide his time between Weimar and Berlin. Though the degree of his influence is still controversial, van Doesburg's presence at Weimar seems to have stimulated important changes at the Bauhaus; from a somewhat expres-sionist mysticism and transcendentalism, the Bauhaus more and more turned toward clarity, discipline and the desire for a uniform and consciously devel-oped style in architecture and the allied arts such as the Dutch movement had already initiated. Doubtless some of this change of direction was self-generated; furthermore, there was surely some French and, after 1922, some Russian influence at the Bauhaus; yet it remains significant that in 1922, for instance, Gropius, who had been engaged in designing a picturesque wooden blockhouse with cubistic decorations and a symmetrical fagade, sent to the *Chicago Tribune* competition an austere, asymmetrical skyscraper project, its facade enlivened by a Stijl-like arrangement of balconies and other accents. The influence of de Stijl upon German architecture may further be seen in Mies van der Rohe's plan for a country house done in 1922, the year after van Doesburg's arrival in Berlin. (MoMA 1952, 10)

Gropius made architectural design the ultimate educational goal in his comprehensive art education. He established his educational system that aimed to integrate all arts. Moreover, many of the instructors who taught at Bauhaus had progressive ideas. Inviting leading artists of the time, such as Paul Klee, Johannes Itten, Wassily Kandinsky, and Moholy-Nagy László, as lecturers laid the foundation for Bauhaus art education.

The Bauhaus education system comprised preparatory education and practical skills (Baumann 2007). Johannes Itten created this preparatory education. Each course had a faculty member called a Meister, who taught in a laboratory-style environment. Students learned philosophy, expression, and composition and attended workshops to learn practical techniques such as woodworking, metalworking, glass, and pottery. Early Bauhaus educational policies were based on the modern ideas of rationalism and functionalism. At Bauhaus, small religious communities were booming during the Weimar period. Johannes Itten believed in the teaching of "Mazdaznan." This is a religious idea with strict dietary restrictions and potential racism. Bauhaus education is also an education that seeks human formation through art, and while Itten sought the essence of education from religion, Gropius sought the technical side. Itten confronted Gropius and left due to this conflict regarding the essential point of view of human education.

Structuralism

Structuralism is the idea that human society and culture have a certain underlying structure. It was introduced in Lévi-Strauss's theory of anthropology, which drew from linguistic theory since the work of Ferdinand de Saussure (Lévi-Strauss 1963). After that, it was developed and extended in fields of the humanities and social sciences, such as philosophy and psychoanalysis. Leading structuralist thinkers include Louis Althusser, Jacques Lacan, Michel Foucault, and Roland Barthes.

In the realm of architecture, Aldo Van Eyck sought to find a prescriptive urban structure within the city as an ambiguous and ambiguous space (McCarter 2015). Van Eyck tried to overcome the unified concept of the city by considering the range of functions required by architecture and cities, making reference to the settlements of the Pueblo people. A movement called Dutch structuralism was formed by Aldo Van Eyck, Herman Hertzberger, Piet Blom and others. Team X was composed of members (Alison and Peter

Smithson, Jaap Bakema, Aldo van Eyck, Georges Candilis, Shadrach Woods and Giancarlo De Carlo) who gathered at CIAM in July 1953, and their first formal meeting took place in Bagnols-sur-Cèze in 1960. Team X criticized CIAM's uniform approach to urbanism and proposed a new structure that captured the process of urban change and growth. (Deyong 2014). They emphasized that urban areas are made up of different communities and that each should be treated as part of the whole, without any difference in treatment. It was important to apply cultural anthropological methods that analyzed the whole structure along with the separated parts, and that relate the functions of a certain place complexly to the form, structure, usage, and so on.

Symbolic Anthropology and Interpretive Anthropology

Victor Turner and David Schneider are representatives of symbolic anthropology. In contrast to structuralism, it is a way of thinking that allows ambiguity by regarding culture as a system of meaning. Whereas structuralism emphasizes the scientific method, it is important in symbolic anthropology to take the hermeneutic method. Turner conducted a detailed study of Ndembu society (Turner 1967) and analyzed specific rites of passage using Arnold van Gennep's theory of rite of passage (1977). Schneider studied ideas about American kinship (Schneider 1967). Clifford Geertz represented interpretive anthropology. Geertz conducted a field survey in Java and grasped religion as a system of meaning from research on Islam, kinship organizations, etc. (Geertz 1976). He also presented a detailed hermeneutic study of the inhabitants of Bali, using his "Thick Description" (Geertz 1973). Symbolic anthropology and interpretive anthropology emphasized the peculiarity and individuality of culture above all else.

Orientalism

Orientalism was proposed by Edward W. Said as a concept to explain the derogatory depiction of the East by the West (Said 1978). Orientalism in France, Great Britain, and the United States since the eighteenth century was analyzed. The Oriental societies and people in this case can be thought of mainly as those who live in Asia, North Africa, and the Middle East. Said critically analyzed Orientalism as racist and imperialist and called it a way of thinking "from the West to the East."

Postmodern

Postmodern means "after modern times" and is a critical attitude toward "modernism" as a general term for modern culture and values. The term "postmodern" was first used in architecture in *Language of Post Modern Architecture* (1977) by Charles Jencks. He cited Ludwig Mies van der Rohe as a leading modernist architect and criticized modernism for its limited function in pursuit of rationality and universality. He criticized modernism for lacking communication, arguing that architecture should have many meanings. In the social sciences in general, academics were urged to reconsider the rational and hierarchical approach to thinking, such as the conventional dualistic idea, the abstract objectification of the world, and the one-sided stratification of the center and the periphery. For instance, Jean-François Lyotard's *The Postmodern Condition: A Report on Knowledge* (1984) influenced the use of postmodernism in the sense of criticizing not only architecture but also modernism in general. Per Lyotard, the postmodern was the end of "grand narratives" or grand ideological systems such as Marxism. In other words, the postmodern can be said to be one of the consequences of a rational worldview, emerging due to the development of democracy and science and technology. From the 1970s to the 1980s, society transformed from an industrial society to a post-industrial society, the bonds of the community came to collapse, and individualism emerged. Therefore, it was necessary to explain the social structure differently than in the past. No clear new value had appeared to replace "modern," but the old value no longer functioned. In the midst of this, postmodernism attempted to create a new value through patchwork, remakes, and mixes of various styles of the past. Postmodernism is a way of knowledge and practice that corresponds to such a mass consumer society and an information society, and it may be said that it has inevitably emerged in response to social changes.

Importantly, postmodernism sees knowledge and value systems as political, historical and cultural products. In short, postmodernism reveals a relative value system, criticizes universal ideas, and affirms pluralism in disciplines such as economics, linguistics, architecture, literature, and art. Postmodernism encompasses the concept of deconstruction, an approach to understanding the relationship between text and meaning, initiated by Jacques Derrida (Derrida 2001). Derrida deconstructed traditional thinking systems in Europe by unraveling their hidden ambiguities and breaking open the binary oppositions underlying meanings of words.

Postmodernism in architecture sought to overcome the modernism of the unified idea, criticizing functionalism and rationalism. Postmodernism affirms the decorativeness denied by modernism and refers back to classical architecture. Deconstructivism in architecture began in 1988 with the "Deconstructivist Architecture" exhibition held at the Museum of Modern Arts (MoMA). Peter Eisenman, Frank Gehry, Zaha Hadid, Coop Himmelblau, Rem Koolhaas, Daniel Libeskind, and Bernard Tschumi are viewed as deconstructivist architects. They created extremely unstable forms by deconstructing the principles of modernist architecture and dismantling their functions and structures. Koolhaas built buildings from programs. Some architects dislike the label of deconstruction, but in the sense of deconstruction as an approach to destroying the hierarchical and traditional system, it has been passed down to the present day.

This glossary has described some of the theories of culture. There are many other cultural theories and criticisms of them. Currently, many theories tolerate multiculturalism, or the idea that multiple communities with different origins, customs, and cultures can respect each other and aim for peaceful symbiosis. Cultural anthropology continues to look for new ways to explain situations from multiple perspectives. Having many ideas that can further the understanding of such history and deepening one's thoughts is of utmost importance in understanding others. Various ideas have been subject to criticism in each era. For example, according to Spivak, pluralism is actually a methodology used to make the dominant culture pretend to accept the opinions of other minority cultures even as it guts them (Spivak 1990). In light of these points, it is necessary to keep in mind the reflections mentioned in chapter 1. In other words, criticizing the absoluteness of the concepts of one's own culture and leading to reflection should help create new values.

Moreover, for one to know things in the truest sense, it will be important to return to the basics of anthropology. In anthropology, we work with people and learn how to learn from people. The cycle of the process of architectural anthropology (reading, presenting, and making) helps create this understanding.

Bibliography

Aalto, Alvar. 1932. Paimio Sanatorium. Paimio, Finland. Architecture.

Alberti, Leon Battista. 1991. *On the Art of Building.* Cambridge, MA: The MIT Press.

Alexander, Christopher. 1965. "A City is Not a Tree (Part II)." *Architectural Forum* 122, no. 2: 58–62.

Anderson, Benedict. 1987. *Imagined Communities: Reflections on the Origin and Spread of Nationalism.* London: Verso.

Asch, Timothy. 1971. *Yanomamo: A Multidisciplinary Study.* Watertown, MA: Documentary Educational Resources. Video.

Bakhtin, Mikhail M. 1981. *The Dialogic Imagination.* Austin: University of Texas Press.

———. 1986. "Response to a Question from the *Novy Mir* Editorial Staff," *Speech Genres, and Other Late Essays.* Translated by Vern W. McCee. Austin: University of Texas Press.

Basch, Linda. 1993. *Nations Unbound: Transnational Projects, Postcolonial Predicaments, and Deterritorialized Nation-States.* Abingdon: Routledge.

Bateson, Gregory. 1972. *Steps to an Ecology of Mind.* Lanham, MD: Jason Aronson Inc.

Baumann, Kirsten. 2007. *Bauhaus Dessau: Architecture Design Concept.* Berlin: JOVIS Verlag.

Bentham, Jeremy. 2007. *An Introduction to the Principles of Morals and Legislation.* Garden City, NY: Dover Publications. https://doi.org/10.1093/oseo/instance.00077240.

Bernabe, Jean, Patrick Chamoiseau, and Raphael Confiant. 1993. *In Praise of Creoleness.* Paris: Gallimard.

Boas, Franz. 1887. "Museums of Ethnology and their Classification." *Science* 9, no. 228: 587–9. https://doi.org/10.1126/science.ns-9.228.587.b.

Boulding, Kenneth. 1956. *The Image: Knowledge in Life and Society.* Ann Arbor: University of Michigan Press. https://doi.org/10.3998/mpub.6607.

Boullée, Étienne-Louis. 1784. Cénotaphe à Newton [Cenotaph for Newton]. In BnF, Prints and Photographs Department of the National Library of France, reserve collection 57. format 4, plate 7–9. Unbuilt Architecture.

Bourdieu, Pierre. 1970. "La maison Kabyle ou le monde renversé" [The Kabyle house or the overthrown world]. In *Echanges et communications: mélanges offerts a Claude Lévi-Strauss a l'occasion de son 60 anniversaire*, edited by J. Pouillon and P. Maranda, 739–58. Paris: Mouton. https://doi.org/10.1515/9783111698281-002.

———. 1973. "The Berber House." In *Rules and Meanings: The Anthropology of Everyday Knowledge*, edited by Mary Douglas, 98–110. London: Penguin Education.

———. 1977. *Outline of a Theory of Practice*. Translated by Richard Nice. Cambridge University Press. https://doi.org/10.1017/CBO9780511812507

Bourdier, Marc J. F. 1992. *Dojunkai apaato genkei: nihonkenchikushi ni okeru yakuwari* [Dojunkai Apartment Original Scenery: Role in Japanese Architectural History]. Tokyo: SUMAI Library Publishing Company.

Campbell, Margaret. 2005. "What Tuberculosis Did for Modernism: The Influence of a Curative Environment on Modernist Design and Architecture." *Medical History* 49, no. 4: 463–88. https://doi.org/10.1017/s0025727300009169.

Carsten, Janet, and Stephen Hugh-Jones, editors. 1995. *About the House: Lévi-Strauss and Beyond*. Cambridge: Cambridge University Press. https://doi.org/10.1017/CBO9780511607653.

Chalk, Warren. 1964. Capsule Homes. In *Archigram*, 1999. edited by P. Cook, 44–7. Chicago: New York: Princeton Architectural Press. Unbuilt Architecture.

Clifford, James. 1980. "Fieldwork, Reciprocity, and the Making of Ethnographic Texts: The Example of Maurice Leenhardt." *MAN* 15: 518–32. https://doi.org/10.2307/2801348.

———. 1982. *Person and Myth: Maurice Leenhardt in the Melanesian World*. Santa Cruz: University of California Press.

———. 1997. *Routes: Travels and Transitions in the Late Twentieth Century*. Cambridge, MA: Harvard University Press.

———. 2002. *Routes: Travels and Transitions in the Late Twentieth Century*. Translated by Yoshitaka Mouri. Tokyo: Getsuyosha.

Clifford, James, and George E. Marcus, editors. 1986. *Writing Culture: Poetics and Politics of Ethnography*. Irvine, CA: University of California Press.

Congress of the Philippines, 1992. *The Urban Development and Housing Act (Republic Act Number 7279)*. Manila: Republic of the Philippines.

Coulter, William L. 1885. The Adirondack Cottage Sanatorium. Saranac Lake, NY. Architecture.

Costa, Lucio. 1956. Brasilia's Pilot Plan. Brasilia, Brazil. Architecture.

Crosby, Donald A. 1998. "Nihilism." In *Routledge Encyclopedia of Philosophy.* London: Taylor & Francis.

Cullen, Gordon. 1961. *Concise Townscape*. Abingdon: Routledge.

Cunningham, Clark E. 1973. "Order in the Atoni House." In *Right and Left: Essays on Dual Symbolic Classification*, edited by R. Needham, 204–38. Chicago: University of Chicago Press.

Damrosch, Leo. 2005. *Jean-Jacques Rousseau: Restless Genius*. New York: Houghton Mifflin Harcourt.

Davis, Mike. 1990. *City of Quartz: Excavating the Future in Los Angeles.* Brooklyn, NY: Verso.

De Josselin de Jong, Patrick E. 1972. "Marcel Mauss et les origines de l'anthropologie structurale Hollandaise" [Marcel Mauss and the origins of Dutch structural anthropology]. Translated by K. Miyazaki. *L'Homme* 11, no. 4 (Oct–Dec): 62–84. https://doi.org/10.3406/hom.1972.367300.

Derrida, Jacques. 2021. *Writing and Difference.* Chicago: University of Chicago Press.

Del Rosario, Eduardo D. 2021. "The Community Mortgage Program: Decent, affordable housing for Filipinos." Scribbr. January 16, 2021. https://business.inquirer.net/315856/the-community-mortgage-program-decent-affordable-housing-for-filipinos#ixzz70kDFHi8A.

De Soto, Hernando. 2000. *The Mystery of Capital: Why Capitalism Triumphs in the West and Fails Everywhere Else.* New York: Basic Books.

Deyong, Sarah. 2014. "An Architectural Theory of Relations: Sigfried Giedion and Team X." *Journal of the Society of Architectural Historians* 73, no. 2: 226–47. https://doi.org/10.1525/jsah.2014.73.2.226.

Donaldson, Alfred L. 1921. *A History of the Adirondacks.* New York: Century.

Droste, Magdalena, and Peter Gossel, editors. 2005. *Bauhaus.* New York: Taschen America LLC.

Dühr, Stefanie. 2007. *The Visual Language of Spatial Planning: Exploring Cartographic Representations for Spatial Planning in Europe.* Abingdon: Routledge. https://doi.org/10.4324/9780203965818.

Durkheim, Émile, and Marcel Mauss. 1903. "De quelques formes primitives de classicication: Contribution a l' etude des représentation collectives" [Some primitive forms of classicication: Contribution to the study of collective representations]. *Anneé Sociologique* 6: 2–72.

Eames, Charles, and Ray Eames. Case Study House No. 8. Pacific Palisades, CA. Architecture, 1949.

Eisenman, Peter. 2003. *Giuseppe Terragni Transformations Decompositions Critiques.* New York: The Monacelli Press.

Ellen, Roy. 1986. "Microcosm, Macrocosm and the Nuaulu House: Concerning the Reductionist Fallacy as Applied to Metaphorical Levels." *Bijdrangen tot de Taal-, Land-en Volkenkunde* 142, no. 1: 1–30. https://doi.org/10.1163/22134379-90003366.

Feldman, Jerome A. 1979. "The House as World in Bawömatalua, South Nias." In *Art, Ritual and Society in Indonesia,* edited by Edward M. Bruner and Judith O. Becker, 127–89. Athens, OH: Ohio University Center for International Studies.

Finke, Ronald A. 1989. *Principles of Mental Imagery.* Cambridge, MA: The MIT Press.

Flaherty, Robert J. 1922. *Nanook of the North.* Les Frères Revillon and Pathé Exchange. Video.

Forester, John. 1989. *Planning in the Face of Power.* Berkeley: University of California Press.

———. 1993. *Critical Theory, Public Policy, and Planning Practice.* Albany: State University of New York Press.

Frobenius, Leo. 1900. "Die Kulturformen Ozeaniens" [The cultural forms of Oceania]. *Petermanns Mitteilungen* 46: 204–15, 234–8, 262–71.

Frazer, James G. 1922. *The Golden Bough: A Study in Magic and Religion: 1890–1936*, Abridged Edition. New York: Macmillan. https://doi. org/10.1007/978-1-349-00400-3.

Friedman, Alice. 1998. *Women and the Making of the Modern House*. New York: Harry N. Abrams.

Fukushima, Shigeru. 1992. "Philippines manila daitoshiken no juutakujijo to juutaku-seisaku" [Housing Situation and Housing Policy in the Manila Metropolitan Area, Philippines: Strategy and Development of National Housing Plan Under the Aquino Administration]. *Jutaku* 41: 57–66.

Fuller, Richard Buckminster. 1930. Dymaxion House. Andover, KS. Architecture, 1930.

Funo, Shuji. 1991. *Kanpon no sekai: jawa no shomin jukyoshi* [Kampung's World: Javanese People's Home Ethnography]. Tokyo: PARCO Publishing.

Furbank, Philip N. 1992. *Diderot:A Critical Biography*. New York: Alfred A. Knopf.

Furuya, Yoshiaki. 1996. "Kindai Eno Betsuno Hairikata" [Another Way to Enter Modern Times: Indigenous Brazilian Resistance Strategies]. In *Iwanami Kouza Bunkajinruigaku 12*, edited by Tamotsu Aoki, 255–80. Tokyo: Iwanami Shoten.

Frampton, Kenneth. 2007. *Modern Architecture: A Critical History*, Fourth Edition. Thames & Hudson.

Gadamer, Hans-Georg. 1996. *Truth and Method*. New York: Continuum.

Geertz, Clifford. 1973. "Thick Description: Toward an Interpretive Theory of Culture." In *The Interpretation of Cultures: Selected Essays*. New York, NY: Basic Books.

———. 1976. *The Religion of Java*. Chicago, Il. University of Chicago Press.

Gilroy, Paul. 1993. *The Black Atlantic*. Cambridge, MA: Harvard University Press.

Graebner, Fritz. 1911. *Methode der Ethnologie* [Method of ethnology]. Kulturgeschichtliche Bibliothek. Erste Reihe, Ethnologische Bibliothek, 1. Heidelberg: Carl Winters Universtatsbuchhandlung.

Greene, David. 1999. "Living Pod." In *Archigram*, edited by Peter Cook. Chicago: New York: Princeton Architectural Press. Unbuilt Architecture.

Guarnizo, Luis E., and Michael. P. Smith. 1998. "The Locations of Transnationalism." In *Transnationalism from Below*, edited by Michael P. Smith and Luis E. Guarnizo, 3–34. Piscataway, NJ: Transaction Books.

Habermas, Jürgen. 1984. *Theory of Communicative Action, Volume One: Reason and the Rationalization of Society*. Translated by Thomas A. McCarthy. Boston: Beacon Press.

Hara Laboratory, Institute of Industrial Science, the University of Tokyo, editor. (1973–1979) 2006. *Fukkokuban: jukyo shugoron* [Reprint: Housing theory] I & II. Tokyo: Kashima Shuppankai.

Hartmann, Nicolai. 1927. "Über die Stellung der ästhetischen Werte im Reich der Werte überhaupt" [About the position of aesthetic values in the realm of values in general]. *Proceedings of the Sixth International Congress of Philosophy*: 428–36. New York: Longmans, Green, and Co. https://doi.org/10.5840/wcp6192776.

Harvey, David. 1989. *The Condition of Postmodernity: An Enquiry into the Origins of Cultural Change*. Thousand Oaks, CA: Sage.

Healey, Patsy. 1997. *Collaborative Planning: Shaping Places in Fragmented Societies*. Vancouver: The University of British Columbia Press.

Heidegger, Martin. 1996. *Being and Time*. State University of New York Press.

———. 1971. "Der Weg zur Sprache" [The Way to Language]. In *On the Way to Language*, 111–38. New York: Harper & Row.

Hobday, Richard A., and John. W. Cason. 2009. "The Open-Air Treatment of Pandemic Influenza." *American Journal of Public Health*, 99, Suppl 2: 236–42. https://doi.org/10.2105/AJPH.2008.134627.

Horkheimer, Max, and Theodor W. Adorno. 2002. *Dialectic of Enlightenment*. Stanford University Press.

Housing and Land Use Regulatory Board. 1977. *Presidential Decree No. 1216 (DC1216)*. Manila: Government of the Philippines.

———. 1995. *Resolution No. 579*. Manila: Government of the Philippines.

———. 2001. *Implementing Rules and Regulations BP220 (IRR BP220)*. Manila: Government of the Philippines.

Howard, Ebenezer. 1965. *Garden Cities of Tomorrow*. London: Faber & Faber.

Hume, David. 2011. *David Hume: A Treatise Of Human Nature: Volume 1*. Oxford: Oxford University Press. https://doi.org/10.1093/oseo/instance.00046221.

Husserl, Edmund. 1970a. *Logical Investigations*. Abingdon: Routledge & Kegan Paul Ltd.

———. 1970b. *The Crisis of European Sciences and Transcendental Phenomenology*. Evanston, IL: Northwestern University Press.

Hutcheson, Francis. 2003. *An Essay on the Nature and Conduct of the Passions and Affections, With Illustrations on the Moral Sense*. Indianapolis: Liberty Fund.

Iijima, Yoshiharu. 1986. *Kamadoshin to kawayashin* [Stove God and Toilet God: The Boundary Between the Other World and This World]. Tokyo: Jinbun Shoin.

Imafuku, Ryota. 1991. *Kureohru syugi* [Creolism]. Tokyo: Seido Sha.

Innes, Judith E. 1998. "Information in Communicative Planning." *Journal of the American Planning Association* 64, no. 1: 52–63. https://doi.org/10.1080/01944369808975956.

IOM (International Organization for Migration). 2017. *Migration in The Caribbean: Current Trends, Opportunities and Challenges*. International Organization for Migration Regional Office for Central America, North America and the Caribbean.

Ito, Chuta. 1894. "'Architecture' no hongi wo ronjite sono yakuji wo senteishi waga 'zouka gakkai' no kaimei wo nozomu" [Discuss the true meaning of the architecture, select its translation, and hope to rename our "home-building society"]. *Journal of Architecture and Building Science* 90: 195–97.

Izumi, Seiichi. 1971. *Sumai No Genkei I* [Prototype of the house I]. Tokyo: Kashima Publishing.

Jacobs, Jane. 1961. *The Death and Life of Great American Cities*. New York: Random House.

———. 1969. *The Economy of Cities*. New York: Random House.

Jencks, Charles. 1977. *The Language of Postmodern Architecture*. New York: Rizzoli International Publications.

Kawada, Makito. 2003. *Inori to matsuri no nichijochi* [Daily knowledge of prayer and worship: ethnography of Bantayan Island in the Visayas Region of the Philippines]. Fukuoka: Kyushu University Press.

Kearney, Michael. 1995. "The Local and the Global: The Anthropology of Globalization and Transnationalism." *Annual Review of Anthropology* 24: 547–65. https://doi.org/10.1146/annurev.an.24.100195.002555.

Kelling, George L., and Catherine M. Coles. 1995. *Fixing Broken Windows*. New York: Simon & Schuster.

Kiesler, Frederick. 1939 "On Correalism and Biotechnique: A Definition and Test of a New Approach to Building Design." In *Rethinking Technology: A Reader in Architectural Theory*, edited by Braham, William W., and Jonathan A. Hale. London: Routledge.

———. 1950. Endless House. In collections of MoMA, Department of Architecture and Design. Unbuilt Architecture.

———. 1965. Temple of the Book. Jerusalem. Architecture.

Kikuchi, Juro. 1958. "Kinseiniokeru 'ARCHITECTURE' No yakugonituite" [About the Translation of "ARCHITECTURE" in the Early Modern Period]. *Transactions of the Architectural Institute of Japan* 60, no. 2: 661–64. https://doi.org/10.3130/aijsaxx.60.2.0_661.

Kikuchi, Yasushi. 1980. *Philippines no shakai jinruigaku* [Social Anthropology in the Philippines]. Tokyo: Keibundo.

———. 1991. *Uncrystallized Philippine Society: A Social Anthropological Analysis*. Quezon City: New Day Publishers.

Kikuchi, Yasushi, and Fuyuki Makino. 1999. "Hyoka chousa houkokusyo: Metro Manila Electrification Project" [Evaluation Survey Report: Metro Manila Electrification Project]. In *Kaigai Keizai Kyoryoku Kikin Enshakkan Anken Jigyohyouka Houkokusho*, by Overseas Economic Cooperation Fund, 178–97. Tokyo: Overseas Economic Cooperation Fund.

Kikutake, Kiyonori. 1958. Tower City. In *International architecture*. 1959(1). Tokyo: Bijutsu Shuppansha. Unbuilt Architecture.

———. 1960. Marine City. In Metabolism 1960 Toshi eno Teian [Metabolism 1960 proposal to the city]. Edited by N. Kawazoe. Tokyo: Bijutsu Shuppansha. Unbuilt Architecture.

Koenig, Pierre. 1960. Case Study House No. 22/Stahl House. Los Angeles, CA. Architecture.

Kon, Wajiro. 1922. Ninon no minka [Japanese Folk dwellings]. Tokyo: Suzuki Shoten.

Le Corbusier. 1922. Modern City and Plan Voisin. In *Oeuvre complète 1910–1929* [Complete Works 1910–1929]. Vol.1. Edited by Le Corbusier and P. Jeanneret. Unbuilt Architecture.

———. 1928. Villa Stein-De Monzie. Garches, France. Architecture.

———. 1929. Villa Savoye. Poissy, France. Architecture.

———. 1930. Radiant City. In *Oeuvre complète 1934–1938* [Complete Works 1934–1938]. Vol. 3. Edited by Le Corbusier and P. Jeanneret. Unbuilt Architecture.

———. 1931. *Toward an Architecture*. London: J. Rodker.

———. 1973. *The Athens Charter*. New York. Grossman Publishers.

———. 1950. Master Plan for Chandigarh. Chandigarh, India. Architecture.

Ledoux, Claude Nicolas. 1804. Project for the Ideal City of Chaux: House of Supervisors. In BnF, Prints and Photographs Department of the National Library of France, RES-V-45. Unbuilt Architecture.

Lequeu, Jean-Jacques. 1800. Gate of a Hunting-Ground. In BnF, Prints and Photographs Department of the National Library of France, RES-V-45. Unbuilt Architecture.

Lerner, Jaime. 1968. The Curitiba Master Plan. Curitiba, Brazil. Architecture.

Lévi-Strauss, Claude. 1963. *Structural Anthropology*. Translated by Claire Jacobson and Brooke Grundfest Schoepf. New York: Doubleday Anchor Books.

———. 1969. *The Savage Mind*. Chicago: University of Chicago Press.

———. 1977. *Tristes Tropiques*. Translated by John and Doreen Weightman. London: Penguin.

———. 1982. "The Social Organization of the Kwakiutl." In *The Way of the Masks*, translated by S. Modelski, 163–87. Seattle: University of Washington Press.

Locke, John. 2013. *Two Treatises on Government: A Translation into Modern English*. Manchester: Industrial Systems Research.

Loos, Adolf, and Adolf Opel. 1997. *Ornament and Crime: Selected Essays*. Riverside, CA: Ariadne Press.

Lyotard, Jean-François. 1984. *The Postmodern Condition: A Report on Knowledge*. Minneapolis: University of Minnesota Press.

Lynch, Kevin. 1960. *The Image of the City*. Cambridge, MA: The MIT Press.

Maekawa, Kunio. 1946–1951. PREMOS. Hokkaido and Kyushu, Japan. Architecture.

Malinowski, Bronislaw. 1922. *Argonauts of the Western Pacific*. Routledge & Sons.

Markgraf, Monika. 2007. *Archaeology of Modernism: Renovation Bauhaus Dessau*. Berlin: JOVIS Verlag.

Marshall, John. 1973. *Men Bathing*. Watertown, MA: Documentary Educational Resources. Video.

———. 2002. *A Kalahari Family*. Watertown, MA: Documentary Educational Resources. Video.

Marshall, John, and Robert Gardner. 1957. *The Hunters*. Cambridge, MA: Peabody Museum of Archaeology and Ethnology.

Matsuda, Motoji. 1996. *Toshi wo kainarasu* [Tame the city: Urban anthropology in Africa]. Tokyo: Kawaideshobo Shinsha.

———. 1999. *Teikou suru toshi* [Cities to resist: From the world of Nairobi immigrants]. Tokyo: Iwanami Shoten.

Matsumura, Shin, Naoko Fukami, Kyota Yamada, and Yuta Uchiyama, editors. 2016. *Mega city no shinka to tayosei* [Evolution and Diversity of Megacities]. Tokyo: Tokyo University Press.

MaCarter, Robert. 2015. *Aldo van Eyck*. New Haven, CT: Yale University Press.

McKellar, Peter. 1957. *Imagination and Thinking*. London: Cohen & West.

Mies van der Rohe, Ludwig. 1945–1951. Farnsworth House. Plano, Il. Architecture.
———. 1972. *Ludwig Mies van der Rohe*. London and New York: Thames and Hudson.
Mitlin, Diana, and David Satterthwaite. 2004. *Empowering Squatter Citizen Local Government, Civil Society and Urban Poverty Reduction*. Abingdon: Routledge.
Miyawaki, Mayumi, and Miyawaki Seminar. 2003. *Ninon no dentoteki toshi kukan: design survey no kiroku* [Japanese traditional urban space: Record of design survey]. Tokyo: Chuo-Koron Bijutsu Shuppan.
MoMA (Museum of Modern Art). 1952. "De Stijl, 1917–1928." *The Museum of Modern Art Bulletin* Vol. 20, no. 2, Winter: 4–13.
Moore, Henrietta L. 2004. *A Passion for Difference: Essays in Anthropology and Gender*. Cambridge: Polity Press.
Morgan, Lewis H. 1877. *Ancient Society*. New York: Holt.
Motohashi, Tetsuya. 2005. *Postcolonialism*. Tokyo: Iwanami Shoten.
Mumford, Eric. 2000. *The CIAM Discourse on Urbanism, 1928–1960*. Cambridge, MA: The MIT Press.
Mumford, Lewis. 1938. *The Culture of Cities*. San Diego: Harcourt Brace.
Muratake, Seiichi. 1971. "Okinawa honto nashiro no decent ie yashiki to sonraku-kuukan" [Decent house, mansion and village space on the main island of Okinawa, Nashiro]. *The Japanese Journal of Ethnology* 36, no. 2: 109–50.
———. 1984. *Saishi kuukan no kouzou* [Structure of the Ritual Space]. Tokyo: Tokyo University Press.
Naomichi, Ishige. 1971. *Juukyo-kuukan no jinruigaku* [Anthropology of Living Space]. Tokyo: Kashima Publishing.
National Home Mortgage Finance Corporation. 1998. *NHMFC Corporate Circular 010 Consolidated Implementing Guidelines for the Community Mortgage Program, Socialized Housing in the Philippines: A Compilation of Housing Laws and Other Reference Materials*, Volume II. Quezon City: Partnership of Philippine Support Service Agencies, Inc. (PHILSSA).
Needham, Barrie. 1997. "A Plan with a Purpose: The Regional Plan for the Province of Friesland 1994." In *Making Strategic Spatial Plans: Innovation in Europe*, edited by Patsy Healey, Abdul Khakee, Alain Motte, and Barrie Needham, 173–90. London: UCL Press.
Needham, Rodney, editor. 1973. *Right and Left: Essays on Dual Symbolic Classification*. Chicago: University of Chicago Press.
Neuman, Michael. 1996. "Images as institution builders." *European Planning Studies* 4, no. 3: 293–312. https://doi.org/10.1080/09654319608720347.
NHA (National Housing Authority). 2000. *Magnitude of informal settlers in Metro Manila summary*. Manila: National Housing Authority.
———. 2002. *Families Relocated/Resettled: August 1982–December 2001*. Quezon City: National Housing Authority.
NSCB (National Statistical Coordination Board). *Philippine Statistical Yearbook*. 2005. Quezon City: NSCB.
Oda, Makoto. 2001. "Ekkyo kara kyokaino sairyodokae" [From crossing borders to re-territorialization of boundaries]. In *Jinruigakuteki Jissen No Saikouchiku*

[Reconstruction of anthropological practice], edited by Takashi Sugiyama, 297–321. Tokyo: Sekaishiso Sha.

———. 2009. "Kyodoutai to daitai fukanosei ni tsuite" [Community and irreplaceability: An essay on the duality of society]. *Nihon Jomin Bunka Kiyo* 27: 219–60.

Oregon University. 1966. *Kanazawa saimachi no dezain sahvei: kokusai kenchiku 11* [International architecture: design survey by University of Oregon in November 1966]. Tokyo: Bijutsu Shuppansha.

Palladio, Andrea. 1965. *The Four Books of Architecture*. Garden City, NY: Dover Publications.

Pallasmaa, Juhani. 1998. "Alvar Aalto: Toward a Synthetic Functionalism." In *Alvar Aalto, Between Humanism and Materialism*, edited by Peter Reed, 21–44. New York: The Museum of Modern Art.

Panofsky, Erwin. 1972. *Studies In Iconology: Humanistic Themes In The Art Of The Renaissance*. Abingdon: Routledge.

Park, Robert E., Ernest W. Burgess, and Roderick. D. McKenzie. 1925. *The City*. Chicago: University of Chicago Press.

Pearson, Roger. 2005. *Voltaire Almighty: A Life in Pursuit of Freedom*. Bloomsbury.

Piranesi, Giovanni B. 1748. Antichita Romanae. In the collections of Victoria and Albert Museum, Department of Prints and Drawings and Department of Paintings. Unbuilt Architecture.

———. 1761. Imaginary Prisons. In the collections of Victoria and Albert Museum, Department of Prints and Drawings and Department of Paintings. Unbuilt Architecture.

Portes, Alejandro, Luis E. Guarnizo, and Patricia S. Landolt. 1999. "The Study of Transnationalism: Pitfalls and Promise of an Emergent Research Field." *Ethnic and Racial Studies* 22: 217–37. https://doi.org/10.1080/014198799329468.

Prouvé, Jean. Tropical House. 1949. Brazzaville, Congo. Architecture.

———. 2011. *Jean Prouve: La Maison Tropical/The Tropical House*. Paris: Centre Pompidou.

Putnam, Hilary. 1975a. "Minds and Machines." *Mind, Language, and Reality*: 362–85. Cambridge: Cambridge University Press. https://doi.org/10.1017/CBO9780511625251.020.

———. 1975b. "The Nature of Mental States." *Mind, Language, and Reality*: 429–40. Cambridge: Cambridge University Press. https://doi.org/10.1017/CBO9780511625251.023.

Putnam, Robert. 1993. *Making Democracy Work: Civic Traditions in Modern Italy*, Princeton University Press. https://doi.org/10.1515/9781400820740.

Racelis, Mary. 1967. "Tagalog Social Organization." In *Brown Heritage: Essay on Philippine Cultural Tradition and Literature*, 134–48. Manila: Ateneo de Manila University Press.

Radcliffe-Brown, Alfred R. 1931. *The Social Organization of Australian Tribes*. New York: Macmillan & Co. https://doi.org/10.1002/j.1834-4461.1931.tb00015.x.

Rampley, Matthewa. 2001. "Iconology of the Interval: Aby Warburg's Legacy." *Word & Image* 17, no. 4: 303–24. https://doi.org/10.1080/02666286.2001.10435723.

Rapoport, Amos. 2005. *Culture, Architecture, And Design*. Chicago: Locke Science Publishing Company, Inc.

Rassers, Willem. H. 1959. "On the Javanese Kris." In *Panji, The Culture Hero: A Structural Stury of Religion in Java*, 219–97. Berlin: Springer. https://doi.org/10.1007/978-94-017-6655-5_4.

Ratzel, Friedrich. 1896. *History of Mankind*. Translated by A. J. Butler. London: Macmillan.

Redfield, Robert. 1941. *The Folk Culture of Yucatan*. Chicago: University of Chicago Press.

Reed, Peter. editor. 1998. *Alvar Aalto, Between Humanism and Materialism*. New York: The Museum of Modern Art.

Richardson, Alan. 1969. *Mental Imagery*. London: Routledge & Kegan Paul. https://doi.org/10.1007/978-3-662-37817-5.

Rietveld, Gerrit. 1924. The Schroeder House. Utrecht, Netherlands. Architecture.

Robbins, Edward. 1994. *Why Architects Draw*. Cambridge, MA: The MIT Press.

Roberts, David. 2006. *Art and Enlightenment: Aesthetic Theory After Adorno*. Lincoln: University of Nebraska Press.

Rosaldo, Renato. 1989. *Culture and Truth: The Remaking of Social Analysis*. Boston: Beacon Press.

Rousseau, Jean-Jacques. 1997. *Rousseau: 'The Social Contract' and Other Later Political Writings*. Cambridge: Cambridge University Press.

Rowe, William L. 1973. "Caste, Kinship, and Association in Urban India." In *Urban Anthropology*, edited by Aidan Southall, 211–249. Oxford: Oxford University Press.

Rudofsky, Bernard. 1964. *Architecture Without Architects*. New York: MoMA Press.

Said, Edward W. 1978. *Orientalism*. New York: Georges Borchardt Inc.

Sander, Thomas H. 2000. "Social Capital and New Urbanism: Leading a Civic Horse to Water?" *National Civic Review* 91: 213–34. https://doi.org/10.1002/ncr.91302.

Sangren, Paul S. 1988. "Rhetoric and the Authority of Ethnography: 'Postmodernism' and the Social Reproduction of Texts." *Current Anthropology* 29: 405–35. https://doi.org/10.1086/203652.

Sassen, Saskia. 1991. *The Global City*. Princeton, NJ: Princeton University Press.

Satoh, Koji. 1988–1989. *Shirizu kenchiku jinruigaku: sekai no sumai wo yomu* [Architectural anthropology series: Read homes in the world]. Vols. 1–4. Kyoto: Gakugei Shuppansha.

———. 1989a. "Minzoku kenchikugaku/jinruigakuteki kenchikugaku (ue)" [Ethnic architecture/anthropological architecture (1)]. *Journal of the Society of Architectural Historians of Japan* 12: 106–32.

———. 1989b. "Minzoku kenchikugaku/jinruigakuteki kenchikugaku (shita)" [Ethnic architecture/anthropological architecture (2)]. *Journal of the Society of Architectural Historians of Japan* 13: 93–115.

Scharer, Hans. 1963. *Ngaju Religion: The Conception of God Among a South Borneo People*. Translated by R. Needham. Koninklijk Instituut voor Taal-, Land-en Volkenkunde Translation Series 6. The Hague: Martinus Nijhoff.

Schildt, Göran. 1984. *Alvar Aalto. The Early Years*. New York: Rizzoli.

Schiller, Nina Glick, Linda Basch, and Cristina Blanc-Szanton. 1992. "Transnationalism: A New Analytical Framework for Understanding Migration." In *Towards a Transnational Perspective on Migration: Race, Class, and Nationalism Reconsidered*, edited by Nina Glick Schiller, Linda Basch, and Cristina Blanc-Szanton, 1–24. New York: New York Academy of Sciences. https:// doi.org/10.1111/j.1749-6632.1992.tb33484.x.

Schindler, Rudolph M. 1921. Kings Road House. West Hollywood, CA. Architecture.

Schmidt, Wilhelm, and Wilhelm Koppers. 1924. *Völker und Kulturen*. Regensburg: Habbel.

Schneider, David M. 1967. *American Kinship: A Cultural Account*. Hoboken, NJ: Prentice Hall.

Sieden, Lloyd S. 2000. *Buckminster Fuller's Universe*. New York: Basic Books.

Sime, James, and John Malcolm Mitchell. 1911. "Winckelmann, Johann Joachim." In *Encyclopædia Britannica 28*, edited by Hugh Chisholm, 707. Cambridge: Cambridge University Press.

Smith, Elizabeth A. T., Julius Shulman, Peter Gssel, Shannon Loughrey, and Peter Loughrey, editors. 2009. Case Study Houses. Los Angeles: Taschen America LLC.

Social Housing Finance Corporation. 2019. *Our Way Forward: Innovating the Community Mortgage Program (2019 Annual Report)*. Makati City: Social Housing Finance Corporation.

Soja, Edward W. 1996. *Thirdspace: Journeys to Los Angeles and Other Real-and-Imagined Places*. Oxford: Basil Blackwell.

Southall, Aidan. 1973. *Urban Anthropology: Cross-Cultural Studies of Urbanization*. Oxford: Oxford University Press.

Sparkes, Stephen, and Signe Howell, editors. 2003. *The House in Southeast Asia: A Changing Social, Economic and Political Domain*. Abingdon: Routledge.

Spencer, Herbert. 1858. "The Development Hypothesis." In *Essays: Scientific, Political, and Speculative,* 389–95. London: Longman, Brown, Green, Longmans and Roberts.

Sperber, Dan. 1974. *Le Symbolisme en general* [Symbolism in general]. Paris: Hermann.

Spivak, Gayatri C. A. 1990. *The Post-Colonial Critic*. London: Routledge.

Steele, James. 2002. *Pierre Koenig*. New York: Phaidon Press.

Sugishima, Takashi. 1988. "Butaisouchi toshiteno kaoku: higashi indonesia niokeru kaoku no symbolism nikansuru ichikousatsu" [Houses as stage sets: A study on the symbolism of houses in East Indonesia]. *Bulletin of The National Museum of Ethnology* 13, no. 2: 183–220.

Sullivan, Louis H. 1896. *The Tall Office Building Artistically Considered*. Los Angeles: Getty Research Institute.

Sumida, Shoji, and NPO Uzo Nishiyama Memorial Library. 2007. *Nishiyama Uzo No Juutaku Toshiron: Sono Gendaiteki Kensyo* [Uzo Nishiyama's Theory of Housing and Urban Studies: Its Contemporary Verification]. Nippon Hyoronsha Co., Ltd.

Sutamo, Papadaki. 1953. *Le Corbusier*. Bijutsu Shuppansha.

Suzuki, Peter T. 1984. "The Limitations of Structuralism, and Autochthonous Principles for Urban Planning and Design in Indonesia: The Case of Nias." Anthropos 79: 47–53.

Tange, Kenzo. 1961. Tokyo Plan 1960. In Shinkenchiku, 1961(3). Tokyo: Shinkenchiku Sha. Unbuilt Architecture.

Thompson, Edward P. 1955. William Morris: Romantic to Revolutionary. London: Lawrence & Wishart.

Tokoro, Ikuya. 1999. Ekkyo: Sulu kaiiki sekai kara [Cross-border: Sulu Sea from the world]. Tokyo: Iwanami Shoten.

Toynbee, Arnold J. 1970. *Cities on the Move*. Oxford: Oxford University Press.

Turner, Victor. 1967. "Betwixt and Between: The Liminal Period in *rites de passage*." In *Forest of Symbols: Aspects of the Ndembu Ritual*, 23–59. Ithaca, NY: Cornell University Press.

Uchida, Yuzo. 1993. "Philippines no communiy teito jigyo ni kansuru chousa kenkyu" [A study on the Community Mortgage Program in the Philippines]. *Journal of the City Planning Institute of Japan* 28: 781–86.

Ueno, Chizuko. 2002. *Kazoku wo ireruhako kazoku wo koeruhako* [A box that accommodates the family and a box that exceeds the family]. Tokyo: Heibonsha, 2002.

———. 2004. *'51C' kazoku wo ireruhako no sengo to genzai* ['51C' postwar and present of the box that holds the family]. Tokyo: Heibonsha.

Uesugi, Tomiyuki. 2004. "Jinruigaku kara mita transnationalism kenkyu: kenkyu no seiritsu to tenkai oyobi tankan" [Transnationalism studies reviewed from an anthropological perspective: The formulation, development and paradigm shift in the concept of transnationalism]." *Nihon joumin bunka kiyo* 24: 126–84.

United Nations. 1987. *Report of the World Commission on Environment and Development: Our Common Future*. New York: United Nations.

United Nations Conference on Environment and Development. 1992. *The Rio Declaration on Environment and Development*. New York: United Nations.

United Nations Conference on Environment and Development. 1992. *Agenda 21*. New York: United Nations.

Urban Poor Associates. 2004. *Community and Household Profile of U.P. Pook Daang Tubo*. Manila: UPA.

Van Gennep, Arnold. 1977. *The Rites of Passage*. East Sussex, UK: Psychology Press. https://doi.org/10.7208/chicago/9780226027180.001.0001.

Van Sande, Hera. 2020. *JA 117, Spring 2020 Kunio maekawa*. Tokyo: Shinkenchiku Sha.

Vertovec, Steven. 1999. "Conceiving and Researching Transnationalism." *Ethnic and Racial Studies* 22, no. 2: 447–61. https://doi.org/10.1080/014198799329558.

Voltaire. 2000. *Treatise on Tolerance*. Cambridge: Cambridge University Press.

Wakakuwa, Midori. 1990. *Toshi no iconology: ningen no kuukan* [Urban iconology: Human space]. Tokyo: Seidosha.

———. 2000. *Imehji no rekishi* [History of images]. Tokyo: Hoso Daigaku Kyouiku Shinkokai.

Warner, William L. 1976. *The Social Systems of American Ethnic Groups.* New York: Greenwood Publishing Group.

Watari, Junkichi. 2010. "The Visual Image of Women Recorded on Move Films and Slides Shows That Have Recorded The Movement for the Improvement of Living in the Post–World War II Era." *Faculty Journal of Komazawa Women's University* 17: 325–60.

Waterson, Roxana. 1990. *The Living House: An Anthropology of Architecture in South-East Asia.* Oxford: Oxford University Press.

Webb, Michael. 1966. "Drive-in Housing." In *Archigram*, 1999. edited by Peter Cook. Chicago: New York: Princeton Architectural Press. Unbuilt Architecture.

Whyte, William F. 1943. *Street Corner Society: The Social Structure of an Italian Slum*, Chicago: University of Chicago Press.

Wright, Frank L. 1922. Hollyhock House. Los Angeles, CA. Architecture.

Yahagi, Kijuro. 2000. *Heimen kukan shintai* [Plane, space, body]. Tokyo: Seibundo Shinkosha, 2000.

Yamaguchi, Masao. 1983. "Kaoku wo yomu: rio zoku (Flores, Indonesia) no shakai kouzou to ucyuukan" [Read houses: Rio (Flores, Indonesia) social structure and space view]. *Annual Report of Social Anthropology* 9: 1–28.

Yoshioka, Masanori. 1994. "'Ba' ni yotte musubitsuku hitobito" [People connected by "place": Residents, ethnic groups, people in Vanuatu]. In *Kokuminbunka ga umarerutoki* [When national culture is born], edited by Teruo Sekimoto and Takeo Funabiki, 211–37. Tokyo: Libro Co, 1994.

Yoshizaka, Takamasa. Editor. 1973. *Sumai No genkei II* [Prototype of the house II]. Tokyo: Kashima Publishing.

Yourcenar, Marguerite. 1984. *The Dark Brain of Piranesi.* New York: Farrar, Straus & Giroux.

Index

Aalto, Alvar, 115
Adirondack Cottage Sanatorium, 115
adjacency, 2, 4
Agenda 21, 117
Ancient Society (Morgan), 14
Anderson, Benedict, 92–93
anthropology: anthropological practice,
    1, 28; house research in, 13–15;
    interpretive anthropology, 166;
    participant observation in, 157;
    range of study, 158; reconstruction
    of framework, 27; symbolic
    anthropology, 166; visualized
    architecture and, 34–36. *See also*
    architectural anthropology; cultural
    anthropology; urban anthropology
Aquino, Corazon, 71, 89n3
Archigram architectural group, 39
architectural anthropology, 1; aims of,
    161; basics of, 2; collaboration in,
    29–30; cyclical process of, 159;
    partners in, 29; platform in, 29–30;
    reading, presenting, making in, 2, 4,
    27, 158; visual images in, 157
architecture: cultural anthropology
    and, 21–22; drawings in, 43–44;
    Enlightenment influencing,
    161–62; ethno-architecture, 22;
    as ethnography, 157–59; images

in, 38–39; in Japan, 27, 158; local
    houses and, 21–22; neoclassical, 162;
    new, 116; reading of, in broad sense,
    31–33; transdisciplinary nature of,
    158; unbuilt, 39–40, 117. *See also*
    visualized architecture
Architecture Without Architects
    (Rudofsky), 21
Argonauts of the Western Pacific
    (Malinowski), 22–23
Arias, Felix, 43
Asch, Timothy, 17
Athens Charter, 128–30, 133
authentic society, 91–93

Bakhtin, Mikhail M., 41, 139
Bateson, Gregory, 38
Bauhaus, 121–23, 161–62, 164–65
Be Better, Build Better Program, 147
Bentham, Jeremy, 163
Black Atlantic (Gilroy), 11
Boas, Franz, 163
Boulding, Kenneth, 41
Bourdieu, Pierre, 9, 17
Brazil, 131–32
bricolage, 36, 68–69, 94, 95, 120
Brundtland Report, 117

About the Author

Fuyuki Makino is associate professor in the Art and Architecture School at Waseda University in Tokyo, Japan. Between 2002 and 2004, Fuyuki took part in the Ethnology seminar, University of Zurich, Switzerland, on policy to improve illegally occupied areas and organize residents. He completed his PhD research on the anthropological study of adjacency and urban communities in Asian cities. Next, he earned a first-class architectural license in Japan. He worked at Waseda University as an assistant professor and at Komazawa Women's University as an associate professor. In 2018, he established an architectural and anthropological social enterprise, the Institute for Architectural Anthropology.

www.ingramcontent.com/pod-product-compliance
Lightning Source LLC
Chambersburg PA
CBHW031133270326
41929CB00011B/1612